CONNECTICUT IN THE MOVIES

Christmas in Connecticut (1945). (Photofest)

For Laura & Leif

Happy Holidays

CONNECTICUT IN THE MOVIES
FROM DREAM HOUSES TO DARK SUBURBIA

Much Love

ILLEANA DOUGLAS

Illeana Douglas

LYONS PRESS
Essex, Connecticut

An imprint of Globe Pequot, the trade division of
The Rowman & Littlefield Publishing Group, Inc.
4501 Forbes Blvd., Ste. 200
Lanham, MD 20706
www.rowman.com

Distributed by NATIONAL BOOK NETWORK

Copyright © 2023 by Illeana Douglas

All photos not otherwise credited are courtesy of the author. All film posters not otherwise credited are courtesy of Photofest.

All rights reserved. No part of this book may be reproduced in any form or by any electronic or mechanical means, including information storage and retrieval systems, without written permission from the publisher, except by a reviewer who may quote passages in a review.

British Library Cataloguing in Publication Information available

Library of Congress Cataloging-in-Publication Data available

ISBN 978-1-4930-7573-7 (hardcover)
ISBN 978-1-4930-8088-5 (e-book)

Printed in India

CONTENTS

INTRODUCTION..VII

1 SILENT FILMS OF CONNECTICUT..1
Sherlock Holmes, The Country Doctor, Way Down East, Cinderella, Romeo and Juliet, Born Rich, The April Fools

2 COUNTRY LIVING COMEDIES..15
The Wedding Night, Theodora Goes Wild, Bringing Up Baby, In Name Only

3 CHRISTMAS IN CONNECTICUT..39
Christmas in Connecticut, Holiday Inn, The Family Stone, Christmas Cornucopia of Hallmark Films

4 THE DREAM OF SUBURBIA...53
Mr. Blandings Builds His Dream House

5 SUBURBAN SEX COMEDIES..69
Rally 'Round the Flag, Boys!, The Tunnel of Love, Wives and Lovers, My Six Loves, The Secret Life of an American Wife

6 DARK SUBURBIA..83
The Man in the Gray Flannel Suit, The Swimmer, Loving, The Stepford Wives

7 LOCATION, LOCATION, LOCATION: THE TOWN IS THE STAR........113
It Happened to Jane, Parrish, Mystic Pizza, Jacknife, Stanley & Iris

8 CRIMES AND MISDEMEANORS...165
Gentleman's Agreement, Boomerang!, The Stranger, The Man in the Net, Man on a Swing, Everybody Wins, Bristol Boys, All Good Things

9   CONNECTICUT CAMEOS..201
Dragonwyck, It's a Wonderful Life, A Connecticut Yankee in King Arthur's Court, All About Eve, Strangers on a Train, Auntie Mame, Wanda, The Other, The Cannonball Run, A Mighty Wind, Indiana Jones and the Crystal Skull, The Haunting in Connecticut, Away We Go

10   HOMEGROWN DRAMA: THE FILMS OF EUGENE O'NEILL.................219
Ah, Wilderness!, Desire Under the Elms, Long Day's Journey into Night

11   CONNECTICUT HISTORY...231
Come to the Stable, Other People's Money, Amistad, Marshall

12   DARK SUBURBIA REDUX..253
The Ice Storm, Far from Heaven, Revolutionary Road, Rachel Getting Married, The Private Lives of Pippa Lee, Thoroughbreds, The Land of Steady Habits

13   CREEPY CONNECTICUT..279
Violent Midnight, The Curse of the Living Corpse, The Horror of Party Beach, Let's Scare Jessica to Death, The Last House on the Left, Friday the 13th Part 2, My Soul to Take, Deep in the Darkness, We Need to Talk About Kevin

14   THE CHANGING LANDSCAPE AND A SEARCH FOR IDENTITY.............301
Rachel, Rachel, One Summer Love, When Every Day Was the Fourth of July, Promises in the Dark, Good Fences, The Life Before Her Eyes, Birds of America, The Big Bad Swim, Peeples, Hello I Must Be Going, Hope Springs, And So It Goes

15   COMING HOME..321
The Green

ACKNOWLEDGMENTS..328
ABOUT THE AUTHOR...330
APPENDIX: LIST OF FILMS WITH CREDITS.....................................332

INTRODUCTION

Two things that have always brought me happiness are movies and Connecticut. Returning to a film set, or returning to the state where I grew up, both have the same effect on me: instant relaxation and a feeling that I am home. In December of 2021 I was living in California and suffering through the isolation of COVID-19. In the throes of homesickness but unable to visit my family, I began to write, more as a coping mechanism, about a subject that has always fascinated me—the history of Connecticut in the movies.

When I was a kid, my ears would perk up if a story was set in Connecticut, or a character was from Connecticut. Often, the filmmakers used it as a kind of shorthand to convey something beyond being just a location, or a description of a man or a woman's home state. It signaled something about that person or place, giving insight, or adding context.

For example, in Alfred Hitchcock's 1948 film *Rope,* Brandon Shaw (John Dall) and Philip Morgan (Farley Granger) have strangled a fellow classmate to see if they can get away with murder. They plan on disposing of the body in a lake on their way to Shaw's family home . . . in Connecticut. Shaw, in full patrician accent, tells his guests—while hosting a dinner party with their dead classmate hidden inside a trunk—that he and Philip are off to "Connecticut" for the weekend. *Rope* was loosely based upon a true story of a murder committed by students Nathan Leopold and Richard Loeb in

Chicago, so why did the "master of suspense" feel Shaw, was more menacing if he was from Connecticut? Just as he did in *Strangers on a Train* (1951), Hitchcock used "Connecticut" as if it were an unseen character.

People are always surprised to learn that, yes, in addition to *Mystic Pizza,* more than two hundred films (and counting), going back to the silent era, have been made in Connecticut, or feature Connecticut as a central location or part of the storyline. Is there such a thing as Connecticut cinema? I think this book will show that there is.

Renowned filmmakers, from D. W. Griffith and Hitchcock to Elia Kazan and Steven Spielberg, have all made movies here, yet no one seems to know that. I always thought that Connecticut's contributions to cinema—beyond the fact that everyone knows Katharine Hepburn was born here—have been overlooked because they were never categorized in any type of genre, yet there has been such a variety of films with Connecticut ties that multiple genres emerge to me as Connecticut cinema. So, I thought maybe I could combine my two favorite topics—movies and Connecticut—and share my expertise about both in an entertaining little guidebook.

Although it was not part of my research (or my life plan), after long days of writing about Connecticut's rich history of films, I found myself up at night scrolling—just for fun, I thought—through the real estate site, Zillow. I shared my potential interest with my friend Linda, who just happens to be a Connecticut realtor. She forwarded me a listing for an 1810 farmhouse on the market, pressing me with the classic realtor's mantra, "location, location, location," hoping I would bite because of its beautiful setting. Now, value is an elusive concept. Something that is valuable to one person might not be valuable to another. What Linda didn't realize is that not only was it a beautiful property, but it was also about a two-minute walk to my mother's house.

Linda had struck the emotional jackpot. I not only knew the house, but I had also been inside it many times. I practically grew up there, having played there as a child. There were memories of sledding down hills in winter, the time my brother lost his front tooth after we crashed into the woodpile, touch football games out on the lawn in the fall, Easter egg hunts in spring, swimming in the pool in summer. I learned how to make a fire in that very fireplace! I kept my horse, Laddie, in their barn, disco-danced to the *Saturday Night Fever* soundtrack album in the converted basement, and played the hiding game "Sardines" in the attic. I had even smoked cigarettes and had some beer with other kids in the pump house at the edge of the property. I knew this house. One thing I was not aware of was that, according to the real estate blurb, there was some historical evidence the house may have been part of the Underground Railroad. Intriguing . . .

There was a huge problem, though. Well, quite a few huge problems. The house, to which so many of my own personal memories were attached, had been severely neglected and fallen into disrepair. A renovation of this size was daunting.

After telling Linda all about my history with the house, she convinced me that I was, in fact, the perfect person to restore it to its former glory. It wouldn't take much, she assured me—just someone to supply their loving touch—and wouldn't it be better, "more authentic," to be writing about Connecticut while I was actually living there?

In autumn, as the leaves began to fall in New England, having now sold my house in California, I purchased my dream house. Once I moved in, I realized what I was up against. I was going to have to do something about that kitchen—there was no functioning stove, the floor was so eaten up by termites that the joists were gone, and mice had made themselves comfortable pretty much everywhere. I needed a new . . . well, everything! The furnace, the boiler, the water heater, every bathroom, anything electric or that had pipes—was shot. An engineer who inspected my basement with its maze of beams and lally columns holding up the living room was impressed the whole thing had not completely caved in.

Either *Connecticut in the Movies* was writing itself or God was playing a literary joke on me. I had just begun writing about the history of *Mr. Blandings Builds His Dream House.* The storyline of the film, as you may have guessed from its title, follows a sophisticated New Yorker, Jim Blandings, who falls in love with his "dream house" in Connecticut, only to discover he's been duped by a sly Yankee realtor who unloaded an unsellable money pit on him. I was writing about the travails of Mr. Blandings and realizing to my horror that I was a real-life Mrs. Blandings. Had I really thought I could supervise a full-scale renovation and write a book—at the same time? Mr. Blandings had a nervous breakdown doing just one of those things!

The renovation began with a bang. Well, lots of bangs, as we began to support the foundation, and found water. Lots of it, running like a stream under the house. The irony of having left California, where there is no water, and coming to a place where there is too much water, was not lost on me.

Making my way to my office to write, I waded through a sea of plastic and dust, stopping to discuss with my various contractors—the carpenter, the electrician, the painter, the plumber—what latest crisis had befallen me. What was it this time? The crooked chimney? The crooked foundation? Cracked pipes? A cracking-up owner? And why did they always want to show you things?

"Illeana, I need to have you look at this . . . So, the mice are living in the hole that the termites made. See that?"

Yeah, Steve, that looks pretty bad. I need to go back and write my book now.

Maybe it was more water in the basement? One day my plumber joked with typical wry New England humor, "Hey, it's not everyone who can brag they have a swimming pool in their basement!" At times like that I tried always to remember that *Mr. Blandings Builds His Dream House* does have a happy ending.

Though my own dream house is not yet complete—will it ever be?—*Connecticut in the Movies* is. Both projects have been a labor of love. I like to think that the same kind of loving care I've put into bringing this house back to life, and giving it a place of honor, I've put into writing about these films. They all deserve to be honored, rediscovered, watched, and talked about. Believe me, every time I thought I was done, I would find just one more great film to write about and include in this volume. Hey, there's a lot to be proud of!

Whether you're a native or just a movie lover, you're about to learn that Connecticut is full of surprises—versatile, scenic, complicated, uptight, and sometimes just plain scary. So, here we go! Consider me your cinematic tour guide as we go on a road trip through the Constitution State. I think by the end of our movie tour, you'll not only have a better understanding of these films, but you'll also have a better understanding of the amazing place I now once again call home: Connecticut.

You can go home again. Me with my ponies Nancy and Laddie at the house where I now live. In a plotline ripped from *Mr. Blandings Builds His Dream House*, I have been fixing it up ever since.

CONNECTICUT IN THE MOVIES

(Courtesy San Francisco Silent Film Festival)

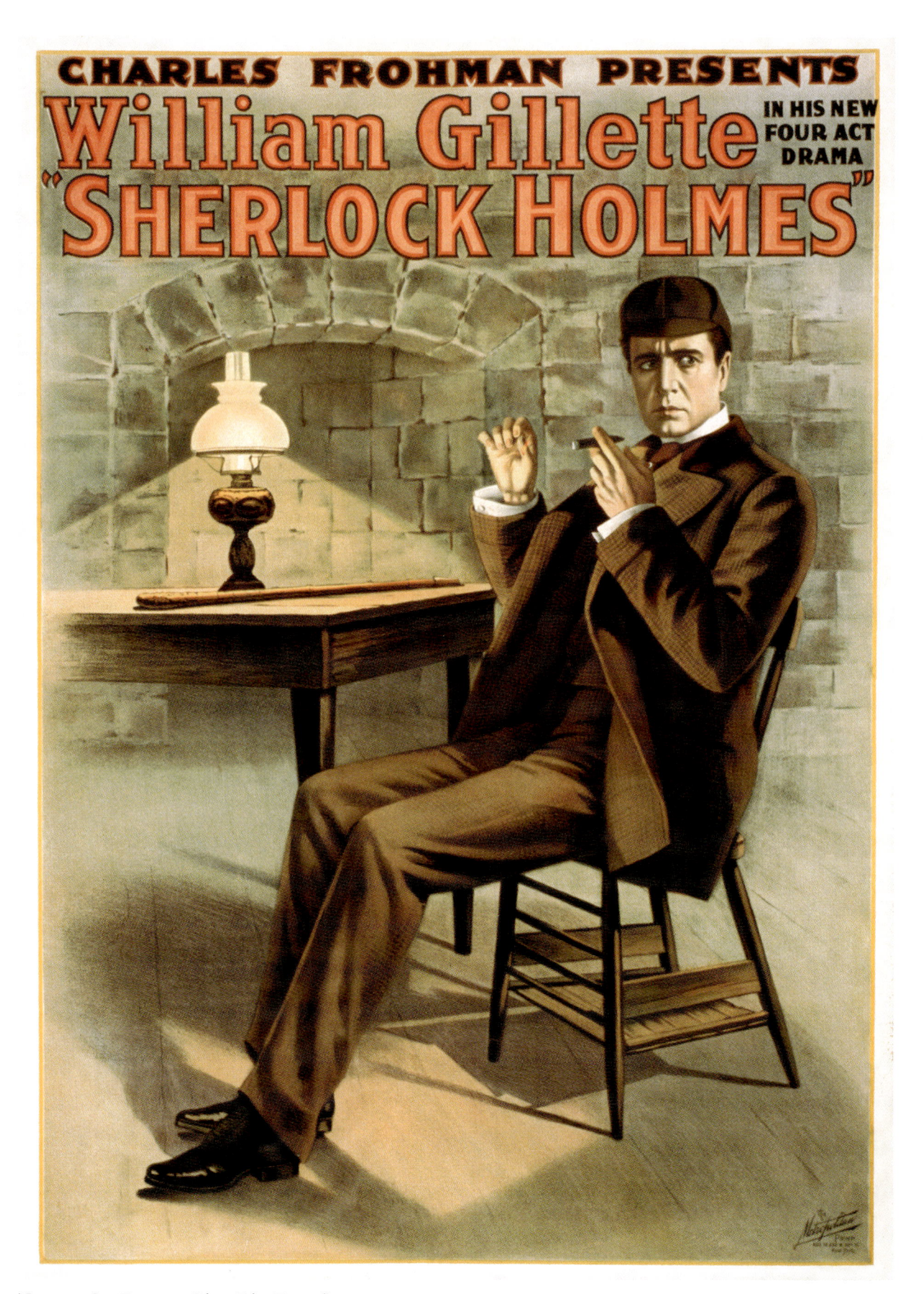

CHAPTER 1

SILENT FILMS OF CONNECTICUT

SHERLOCK HOLMES (1916)

Though it was made in Chicago by the Essanay Film Manufacturing Company, *Sherlock Holmes: A Drama in Four Acts* (1916), directed by Arthur Berthelet, is a silent film of great significance to Connecticut because of its star, William Gillette. Gillette was born in 1853 and lived with his family at Nook Farm in Hartford, Connecticut. The artistic enclave was also home to Mark Twain and Harriet Beecher Stowe. It was Twain himself who recommended that Gillette, who left Hartford at the age of twenty to become an actor, star in his play *The Gilded Age* at the Globe Theatre in Boston in 1875. Gillette would go on to become one of the biggest stars in turn-of-the-century American theater in a career that spanned more than sixty years.

Although barely remembered today, William Gillette created what would become the first and most widely

Basil Rathbone in *The Hound of the Baskervilles* (1938) in signature Sherlock Holmes attire, based on Gillette's conception. (Photofest)

accepted version of the character Sherlock Holmes. He obtained permission from the author, Arthur Conan Doyle, for the first authorized stage adaptation of a Sherlock Holmes story. Along with writing the play, it was Gillette who added the props we have come to recognize for the inquisitive detective. The cape, the deerstalker hat, the magnifying glass, and the curved calabash pipe were all conceived by Gillette. He chose a curved pipe out of necessity after discovering he was not able to say his lines with a straight pipe in his mouth. It was also Gillette, not Doyle, who said, "Elementary, my dear fellow," which morphed over time into Sherlock Holmes's most iconic line, "Elementary, my dear Watson."

Sherlock Holmes: A Drama in Four Acts (1916). (Courtesy San Francisco Silent Film Festival) Actor and Connecticut native William Hooker Gillette created the persona of Sherlock Holmes and built a cultural treasure—Gillette Castle in East Haddam, Connecticut.

Gillette and Doyle corresponded about the play but had not actually met. When Doyle came to America, Gillette decided to meet him at the train station in his complete Sherlock Holmes costume. Upon seeing Doyle at the station, Gillette approached him in character, whipped out his magnifying glass, put it up to Doyle's face, examined him, and exclaimed, "Unquestionably an author." With that, a character, a partnership, and a lifelong friendship were born. Gillette would go on to play Sherlock Holmes over fifteen hundred times onstage in America and England. He filmed *Sherlock Holmes: A Drama in Four Acts* when he was sixty-three years old. The film, long presumed lost but rediscovered in 2014, offers definitive proof not only that William Gillette conceived of the Holmes character in looks and manner, but that his unique persona became the model for all future portrayals.

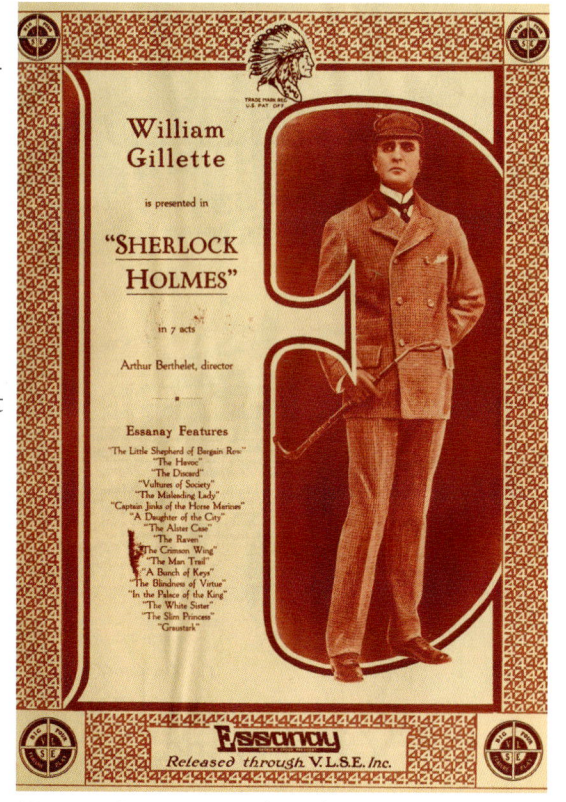

(Courtesy San Francisco Silent Film Festival)

SILENT FILMS OF CONNECTICUT

Gillette Castle State Park in East Haddam, Connecticut.

Gillette would often don conductor attire, driving passengers around his property. In the 1940s, the tracks and train were sold to Lake Compounce in Bristol. They donated it back to Gillette Castle in the 1990s. As of this writing, you can see a restored car on display in the main lobby.

Gillette's original Sherlock Holmes props on display at Gillette Castle.

As an actor, William Gillette lived a nomadic life. His wife had died after only six years of marriage and no children. In the 1900s, he began looking for a place to retire from the stage. Traveling by houseboat up the Connecticut River, he spotted a beautiful piece of land high up on a hill in an area called Seven Sisters in East Haddam, Connecticut. It was here that he would design and build his home.

For most people, the phrase "A man's home is his castle" is a metaphor, but in Gillette's case, it was actually true. Gillette built his medieval-style castle out of local fieldstone designed to look as if it were partially a ruin. Construction began in 1914 and took five years to complete, at a cost of $1,000,000. The house was set on a one-hundred-acre property that extended into wooded areas accessible by a miniature train on three miles of track. The interior was in the Arts and Crafts style and had modern features of the day, including electricity. Another notable detail is that there were forty-seven unique, hand-carved oak doors.

Gillette was a jokester and devised a trick service bar that guests had to figure out how to unlock before they could use it. Gillette would invite guests to make themselves a drink and then mischievously excuse himself so he could watch from a one-way mirror to see if they were able to work it out. To his delight, even Albert Einstein was stumped. Gillette would then appear as if by magic to assist his guests in their libations.

William Gillette left his estate to a surviving niece. In 1943, the state purchased the entire property and turned it into a park and museum. Listed as a historic landmark, Gillette Castle holds a dear place in my heart; I have visited it many times over the years and throughout the seasons. It's especially picturesque in the fall, when you can appreciate the sweeping views of the Connecticut River and imagine Gillette himself declaring, "Why, it's elementary," when describing its beauty.

THE COUNTRY DOCTOR (1908) AND *WAY DOWN EAST* (1920) —D. W. GRIFFITH'S TIES TO CONNECTICUT

In her book, *The Movies, Mr. Griffith, and Me* (1969), actress Lillian Gish calls director D. W. Griffith "the father of film," recalling his legacy as a pioneer in the early days of motion pictures. Griffith invented much of the language of film and film technique. He became the most important director of his generation, making over five hundred films, including *The Birth of a Nation* (1915) and *Intolerance* (1916). He revolutionized film financing and, in 1919, helped form the studio, United Artists, with Mary Pickford, Douglas Fairbanks, and Charlie Chaplin. Sadly, Griffith's accomplishments were largely forgotten by the film industry, and he died in relative obscurity in a room at the Knickerbocker Hotel in Hollywood.

Before moving to California in 1912 to make *The Birth of a Nation*—the film that catapulted

Postcard of Sound Beach in Greenwich, Connecticut, where filmmakers like D. W. Griffith and others made silent films.

Postcard of Laddins Rock in Old Greenwich, where D. W. Griffith shot *Adventures of Dollie* (1908).

CONNECTICUT IN THE MOVIES

Postcard of Commodore Elias C. Benedict's estate, early 1900s.

his career—D. W. Griffith got his start making movies right here in Greenwich, Connecticut. Much as independent filmmakers working on the cheap would do today, Griffith, accompanied by his cameraman, actors, and equipment, would board the train from New York to make the forty-five-minute journey to the Greenwich countryside. Old Greenwich and Greenwich, also known as Sound Beach, were where Griffith directed his first short film, *The Adventures of Dollie* (1908), filmed at Binney Park and Laddins Rock.

Griffith directed one-reelers for the American Mutoscope and Biograph Company at the home of Commodore Elias C. Benedict in Indian Harbor. Benedict enjoyed having Griffith use his property to make films, and supplied the director and his actors with champagne and cigars. Griffith made quite a few short films using the Indian Harbor location, including *The Country Doctor* (1909), with the actress who would become known as "America's sweetheart," Mary Pickford. Others included *The Cardinal's Conspiracy* (1909), *What Daisy Said* (1910) (also starring Mary Pickford), and *The Golden Supper* (1910). Griffith used the

The Country Doctor (1908), directed by D. W. Griffith, was filmed at the Commodore Elias C. Benedict estate in Indian Harbor in Greenwich. (Library of Congress)

SILENT FILMS OF CONNECTICUT

What Daisy Said (1910). Production logs in cameraman Billy Bitzer's handwriting list Biograph films, *The Message* (1908), *The Cardinal's Conspiracy* (1909), and *The Adventures of Dollie* (1908), filmed in Greenwich. (Courtesy Film Preservation LLC)

location of Stamford to shoot a sixteen-minute film entitled *The Impalement,* released in 1910.

In 1919, Griffith purchased a home in Mamaroneck, New York, called the Flagler Estate. It was while living here that Griffith used Farmington, Connecticut, to film part of a very memorable scene in *Way Down East* (1920), starring Lillian Gish and Richard Barthelmess. *Way Down East* has one of the most daring action sequences ever filmed, with camera work performed by G. W. "Billy" Bitzer. The sequence may well have been inspired by the damsel-in-distress serial *The Perils of Pauline* (1914), starring Pearl White, parts of which had been shot in a section of Greenwich called Belle Haven.

The plot of *Way Down East* has Anna Moore (Lillian Gish) as a simple country girl who is tricked into marriage, then abandoned when she becomes pregnant. Anna has the baby, the baby dies, and Anna moves to another town to start over. She falls in love with David (Richard Barthelmess), but David's father, Squire Bartlett (Burr McIntosh), finds out about her past and casts her out in a snowstorm. While David searches for her, Anna, lost in the blizzard, falls into an icy river. Now unconscious, Anna floats toward a waterfall on a large piece of ice. Her hair and hand float in the water. Right before the ice goes over the edge, David is able to rescue her.

Way Down East is an example of how actors of the silent era were truly willing to suffer for their art, some even risking their lives. While Bitzer was filming the blizzard scenes, the temperature never rose above zero. A fire had to be built underneath his camera to prevent it from freezing. Griffith sustained frostbite on one side of his face, from which he never recovered. It was Gish's idea to have her right hand and long hair trail in the water as she lay on the ice floe drifting toward the falls—the image most closely associated with the film. Gish's hand froze while shooting the scene, as did her hair, which cracked off. In her autobiography, *The Movies, Mr. Griffith, and Me,* Lillian Gish describes having problems with her hand for the rest of her life. She was once asked about the small sum of money she received for risking her life on the film. Her answer was heartfelt: "We didn't do it for money, we did it for love."

The bulk of the harrowing ice floe sequence was filmed at White River Junction in Vermont, but later in the summer the crew filmed pickups of the scene on the Farmington River in Farmington. The ice floe was built out of plywood, painted white, and covered in cotton batting to mimic

CONNECTICUT IN THE MOVIES

8 SILENT FILMS OF CONNECTICUT

No stunt doubles! That is actually actress Lillian Gish risking her life for her art in *Way Down East*.

D. W. Griffith shooting *Way Down East*. Next to him is his famous cameraman, G. W. "Billy" Bitzer. (Photofest)

Way Down East being shot. While some of the blizzard scenes were filmed in Vermont, Griffith came to Connecticut to film additional scenes on the Farmington River. (Courtesy San Francisco Silent Film Festival)

CONNECTICUT IN THE MOVIES

Postcard of Millstreams around the time of the filming of *Way Down East*. Winchell Smith is buried in Riverside Cemetery in Farmington.

Millstreams is a private residence today.

snow. The cast stayed at the Elm Tree Inn in Farmington during filming.

The other Connecticut location in *Way Down East* is Millstreams, the home of the actor and playwright Winchell Smith, best known for co-writing the play *Brewster's Millions* (1906), based on the novel by George Barr McCutcheon. Smith was born in West Hartford and got his start in the theater company of his uncle, who was none other than William Gillette. Smith convinced Griffith to shoot at Millstreams, built in 1917 along a bend in the Farmington and Pequabuck Rivers, to showcase his grain-milling operation. In what sounds like early product placement, Smith's gristmill appears prominently in the film. Smith milled whole-grain wheat, rye, and buckwheat and sold the flour to bakeries in Hartford. He expanded his milling business in 1925, and had the intention of building a film studio and theaters, but his grain business folded in 1931, and Smith himself died in 1933. The mill is no longer on the property, but the house retains the original front gates Smith obtained from the Lambs Club in New York City.

CINDERELLA (1914)

Griffith was not the only silent filmmaker to make movies in Connecticut. In 1914, Timothy Crowley, a wealthy merchant, commissioned the architect James C. Green to build his estate, Crowley Castle. It's located on Brookside Drive in Greenwich. The medieval-style castle, complete with a drawbridge and moat, was completed in 1917. Some of its quirky features included a bowling alley in the basement and a large pipe organ in the great hall. Outside the castle there were waterfalls, lush gardens, and a large swimming pool.

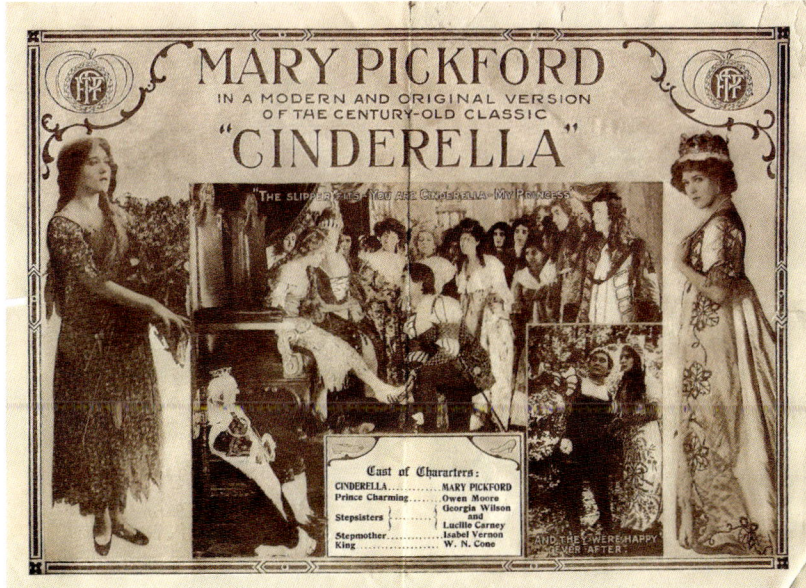

Cinderella (1914) was the first movie to be made at Crowley Castle in Greenwich.

Advertisement for *Cinderella*, filmed in Crowley Castle, Greenwich. (Photofest)

The first use of Crowley Castle in films came quickly, in 1914, with *Cinderella*, released by the Famous Players–Lasky Corporation (which later became Paramount Pictures). It starred husband and wife Mary Pickford and Owen Moore as Cinderella and Prince Charming, and you can see Mary, America's sweetheart, frolicking through the estate's gardens on-screen. It was rumored that Pickford, though married to Moore, was secretly involved with Cinderella's director, James Kirkwood. While she was at the height of her career, Moore's career was in decline. His dependence on alcohol and his abusive behavior led to their divorce in 1920. Pickford soon thereafter married swashbuckling screen idol Douglas Fairbanks.

ROMEO AND JULIET (1916)

In 1916, Crowley Castle became the backdrop for the *film Romeo and Juliet*, starring another soon-to-be husband-and-wife team, Beverly Bayne and Francis X. Bushman (married in 1918). Still photographs highlighting the interiors of the castle, filled with Crowley's own personal antiques, are all that remain of *Romeo and Juliet*, which is now considered lost. Bushman would go on to star as Messala in the classic 1925 version of *Ben-Hur*.

BORN RICH (1924)

In 1924, the comedy *Born Rich*, starring yet another soon-to-be wed couple, Claire Windsor and Bert Lytell, used Crowley Castle's great hall for a scene of flappers dancing the Charleston. Sadly, this film, too, is considered lost, but, again, surviving stills showcase the great hall in all its splendor. Not long after the stock market crash of 1929, John L. Grey purchased the castle from Crowley and renamed it Belle Caro, although the original Crowley Castle name was later restored.

THE APRIL FOOLS (1969)

More than four decades later, in 1969, Crowley Castle was once again utilized as a film location, this time for the romantic comedy *The April Fools*, starring Jack Lemmon, Catherine Deneuve, Myrna Loy, and Charles Boyer. A long way from silent films, *The April Fools* was made at the height of the swinging sixties and has a groovy Pop Art feel. This time the castle's various stunning rooms were used to display a comedic fencing duel featuring Boyer and Lemmon, and there's a lovely scene where Lemmon and Deneuve dance at night on the floor of the castle's drained swimming pool, surrounded by all the ornate statuary. Short on substance, *The April Fools* is high on style, and you will get quite a few glimpses of the castle.

Catherine Deneuve and Myrna Loy in *The April Fools* (1969). It was the last time Crowley Castle was featured in a motion picture. (Photofest)

SILENT FILMS OF CONNECTICUT

Many movie legends have come and gone through the gates of Crowley Castle in Greenwich.

CONNECTICUT IN THE MOVIES

IRENE DUNNE
RIOTOUS
ROMANTIC
COMEDY!
THEODORA
GOES WILD
MELVYN
DOUGLAS
SCREEN PLAY BY SIDNEY BUCHMAN
Directed by RICHARD BOLESLAWSKI
A COLUMBIA
PICTURE
THOMAS MITCHELL • THURSTON HALL
ROSALIND KEITH • SPRING BYINGTON

CHAPTER 2
COUNTRY LIVING COMEDIES

The first appearance of Connecticut not just as a destination but emerging as a character or as part of the narrative of a story came in a series of "country living" comedies from the 1930s: *The Wedding Night* (1935), *Theodora Goes Wild* (1936), and *Bringing Up Baby* (1938). A fourth film, *In Name Only* (1939), is a melodrama but follows a similar transformational country living plot. The country living comedies share the same general storyline: A man—almost always a New Yorker—at a crossroads in his life, finds happiness in Connecticut after meeting the girl of his dreams.

The authenticity of the environment, combined with the authenticity of

Alice DeLamar's estate, once called Stonebrook, was located in Weston. The socialite and heiress was a patron of the arts responsible for bringing many artists to the area, including actress Eva Le Gallienne and choreographer George Balanchine. (Library of Congress)

the girl, brings about the realization that there is a better way to live. Since none of these movies were actually made on location in Connecticut, it was up to Hollywood writers, directors, production designers, art directors, and costumers to create Connecticut for moviegoers. Though the films were made at different studios—Goldwyn, Columbia, and RKO—they share a remarkably similar vision of on-screen Connecticut. The fictional towns, with names like Lynnfield or Bridgefield, became a kind of accepted version of what Connecticut was perceived to look like. The exteriors were a Currier and Ives meets 1930s Beverly Hills Colonial Revival mash-up.

The interiors were more emotionally complex. Connecticut as interpreted by Hollywood had an aesthetic beyond the stone cottages, picket fences, wood-beamed living rooms, and massive fireplaces. It was a place to get in touch with nature, see a new perspective, find true love. It was a place to uncover a more authentic version of yourself, away from the noise of the city. In other words, Connecticut could *cure* you.

The country living comedies had organic roots. Connecticut's proximity to New York and emergence as a country getaway made it a logical place for screenwriters to begin to mine, with a whole host of New England character types and stories to draw from. In the 1920s and 1930s, writers, directors, and actors working on Broadway began to migrate to Connecticut, purchasing summer homes or permanent country getaways.

F. Scott Fitzgerald and his wife Zelda summered in Westport, where he penned *The Beautiful and the Damned* (1922). Some believe that "West Egg," the setting of Fitzgerald's novel *The Great Gatsby* (1925), is actually based on Westport.

In the 1930s, playwright Noel Coward was working on his Broadway productions of *Private Lives* and *Design for Living* while staying at his Connecticut retreat in Fairfield called Sasco Manor, which was owned by his lover and manager, theatrical producer Jack Wilson.

Katharine Hepburn, star of *Bringing Up Baby*, grew up in Hartford. She could be called an ambassador of the Connecticut brand. The family was well connected with artists, doctors, and members of Connecticut society. They purchased an additional property in the Fenwick section of Old Saybrook in 1913 as a summer retreat. Hepburn said of the estate, "This isn't a dream, it's Fenwick—or is it paradise?" While working on Broadway, Hepburn entertained many of her famous friends at Fenwick. That continued as her career took her to Hollywood. While she was in a relationship with Howard Hughes in the 1930s, he once landed his seaplane in the Long Island Sound, right near her house. When the family property was lost the great storm of 1938, she rebuilt a house the same land. She would live there until her death in 2003.

In 1926, another one of the most celebrated actresses of her day, Eva Le Gallienne, purchased a two-hundred-year-old farmhouse on Hillside Road in Weston, which she called her sanctuary. She

Cobb's Mill in Weston was built in 1749. Alice DeLamar turned it into the Cobb's Mill Inn, a popular spot in Weston for years. The property, at 12 Old Mill Road, is now closed, but there are plans for a possible restoration.

F. Scott Fitzgerald and his wife Zelda outside their house on Compo Beach Road South in Westport.

Actress Eva Le Gallienne settled in Weston in 1926, buying a farmhouse on Hillside Road. (Photofest)

Fredric March and wife Florence Eldridge moved to New Milford in the 1930s and they helped found the Merryall Community Arts Center, which is still open today. March asked for his ashes to be spread under his favorite tree on their farm. Part of his estate was left to the Weantinoge Land Trust.

Katharine Hepburn outside her home in Fenwick—perhaps the greatest ambassador of the Connecticut brand. With her signature voice, chiseled features, slim figure, love of the outdoors, and unmatched individuality, she stood apart from other glamorous actresses who came out of the studio system. (Photo by John Bryson, Courtesy Old Saybrook Historical Society)

would later leave part of her property to the Aspetuck Land Trust. Le Gallienne's close friend, the wealthy socialite and patron of the arts, Alice DeLamar, had previously purchased a home and various properties in Weston, creating an artistic haven for Le Gallienne and a steady stream of Broadway visitors, such as George Balanchine, to her estate, Stonebrook.

In 1934, Alice DeLamar purchased Cobb's Mill, also in Weston. The sawmill was built in 1749. In 1936, Alice turned it into a restaurant, the Cobb's Mill Inn, which became one of the hottest gathering spots in town, thriving for many years.

Actor Fredric March and his wife, actress Florence Eldridge, purchased a forty-acre farm in New Milford. Westport became a major hub when summer cottages sprang up on Compo Beach. The

Actress and Connecticut native Katharine Hepburn's family summer home in Fenwick. Kate would remember the family's life there as a kind of "paradise." The house was destroyed in the hurricane of 1938. (Courtesy Old Saybrook Historical Society)

COUNTRY LIVING COMEDIES

The theatrical revolution known as the Group Theatre had its roots in Connecticut. Elia Kazan, Harold Clurman, and Sanford Meisner moved the Group Theatre to Pine Brook Country Club at 33 East Lake Road in Trumbull in the 1930s, having previously rehearsed in Brookfield. Other members who rehearsed at Pine Brook include actor John Garfield, playwright Clifford Odets, actors Lee J. Cobb and Arthur Kennedy, both of whom appeared in *Boomerang!* (chapter 8), which Kazan directed, and director Richard Boleslawski, who directed *Theodora Goes Wild*. (Courtesy Wesleyan University Reid Cinema Archives)

The Westport Country Playhouse opened in 1931. Husband-and-wife producers Lawrence Langner and Armina Marshall were residents of Weston and wanted a theater near their home. It has been in continuous operation since then. My grandfather Melvyn Douglas was one of many luminaries who performed here, and in 1951 starred in *Glad Tidings*. Connecticut resident Paul Newman and Robert Redford performed together at the Playhouse in 2004. (Photofest)

CONNECTICUT IN THE MOVIES

opening of the Westport Country Playhouse in 1931 brought actors such as Henry Fonda and Paul Robeson to the state. Robeson moved to Enfield in 1941, and Fonda rented a house in Greenwich.

In the 1930s, first Brookfield Center, and later, the Pine Brook Country Club in the Nichols section of Trumbull, became the home of the Group Theatre, formed loosely by members Harold Clurman, Cheryl Crawford, Sanford Meisner, Lee Strasberg, and others. The actors, directors, playwrights, and producers of the Group Theatre, including Elia Kazan, Clifford Odets, Harold Clurman, and Arthur Miller, would change the face of American theater and film. It was here that Richard Boleslawski, director of *Theodora Goes Wild*, may have drawn inspiration in teaching the craft of acting, sharing insights he received from the great Russian master Konstantin Stanislavsky and the Moscow Art Theatre.

One of Connecticut's most famous future residents, actress Marilyn Monroe, and the Pulitzer Prize–winning playwright Arthur Miller, chose the picturesque background of his farm in Roxbury to announce to the world in 1956 that they were in love and going to be married. Posing for pictures outside Miller's colonial farmhouse, Monroe greeted the press wearing a rumpled blue skirt and a simple cotton blouse. She never looked more wholesome, more radiant, or as happy. Had Connecticut's transformational powers worked their magic—or had she just seen too many country living comedies with happy endings?

Marilyn Monroe and Arthur Miller announce their engagement with his parents at Miller's farmhouse in Roxbury, Connecticut, in June 1956. The colonial home was built in 1783 and included 325 acres of land. Initially Monroe felt she had at last found true happiness and a sense of belonging. In what sounds like a line from a country living film, the glamorous movie star reportedly told Miller, "I hate Hollywood; I don't want it anymore. I want to live quietly in the country and just be there when you need me." (Photofest)

Tophet Road in Roxbury, where Arthur Miller lived and worked. In all my travels throughout Connecticut, this is one of the most magical places I visited.

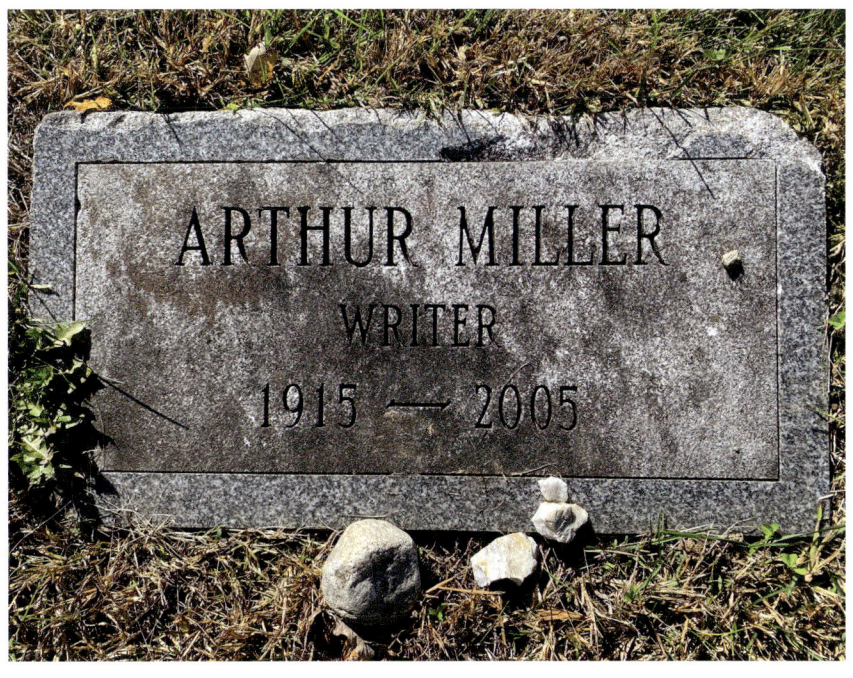

Arthur Miller died in 2005 and is buried at Great Oak Cemetery in Roxbury, near his home. Part of his estate was left to a land trust.

The Wedding Night (1935). A New York writer, Tony Barrett (Gary Cooper), with Anna Sten (Manya), is inspired to write again after moving to his family's Connecticut farm. Though the movie was not filmed in Connecticut, director King Vidor used a rear-screen projection of an actual Connecticut tobacco farm. Dora (Helen Vinson), on the left, spends an unhappy first night with her husband at the farm. Character actress Hilda Vaughn was Hollywood's version of a typical Yankee maid. Walter Brennan, with full-tilt Maine accent, played Bill Jenkins, a typical Yankee farmer. Country living comedies were filled with countrified yokels who usually had more common sense than their New York guests. (Photofest)

THE WEDDING NIGHT (1935)

The Wedding Night (1935) celebrates Connecticut as a transformational haven for a writer who has lost his artistic way. Tony Barrett (Gary Cooper) has been living the high life in Manhattan since the success of his first novel. Once a sparkling talent, he's gone years without writing another book. He spends his time seeking idle pleasures or trying to please his beautiful but shallow wife, Dora (Helen Vinson). Dora enjoys the success and entrée that Tony's name has brought her. As long as the champagne flows, she doesn't notice his dwindling bank account. Looking for an advance from his publisher (Douglas Wood), Tony instead gets some sobering news. His publisher suggests he might want to leave the city and dry out before he attempts to write again; if this next book is a failure, he will drop Tony as a client.

To begin his journey of redemption, Tony convinces Dora to leave their New York life behind and move to the family's ramshackle tobacco farm in fictional Pembrook, Connecticut. The broken-down, unheated farmhouse, far from the glamour of New York society, is not for Dora. She abandons Tony and heads back to Manhattan and her partying ways.

Alone and feeling desperate, Tony wants to sell his family's land to his Polish dairy farmer neighbor, Jan Novak (Sig Ruman), and head back to New York to be with Dora. After meeting Novak's daughter, the beautiful Manya (Anna Sten), he changes his mind. Manya becomes a kind of muse and part-time wife. She brings him fresh milk every day, and then Tony hires her to cook his meals. Manya's warm personality soon brightens Tony's lonely life. There are numerous down-on-the-farm motifs, such as chopping wood and milking the cows together, and Tony is able to stay sober and complete his novel, which he dedicates to Manya. After a few months, he comes to a realization, telling Manya, "I've been running all over looking for life, and I've found it right here."

Gary Cooper had recently moved into talking pictures after success as a silent-film cowboy star. His fascinating inner personality and charm translated well to talkies, and he was able to use minimal dialogue and understated acting to convey deep feelings. He was also adept at comedy, and his lanky six-foot-three-inch frame was put to good use learning a Polish wedding dance and attempting to make breakfast in a cramped farm kitchen.

When a blizzard keeps Manya from returning home, she's forced to sleep in Tony's striped pajamas. The diminutive Anna Sten stumbling around in Gary Cooper's oversized pajamas adds a nice screwball element to their love story.

Because Manya is Polish, her father wants her to marry a fellow Polish farmer, the brutish Fredrik Sobieski (Ralph Bellamy). Manya has gained a kind of independence after spending time with Tony and now sees an arranged marriage as an old-fashioned, out-of-date custom. Ralph Bellamy would later have roles in classic screwball comedies like *The Awful Truth* (1937) and *His Girl Friday* (1940), but here he's the villain.

Tony asks a visiting Dora for a divorce, but she is not about to give up her meal ticket. After reading Tony's new manuscript and its dedication to Manya, she surmises the truth. She tells Manya she will never give Tony up, and Manya reluctantly marries Fredrik. On their wedding night she refuses to consummate the marriage because of her love for Tony. Fredrik, drunk and humiliated, goes to Tony's farm to confront him, and Manya follows. As they fight, Manya gets between them and Fredrik accidentally knocks her down the stairs. As Manya lies dying, Tony reassures her that their love will live on in the novel that she inspired. Tony has learned to love again, to write again, and he decides to stay in Connecticut, where he has found, as Eva Le Gallienne once said, his "sanctuary."

King Vidor had been working as a highly respected director since Hollywood's inception, and specialized in important social dramas like *The Big Parade* (1925) and *Street Scene* (1931). *The Wedding Night* was an assignment for Vidor, and he resented the constant set visits from studio chief Sam Goldwyn, who was checking on the progress of his recently signed star, Anna Sten. Goldwyn had hoped *The Wedding Night* would be a vehicle for the Russian-born Sten to become the next Garbo or Dietrich, but it was not to be.

In Vidor's autobiography, *A Tree Is a Tree* (1953), he writes of *The Wedding Night*, "The picture was referred to as 'Goldwyn's last Sten.'" He goes on to write of the difficulty Anna Sten had with dialogue. "Sten hadn't been speaking English long. The words and syllables came into being just a little bit after the gesture, so that the two were never in perfect synchronization. Rather than a director, I felt like a dentist pulling syllables out her mouth before the parallel gesture had passed by."

Once, while a love scene was being filmed, Goldwyn came by to offer encouragement. Sten was reading the dedication in the novel that Cooper's character had written. The scriptwriter had chosen a verse with the phrase "Earth's returns," from Robert Browning's "Love among the Ruins," which Sten pronounced "Earse returzs." Goldwyn interrupted, yelling, "If this scene isn't the greatest love scene ever put on film, the whole goddamn picture will go right up out of the sewer," and he turned and walked off the set.

Cooper turned to Vidor and asked, "Did he say it or didn't he?"

"He said it," Vidor answered. The cast and crew exploded into laughter. Vidor could not restore order. Every time Sten now said, "Earse returzs," everyone started to howl. Vidor called it a day and was forced to shoot the love scene on another day.

When the picture was previewed in Glendale a few weeks later, Goldwyn emerged from the theater and signaled to Vidor that he needed to speak to him. He told Vidor, "You'll have to shoot the big love scene over." The reason? "That girl can't say 'earse.'"

THEODORA GOES WILD (1936)

Theodora Goes Wild opens on a sign, welcoming visitors to Lynnfield, "The biggest little town in Connecticut—Population 4,426." You could imagine Lynnfield (sounding very much like Litchfield) would be just about the size of a Bridgewater or Cornwall. The editor of the local paper, the *Lynnfield Bugle*, is named Jed Waterbury, also an allusion to Connecticut.

Lynnfield is a town where neighbors look out for neighbors, and everyone knows everyone's business. Therein lies the trouble, which comes when a group of small-minded busybodies headed by the town gossip, Rebecca Perry (Spring Byington), tries to stop Jed Waterbury (Thomas Mitchell) from serializing the sexy bestseller *The Sinner* in the *Lynnfield Bugle*, because it's obscene—even though they have all secretly read it.

She may play the organ in church on Sunday, but the author of *The Sinner* is none other than Lynnfield's own Theodora Lynn (Irene Dunne), writing under the pseudonym of Caroline Adams. Theodora is a direct descendant of the founders of Lynnfield, and if the town discovered she was the author, it would bring disgrace to her family, especially her two puritanical aunts, Aunt Mary (Elisabeth Risdon) and Aunt Elsie (Margaret McWade), with whom Theodora resides.

She travels to New York to visit with her uncle John (Robert Greig), and to tell her publisher, Arthur Stevenson (Thurston Hall), that the charade must end. Stevenson introduces her to the artist who has designed her book jacket, Michael Grant (Melvyn Douglas). Michael presumes she's

Caroline Adams and up for a night on the town. Attempting to live up to her image as a sexually liberated woman, Theodora goes out drinking with him.

A now-tipsy Theodora returns with Michael to his apartment, where he plays soft music and shows her his etchings and a risqué painting of Eve and the Serpent. Theodora is a writer who writes about sex but has never experienced it, so she runs from the apartment with her honor intact. The Production Code's director, Joseph I. Breen, was unhappy that the "decent" and "churchgoing" characters in *Theodora Goes Wild* were "made to appear ridiculous, stupid, and silly," while their city counterparts and Theodora (who engages in "extra-marital activities, drunkenness, and debauchery") were "made to look attractive."

The small-town values of Connecticut transform shallow playboy Michael Grant (Melvyn Douglas), who turns his back on New York society after meeting Lynnfield's own Theodora (Irene Dunne) in *Theodora Goes Wild* (1936). (Photofest)

On a hunch, Michael follows Theodora to Lynnfield and is amused to discover her secret. Theodora, however, is not amused to find Michael in full hobo gear, mowing her front lawn, masquerading as a tramp looking for work (I guess if you're as handsome as Melvyn Douglas, that works), and accompanied by a stray dog named Jake. Theodora pleads with Michael to leave her alone, but Michael is enjoying his own charade. After threatening to reveal Theodora's sideline career as an author, unless he can stay, Theodora reluctantly lets him take up residence with her and her aunts, as their handyman.

Michael spends his first morning filling up on a large breakfast courtesy of Theodora's spinster aunts, who are naturally wary of this strange man and his dog living under the same roof with them. Meanwhile, Michael is happy to be away from New York and warms to the ambience of small-town Lynnfield. Theodora takes him fishing and berry picking. Country living clearly appeals to Michael, and soon, the two realize they are in love. Still, he teases Theodora that he's not leaving town until she reveals to her aunts that she is Caroline Adams. As they picnic by a stream, in order to give her courage, Michael recounts to Theodora how he refused to follow in the footsteps of his father, a banker who didn't want him to pursue a career as an artist. Michael intuits her true feelings, telling her, "Everything Lynnfield doesn't want you to feel, you write about."

Meanwhile, the unusual housing arrangement is making town tongues wag. Rebecca Perry and the other women of Lynnfield confront Theodora with her immoral behavior and ask that Michael leave town. Theodora, inspired by Michael's words, finally rebels, not only telling Rebecca Perry she's in love with Michael, but revealing that she is Caroline Adams, the trashy author they are all obsessed with. Michael has given Theodora the courage to declare her independence, but he now confesses that he is not completely free himself; he is trapped in a loveless marriage to a wealthy society woman, a marriage his banker father arranged. Michael returns to New York, but Theodora decides to turn the tables on him, setting up camp in his apartment as Caroline Adams until he, too, declares his independence.

Theodora Goes Wild. Lynnfield, Connecticut, as imagined by Columbia's art director Stephen Goosson, on the studio's backlot. (Photofest)

Theodora assembles a group of reporters to reveal the plot of her next book, "How love came to a girl in a small New England town and the man who would call her 'Baby.' " Back in Lynnfield, Jed Waterbury and the *Bugle* are having a heyday writing about her antics. Uncle John Lynn brings news from Theodora's aunts that what they have always feared has happened: "Theodora has gone wild." Michael finally declares his independence, leaving his wife and his banker father back in stuffy New York society and returning to Theodora in Lynnfield, where he thanks her for giving him the courage to finally be free. The town of Lynnfield welcomes the couple, having learned a valuable lesson about tolerance.

Theodora Goes Wild is a terrific social comedy that punctures small-town hypocrisy and, as the title suggests, celebrates

Theodora Goes Wild. Aunt Mary (Elisabeth Risdon) and Aunt Elsie (Margaret McWade) keep a watchful eye on their niece, Theodora (Irene Dunne). Though neither actress was from Connecticut, they helped create the stereotype of the quintessential flinty Yankee spinsters, a concept that became ingrained with moviegoers. (Photofest)

Theodora teaching Michael how to fish is a metaphor for city dweller Michael, who is truly a fish out of water in the tranquil country setting. Irene Dunne's distinctive laugh and haughty way of speaking in *Theodora Goes Wild* may have been an imitation of Katharine Hepburn. Dunne was reluctant to do a comedy, but her entrée into the screwball genre garnered her a second Academy Award nomination and led to her starring with Cary Grant in *The Awful Truth* (1937), which was a smash hit. (Photofest)

CONNECTICUT IN THE MOVIES

Theodora's right to love whomever she wants with complete and utter abandon.

My grandfather, Melvyn Douglas, cited the director, Boleslawski—who had worked with the Group Theatre in Connecticut and followed the Stanislavsky acting method, which strove for realism—as a director who created an atmosphere in which actors felt free to experiment. An example of this is a scene in which Theodora is supposed to be romantically feeding Michael berries; instead, Dunne appears to intentionally keep stuffing his mouth with the fruit. Both actors appear to break, stifling their laughter as Michael starts choking—but the scene continues, Michael's face now completely stained with berries. It's messy and fun and out of character for studio films in which leading ladies and men were supposed to look perfect, but Boleslawski captured their playfulness. This naturalism sets it apart from other screwball comedies. In another scene, to achieve just the right shocked reaction from Irene Dunne, Boleslawski crept up behind her and shot off a blank cartridge from a handgun, getting what my grandfather called "the most breathless and bewildered on-screen entrance ever recorded." *Theodora Goes Wild* was Boleslawski's final completed film. He died just shy of turning forty-eight, and Hollywood lost what would surely have been one of its greatest directors.

Director Richard Boleslawski, Melvyn Douglas, and Irene Dunne with Aunt Elise's cat on the set of *Theodora Goes Wild*. (Photofest)

One of my great memories of watching my grandfather on-screen was at the 2017 TCM Classic Film Festival. The organizers had a nitrate print of *Theodora Goes Wild* scheduled for a late-night ten o'clock screening at the Egyptian Theatre, and they asked me to introduce the film and say a few words. I was not sure how many people would show up, but—lo and behold!—it was a packed house.

Many in the audience had not seen the film, and I was not sure what the reaction would be; I hoped it would be as funny as my introduction had touted it to be. The lights went down, and I took a seat in the balcony. I was instantly transported, feeling as if we were an audience in 1936 watching the film for the first time.

Laughter filled the theater as one of my favorite scenes played out: Michael is getting ready for bed. To tease Theodora from his bedroom, he whistles the song that was playing in his apartment the night he attempted to make love to her, a reminder of their past tryst. Theodora's aunts begin to chastise her for Michael's "infernal late-night whistling." An embarrassed Theodora tries to make him stop by loudly playing the piano and belting out, "Be still my heart!" But the louder she pounds and sings menacingly, "Be still my heart!" the louder he whistles his tune. A frustrated Theodora bangs on the keys nonstop as one aunt slams a door, shattering the glass, while the other slams the other door on the cat's tail, causing even more of a cacophony. The scene fades on Theodora pounding away like a madwoman on the piano while presumably Michael just goes to sleep.

There was an avalanche of laughter, cheers, and applause in the theater that brought tears to my eyes. Here was a film my grandfather had made eighty years earlier, still producing belly laughs! As we walked out of the theater after the screening, there was a sense of exhilaration from our shared late-night experience.

BRINGING UP BABY (1938)

Happiness and a million-dollar grant for his museum when a New York paleontologist, David Huxley (Cary Grant), meets a carefree heiress from Connecticut, Susan Vance (Katharine Hepburn), in *Bringing Up Baby* (1938). (Photofest)

Professor David Huxley has spent years assembling a brontosaurus skeleton at the Stuyvesant Museum of Natural History in New York City. Helping him has been his workmate, Miss Alice Swallow (Virginia Walker), to whom the professor is engaged. Theirs is not in any way a romantic pairing. Alice will hardly even let David kiss her, and keeps reminding him that theirs is a work relationship. There are no children, or even a honeymoon, in the couple's future. On the eve of their wedding, Huxley learns that the final bone needed to complete the dinosaur—an intercostal clavicle—has been

Postcard of the Yale Peabody Museum of Natural History at 170 Whitney Avenue in New Haven.

discovered, but he needs $1,000,000 to see the project through. Huxley is set to meet with an attorney, a Mr. Peabody (George Irving), who works for a wealthy Connecticut benefactress named Mrs. Carleton Random (May Robson), who just happens to be considering making a $1,000,000 grant to the museum.

The inspiration for the paleontologist, Huxley, came straight out of Connecticut. In fact, he's based on a Yale paleontologist, O. C. (Othniel Charles) Marsh. In 1879, Marsh was the first to name the genus Brontosaurus. The attorney representing Aunt Elizabeth in *Bringing Up Baby* is named Mr. Peabody, which is no coincidence. O. C. Marsh founded the Peabody Museum of Natural History in New Haven, Connecticut, thanks to an endowment from a wealthy uncle, George Peabody, and his skeletal dinosaur specimen can still be seen on display there.

Yale paleontologist O. C. (Othniel Charles) Marsh (1831–1899). Yes, Cary Grant's character in *Bringing Up Baby* was partially inspired by him. Hmm . . . I do *kind of* see a resemblance.

30   COUNTRY LIVING COMEDIES

Bringing Up Baby was modeled on the brontosaurus housed at the Peabody Museum in New Haven. (Photofest)

Katharine Hepburn's portrayal of heiress Susan Vance in *Bringing Up Baby* and her clipped, patrician way of speaking became synonymous with other screen portrayals of wealthy Connecticut heiresses, like Gloria Upson (Joanna Barnes) in *Auntie Mame* (1958). (Photofest)

Huxley meets Mr. Peabody on the golf course, where he unknowingly crosses paths with Mrs. Random's niece, Susan Vance. He's unable to make a good impression on Peabody because Susan keeps causing problems for him. She steals his golf ball and drives off in his car. Later, at another meeting between Huxley and Peabody, Susan trips him with a loose olive, smashes his top hat, rips his tailcoat up the back, and gets him accused of stealing a women's purse. Grant, who had been an acrobat and was a skilled comedian, taught Hepburn that the more depressed she looked when she went into a prank, the more the audience would laugh. Though the professor is completely frustrated with her—he calls her a "spoiled, conceited little scatterbrain"—Susan interprets his anger as proof of his love for her (which he, himself, will soon come to realize). Susan tricks David into driving with her to Connecticut in a ruse to stop him from marrying Alice Swallow. She neglects to tell him she's also bringing along a leopard named Baby that her brother has sent from Brazil as a gift for her aunt Elizabeth (although, of course, leopards are not native to Brazil). Baby responds to hearing his name in the song "I Can't Give You Anything but Love, Baby."

Susan's bad driving causes a crash with a truck filled with chickens. Baby jumps out of the car and eats most of the cargo (off-screen, thankfully), consequently leaving David covered in feathers when he and Susan arrive at her aunt's house in fictional Westlake (which I'd like to think pays homage to lovely Westport).

Mr. Gogarty (Barry Fitzgerald), the Irish caretaker who likes the bottle, leaves the barn door open, and Baby escapes. Meanwhile, a nearby circus has a vicious leopard that needs to be taken to

Charles Ruggles as Major Horace Applegate, May Robson as Aunt Elizabeth, and Skippy as George the dog join Cary Grant as Dr. David Huxley and Katharine Hepburn as Susan Vance in *Bringing Up Baby* (Photofest). The *Bringing Up Baby* country house was what moviegoers imagined all Connecticut houses to look like. This "Connecticut style" featured stone walls, a large fireplace, beamed ceilings, Colonial Revival furniture, Windsor chairs, a Dutch door, and lots of chintz. It was designed by art director Van Nest Polglase. When Howard Hawks's wife saw the film, she redecorated the interior of their Bel Air home in the same "Connecticut" style. (Photofest)

Bridgeport and, by the kind of coincidence that only happens in movies, that leopard escapes as well. Now two leopards are on the loose. (The trained leopard Nissa played both parts, by the way. Hepburn had no problem working with Nissa, but Grant chose to shoot his scenes in cutaways and had a stand-in for one scene in which the cat rubs against his leg.)

David fares no better in the country than in the city. Aunt Elizabeth's dog, George (played by Skippy, also known as Asta, the wire-haired fox terrier from MGM's *Thin Man* films), steals his rare, historically important bone and runs away with it, while Susan takes his clothes to prevent him from returning to New York. As David mumbles to himself, "I'm losing my mind, that's all. Roaming around Connecticut without any clothes on!" he emerges from Susan's bedroom wearing her frilly peignoir and, naturally, meets Susan's aunt Elizabeth for the first time.

After a back-and-forth ("Who are you?"), she asks him why he's dressed that way. David jumps up in the air and shrieks, "Because I just went gay all of a sudden!" In addition to being an ad-lib by Grant and the first time the word "gay" was used on-

CONNECTICUT IN THE MOVIES 33

screen in a major motion picture to connote homosexuality, it demonstrates how Hawks was able to visually convey the complete role reversal David and Susan have undergone. Susan is literally driving the courtship when she drives him to Connecticut. Once there, she suggests he would look more handsome without his glasses and removes them, something a man might do to an uptight but sexy spinster. After dubbing him "Mr. Bone," an obvious double entendre, she tells her aunt, "If he gets some clothes, he'll go away, and he's the only man I want to marry."

In New York, David's life was orderly and neatly planned out. Now Susan has completely emasculated him, making him the "woman" in the relationship and forcing him to see his life from her perspective, while wearing her clothes. It's at this point that David begins his transformation. "I'm not quite myself today," he tells Aunt Elizabeth, and that's true; his identity, his life's work, his bone, and now even his clothes have been taken by this incorrigible woman. Before it's all over, Susan even finds a way to land Huxley, herself, and their Connecticut neighbor, Major Applegate (Charles Ruggles), a big-game hunter, in the Westlake jail. Huxley finds he is no longer angry; Susan's unbridled spirit, audacity, and disdain for what people think, have broken him, and he realizes he's having the time of his life.

Howard Hawks's first assignment for RKO Studios, where he had recently signed a six-picture deal, was meant to be the prestigious film *Gunga Din*, loosely based on the Rudyard Kipling poem, not a rather slight screwball comedy with an actress RKO was trying to rid itself of. Because of a delay in casting on *Gunga Din*, Hawks read through a pile of RKO-optioned material, choosing something the studio had purchased from *Collier's* magazine for a mere $1,000—a short story by female writer Hagar Wilde, entitled "Bringing Up Baby," about a panther on the loose in Connecticut.

Wilde, a complete unknown, was suddenly flown to Hollywood and partnered with the seasoned writer Dudley Nichols to begin work on the screenplay. Soon a love story was happening on-screen and off- as Wilde and Nichols began a romance that continued through the writing of the film *Carefree* (1938), with Ginger Rogers and Fred Astaire. Wilde worked with Hawks again when she wrote the screenplay for *I Was a Male War Bride* (1949), starring Cary Grant. As for *Gunga Din* (1939), it was not Hawks but George Stevens who ended up making that picture for RKO.

Hawks had issues with Hepburn, who was trying to "act" funny, so Hawks called on vaudevillian comic actor Walter Catlett to work with her. Hepburn was so pleased with Catlett that she asked Hawks to create a part for him, which set the stage for the extended scene with the entire cast at the Westlake jail. Catlett's character, Slocum, is priceless as the befuddled constable who mistakenly thinks he's uncovered a crime ring. This vignette—in which all the characters end up in the same place—was re-created by Peter Bogdanovich in *What's Up, Doc?* (1972), a tribute to Hawks and *Bringing Up Baby*.

Eventually Mr. Peabody and Aunt Elizabeth straighten everything out. David's identity as "Mr.

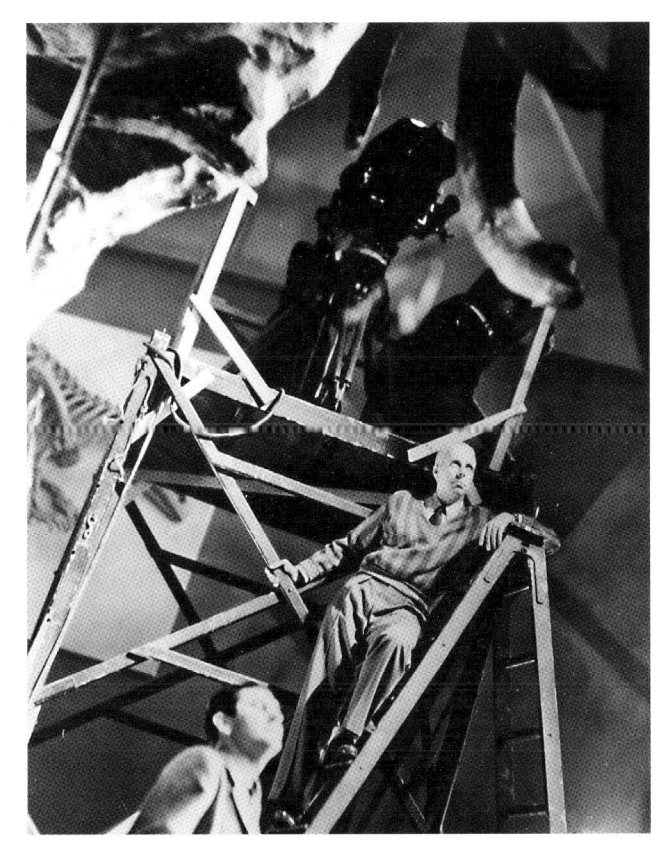

Director Howard Hawks on the set of *Bringing Up Baby*. (Photofest)

Bone" is resolved, Baby is returned, George the dog brings back the intercostal clavicle, and David receives the $1,000,000 grant. More crucial is his realization that there is something more important in life than work. He was having fun in Connecticut, which proves once again that Connecticut cures you! After breaking it off with Alice Swallow, David is reunited with Susan when she brings him news that her aunt has let her give him the endowment. "I've just discovered that was the best day I ever had in my whole life!" he tells her. "Did you really have a good time?" she asks with delight. "Yes, I did!" he says, and they kiss.

Susan's attitude and Hepburn's personality are interchangeable. In Todd McCarthy's book *Howard Hawks: The Grey Fox of Hollywood* (1997), he writes, "There was never any real doubt that anyone other than Katharine Hepburn would play Susan . . . Hawks had imagined that she'd have no problem because the role was a close fit to her own background as a clever, imaginative, outspoken New England heiress."

As RKO honchos began to see the dailies, however, they were unhappy with her. They complained that her hair was out of control, that she lacked glamour and sex appeal. She wears pants in many scenes—a trademark Hepburn look. Hawks disregarded notes for her to be sweeter, more romantic, and less hard. In fact, it's Hepburn's jaunty, confident manner, the hair, the pants, her look, the famous patrician speaking voice, that help to sell the premise that we are in Connecticut, not on the RKO ranch in Encino where the "Connecticut" scenes were filmed.

Like Susan, she had the last laugh. After Hepburn was dropped by RKO after *Bringing Up Baby* and labeled "box office poison," she returned to New York to star in Philip Barry's play *The Philadelphia Story*. With Howard Hughes's help, she purchased the film rights and returned to Hollywood in triumph, starring in the 1940 film, directed by George Cukor, and choosing Grant as her costar.

CONNECTICUT IN THE MOVIES

Alec Walker (Cary Grant) is stuck in a marriage to a New York society wife. While living away from her at his country house in Connecticut, he meets and falls in love with his neighbor, a widow named Julie Eden (Carole Lombard), with a daughter, Ellen (Peggy Ann Garner). In 1946, Garner would receive an Academy Juvenile Award for her performance in Elia Kazan's *A Tree Grows in Brooklyn* (1945). (Photofest)

IN NAME ONLY (1939)

An unhappily married New Yorker, Alec (Cary Grant), purchases his childhood home in Connecticut after meeting the beautiful and innocent Julie (Carole Lombard) in fictional Bridgefield, Connecticut (sounding very much like a combination of Bridgeport and Ridgefield). Ironically, *In Name Only* (1939), based on the novel *Memory of Love* by Bessie Breuer (1934), was conceived as a follow-up for Cary Grant and Katharine Hepburn, reuniting them after *Bringing Up Baby*, but that picture's disappointing box office led RKO to drop Hepburn's contract and the part was rewritten for Carole Lombard, an actress with whom Grant had made two other films—*Sinners in the Sun* (1932) and *The Eagle and the Hawk* (1933). With Lombard on board, the script became more serious, although there are comic moments revolving around—you guessed it—country living.

Now essentially a melodrama, *In Name Only* follows a similar country living plot of a man transformed after finding true love in Connecticut. Alec Walker (Grant) is a wealthy New Yorker spending time at his Connecticut estate, away from his wife Maida (Kay Francis) and their unhappy marriage. One day while out horseback riding, he meets his Connecticut neighbor Julie Eden (Carole Lombard). Julie is a recently widowed commercial artist. In addition to being beautiful, Alec can sense that she is simple and pure—everything his Maida is not. Julie's values and her lifestyle attract Alec, and he falls in love with her, determined that they will spend their life together at his estate.

Cunning Maida, however, is willing to go to any length to keep her wealthy husband and her position in New York society, and refuses to give Alec a divorce so he can marry Julie. A distraught Alec goes on a drinking binge and almost dies after catching pneumonia. Julie selflessly nurses Alec back to health, convincing him he has something to live for, even if they can't be together. Alec recovers and Maida relents, so he and Julie can begin to build a future life in Bridgefield.

Elizabeth Lane (Barbara Stanwyck) and Jefferson Jones (Dennis Morgan) fantasize about a house in the country in *Christmas in Connecticut* from Warner Bros. The postwar romantic comedy symbolizing home and family became a holiday classic. (Photofest)

CHAPTER 3
CHRISTMAS IN CONNECTICUT

CHRISTMAS IN CONNECTICUT (1945)

Christmas in Connecticut (1945) ups the ante of country living comedies, setting the action in a magical Connecticut winter wonderland farmhouse central to the plot. It marks the first time the word "Connecticut" was used in a movie title, and was inspired by the writing of Gladys Taber, a Southbury resident who lived at a real-life magical residence called Stillmeadow Farm.

Warner Bros. released *Christmas in Connecticut* in August 1945, just before World War II officially ended. The war-themed love story about a girl, a boy, and the special house where they meet was a surprise hit for the studio. One of its premieres, which included a Christmas parade, was even held in Norwalk. Over the years, *Christmas in Connecticut* has also become a much-loved holiday film—in part because of the presence of a Connecticut country house.

The fictional town of Stanfield (sounding very much like Stamford and Litchfield put together) was created on a Hollywood soundstage by Stanley Fleischer and Casey Roberts, art director and set decorator, respectively. They managed to build a house in Connecticut that feels so real and cozy, you'd like to look for it on a map and move there. Fleischer worked on more than one hundred films while at Warner Bros., many of them horror movies, such as *The Beast with Five Fingers* (1946),

House of Wax (1953), and *Them!* (1954). In *Christmas in Connecticut* his sets serve as a main character, at times upstaging the actors who stand in front of them with their beauty. Hollywood's interpretation of Connecticut is once again idyllic—Currier and Ives on steroids.

Stanfield is a tucked-away little haven where folks get around by horse and sleigh because it's always snowing. They arrive to see a stone farmhouse fronted by a circular driveway. There's a barn, complete with perfectly placed straw and a large, happy, brown-eyed cow. Inside the home there's a cavernous living room with wood-beamed ceilings and the largest fireplace I have ever seen. The colonial design features lots of pine paneling, bedrooms with four-poster beds, and braided wool rugs on the wide-planked floors. The eat-in kitchen is cozy but features the latest in modern appliances, and you can bake all the pies and cakes you want. In the living room a grand piano awaits someone to play beautiful music. Time stands still in Stanfield until you can discover who you are, whom you love, and what you really want.

Paramount's Edith Head had done Stanwyck's wardrobe for *Double Indemnity* (1944), which she loved, and so Stanwyck requested that Head be hired for *Christmas in Connecticut*. Studio head Jack Warner agreed, but to save money he insisted they recycle the same fur coat Joan Crawford had famously worn in *Mildred Pierce* (1945). The fur coat story is especially funny when juxtaposed against an early scene in the movie, in which Stanwyck's character declares, "What a girl won't do for a mink coat!" (Photofest)

Although never seen or mentioned, the other main character in *Christmas in Connecticut* is a homemaker, author, cookbook writer, and professor named Gladys Taber, a columnist for *Ladies' Home Journal*. Taber was the real-life inspiration for the Elizabeth Lane (Barbara Stanwyck) character, a homemaking columnist for the fictional *Smart Housekeeping* magazine. The difference is that Lane is only pretending to live on a Connecticut farm!

Elizabeth Lane's homespun column, "Diary of a Housewife," is central to the plot of *Christmas in Connecticut*. Her column is so beloved that when Lane writes about searching for a perfect rocking chair in an antique store—"just like Granny had"—readers start sending her rocking chairs, until she's amassed thirty-eight of them! It's also been noted that Elizabeth Lane bears a similarity to the future homemaking guru Martha Stewart, who lived on a farm in Connecticut called Turkey

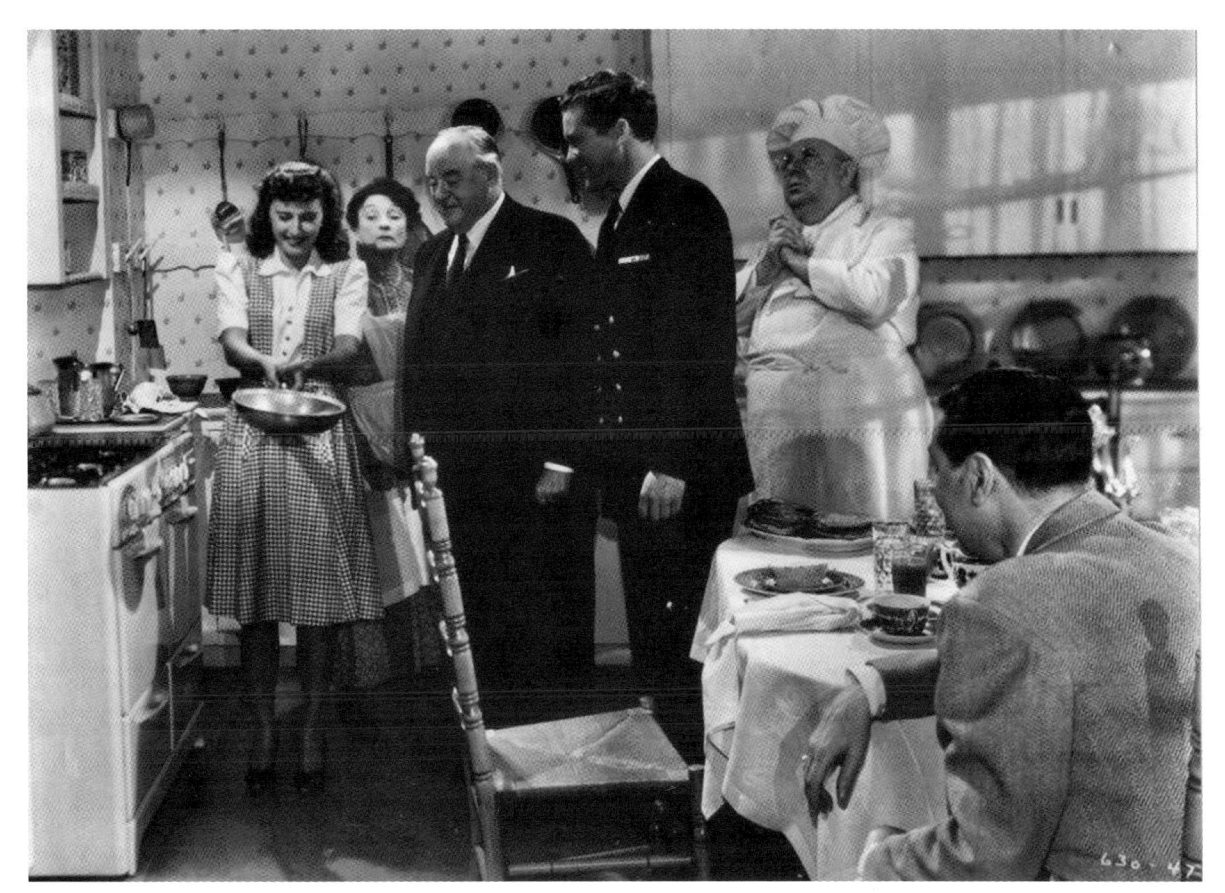

Elizabeth Lane (Barbara Stanwyck) flips flapjacks for her guests (Sidney Greenstreet, Dennis Morgan, S. Z. Sakall, and others) in her perfect Connecticut kitchen. The Elizabeth Lane character was based on Connecticut author and homemaker Gladys Taber. (Photofest)

Hill, but Gladys Taber was making "country living" chic way back in the 1930s.

Taber was herself a Connecticut resident, living with her husband and daughter in a 1690 farmhouse in Southbury called Stillmeadow Farm. It was at Stillmeadow that Taber began penning her column, "Diary of Domesticity," for *Ladies' Home Journal*, beginning in 1937, dispensing tips about homemaking. A sample of her musings: "For no matter what heaven may be like, there is no use just waiting for it. I'll take mine now, with an open fire, and apples toasting on a stick and good friends gathered around the hearth."

This kind of heartfelt sentiment also aligns with the plot of *Christmas in Connecticut*, which revolves around a sailor named Jefferson Jones (Dennis Morgan) who is away at war and dreaming of a home-cooked meal while reading *Smart Housekeeping*. In the real world, copies of *Ladies' Home Journal* were regularly sent out in care packages to overseas GIs. Gladys Taber corresponded with soldiers and even included recipes in some of her letters. Taber wrote an astonishing fifty-nine books, many of them about life at Stillmeadow Farm, including *Harvest at Stillmeadow* (1940) and

Stillmeadow Farm, where Gladys Taber lived, in Southbury.

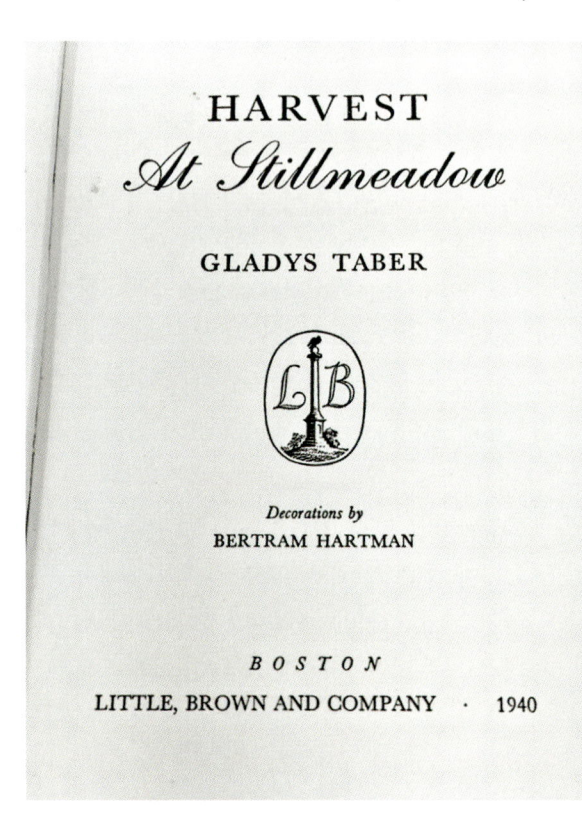

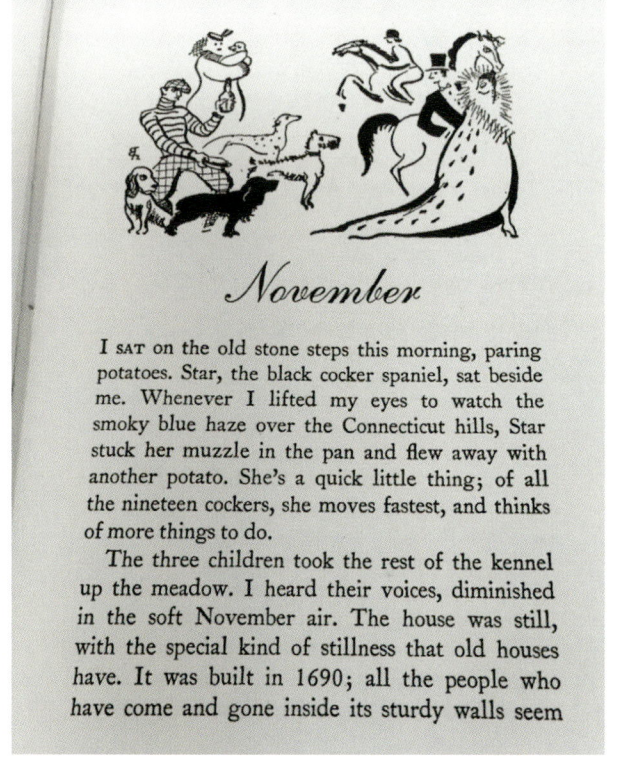

HARVEST
At Stillmeadow

GLADYS TABER

Decorations by
BERTRAM HARTMAN

BOSTON
LITTLE, BROWN AND COMPANY · 1940

November

I SAT on the old stone steps this morning, paring potatoes. Star, the black cocker spaniel, sat beside me. Whenever I lifted my eyes to watch the smoky blue haze over the Connecticut hills, Star stuck her muzzle in the pan and flew away with another potato. She's a quick little thing; of all the nineteen cockers, she moves fastest, and thinks of more things to do.

The three children took the rest of the kennel up the meadow. I heard their voices, diminished in the soft November air. The house was still, with the special kind of stillness that old houses have. It was built in 1690; all the people who have come and gone inside its sturdy walls seem

Harvest at Stillmeadow, one of Gladys Taber's many homemaking books, written at her Southbury farm. A page from the book, which is similar to the words of the movie's "Elizabeth Lane."

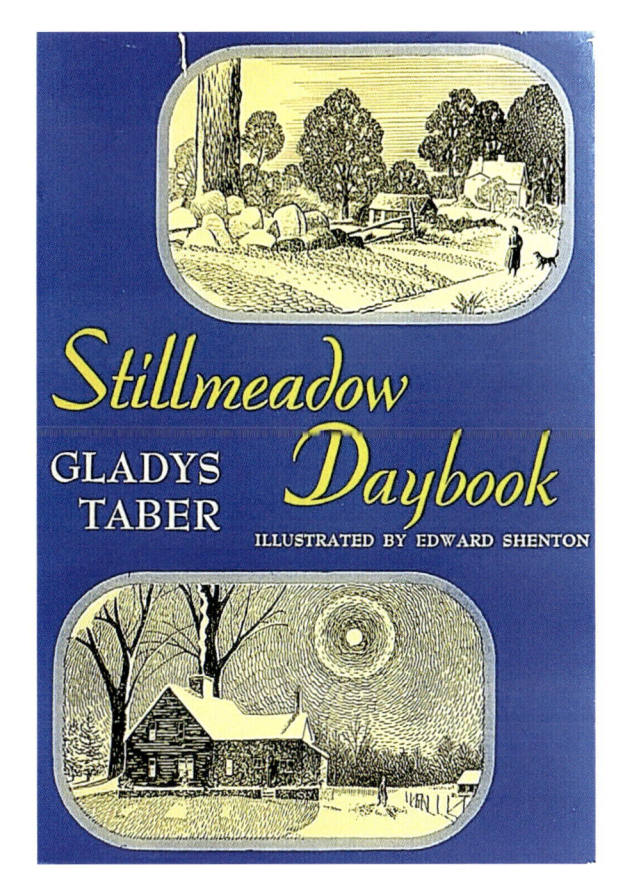

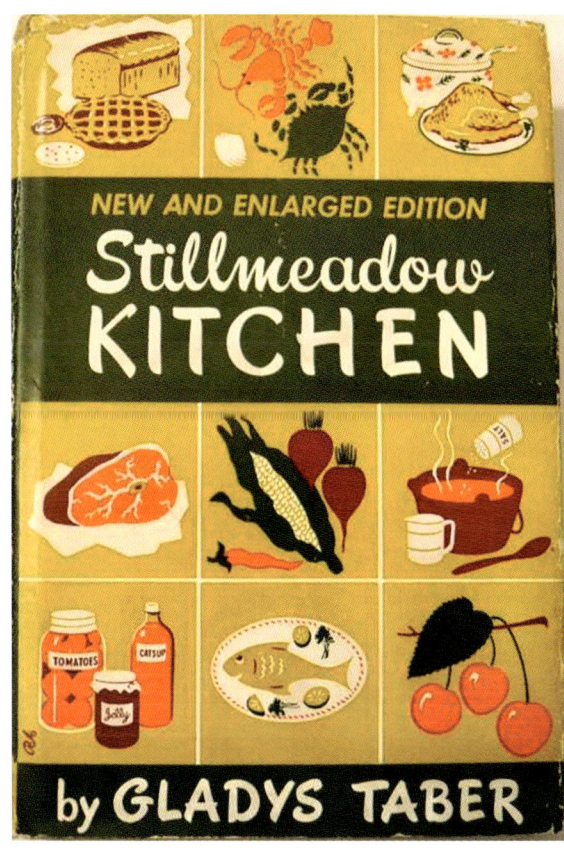

Stillmeadow Kitchen (1947). In 1959, Taber began writing another homemaking column, "Butternut Wisdom," for *Family Circle* magazine.

"Christmas is a bridge," wrote Gladys Taber. "We need bridges, as the river of time flows past. Today's Christmas should mean creating happy hours for tomorrow and reliving those of yesterday." Elizabeth Lane's observations in the movie are similar in spirit; for example, she says: "From my living room window as I write, I can look out across the broad front lawns of our farm, like a lovely picture postcard of wintry New England." Gladys Taber died in 1980 and is buried in the graveyard of Southbury Congregational Church.

And now back to our movie.

Publisher Alexander Yardley (Sydney Greenstreet) is looking for a good publicity story. When he hears that a war hero, Jefferson Jones, wants his first home-cooked meal to be one of star columnists Elizabeth Lane's recipes, he arranges for Jones to spend Christmas with Lane and her family at their farm in Connecticut, knowing it will be great PR for the magazine. He even invites himself along.

The problem is that Lane has not been entirely truthful about her status as a homemaker. In fact, Elizabeth Lane's perfect life as a Connecticut farm wife and mother has been complete fiction.

CONNECTICUT IN THE MOVIES

She is actually a single career gal living in a cramped New York apartment. She can't even cook! It's Lane's friend, Felix Bassenak (S. Z. "Cuddles" Sakall), who runs a Hungarian restaurant, who has been providing her with recipes for her column. (Sakall himself loved to cook in real life.) When we first meet Felix, he's feeding Lane a mushroom omelet. She asks him, "Did you write up those recipes for next month's article? What am I cooking?" Felix recites his menu, "Breasts of gray dove sautéed with peaches grenadine and chicken soup." (Warning: If you are seeing the film for the first time, I suggest you make a few snacks, because it's going to make you very hungry. The pancakes look especially tasty, and you'll learn how to flip flapjacks along with Felix.)

Sakall and Stanwyck had worked together previously in *Ball of Fire* (1941) and enjoyed great on-screen chemistry. Along with being Elizabeth's alter ego here, Felix is not afraid to steer her away from marrying her long-suffering boyfriend, dour architect John Sloan (Reginald Gardiner). It is Sloan who owns the country house in Connecticut, but Lane has no interest in giving up her career to marry him.

Fearing she will lose her job if Yardley discovers her lie, Lane asks Sloan to use his Connecticut farmhouse to pull off the stunt. Sloan agrees, but only if Lane will finally marry him, to which she consents. Needless to say, the arrival of the handsome and affable sailor Jefferson Jones quickly gives her second thoughts.

Jones changes Elizabeth's feelings about city living. Looking around the house, he says, "This is the kind of place I always wanted to be in. A home." It's through his eyes that Lane begins to imagine herself settling down here—with Jones and Felix, not Sloan. While Jones is entirely at home here raiding the kitchen for a late-night snack of cold chicken or bathing the neighbor's baby and changing its diaper, stuffy Sloan looks out of place in his own house. Jones mentions that he was an artist before the war. In many of the country living comedies, it's "an artist" who finds serenity in Connecticut.

As Christmas approaches, Jones plays the piano and sings "O Little Town of Bethlehem" while Lane decorates the Christmas tree. They are the picture of postwar domesticity, as Lane comes to the realization that she has found what had been missing in her life. In another scene, as she descends the stairs, we see behind her old family portraits, a grandfather clock, lots of wide-plank pine paneling—all symbols of the history of the house. After a country hoedown and a sleigh ride with Jones, she says dreamily, "What a night. Moonlight, snow . . . and a cow." Sounds like yet another New Yorker has fallen under the spell of country living.

After her Oscar-nominated role as a cold-blooded femme fatale in *Double Indemnity* (1945), Barbara Stanwyck was looking for a comedy, so when Bette Davis passed on *Christmas in Connecticut*, Stanwyck stepped in. It was the first of three films she made with British director Peter Godfrey,

One detail about the John Sloan (Reginald Denny) architect character that's interesting is that he is designing "multiple dwelling units" in Connecticut—basically, prefab housing for the postwar generation. Connecticut was, in fact, home to a unique experiment in prefab housing called the Lustron house, invented by Carl Strandlund and dubbed, "The House America Has Been Waiting For." The cost for a porcelain-enameled-steel unit was about $3,000, and it came in four different models, called The Westchester, The Westchester Deluxe, The Newport, and The Meadowbrook. Only forty-two Lustrons were built in Connecticut before Strandlund went out of business. A few remain, including one in Berlin and one in Meriden, pictured below. (Photofest)

who was able to bring out Stanwyck's softer side. They followed it up with *The Two Mrs. Carrolls* (1947) and *Cry Wolf* (1947).

Stanwyck was herself a career woman, often choosing work over family life. *Christmas in Connecticut* is significant in its depiction of working women. Throughout the film, working women are seen as the motor that is making America run. Elizabeth Lane is a successful magazine columnist. While she is working from home on her column, a Black delivery girl delivers Lane's fur coat, which she had purchased for herself. Later, at the farm, there are two working moms who leave their babies for Lane to watch while they head off for a long day at the local war plant. There's also the VA nurse, who has my favorite inside-joke line: "I took the wrong train and landed in Bridgeport."

The film also never implies that once men returned from war, women would have to return to traditional roles as housewives. It's refreshing that Lane doesn't even have to choose love over her career. Yardley tells Sloan that he wants the prestige of a husband-and-wife team on his magazine—Sloan in the home-planning department and Lane in the homemaking department, thus depicting a world where men and women are working side by side at the same jobs.

A lot of the comedy—scripted by Lionel Houser and Adele Comandini—is about Lane's indifference to marriage and her ineptitude as a homemaker. Lane doesn't know how to change or bathe a baby. The film pokes fun at things women were supposed to be good at, like being a nurturing parent or a good cook, or supposed to want, such as a nice home and a husband to provide for them. The film even surprises with a feminist happy ending. Lane can "have it all." She doesn't marry Sloan; she ends up with Jones, and she gets to keep her job at the magazine. But my question is: Who ended up living in that fabulous house in Stanfield?

HOLIDAY INN (1942)

Holiday Inn (1942) takes place in another fictional town of Connecticut, this one called Midville (much like Milford). The film centers around a house that will take center stage as a supper club. Jim Hardy (Bing Crosby), Ted Hanover (Fred Astaire), and Lila Dixon (Virginia Dale) are a popular New York song-and-dance team, but after being spurned in love, Jim decides to get out of the rat race and retire to Connecticut. After a few months and a few mishaps with cows—there are lots of cow gags in country living comedies—Jim gets the idea to turn his Connecticut farmhouse into a nightclub, open only on holidays.

Soon, people from all over are visiting Jim's nightclub, now called Holiday Inn, to enjoy its holiday-themed musical numbers. Jim has achieved a kind of bliss living in the country, but love has eluded him. Then Linda Mason (Marjorie Reynolds) comes to work at Jim's club. As Christmas approaches, they get cozy by the roaring fire and—in a scene reminiscent of the one

Jim Hardy (Bing Crosby) serves up some holiday punch to his love, Linda Mason (Marjorie Reynolds), in the homespun Christmas film, *Holiday Inn*. Kemmons Wilson, the founder of Holiday Inn Hotels, named his chain after this movie. (Photofest)

in *Christmas in Connecticut*, in which Jones sings a carol while Lane decorates the Christmas tree—Jim sings Linda a little tune he was inspired to write while living at his Connecticut farm, a seasonal ditty called . . . "White Christmas."

The original concept for the story was actually songwriter Irving Berlin's. Berlin wrote a dozen songs for the film, including "White Christmas," which would go on to win the Academy Award that year for Best Original Song, as well as instantly becoming one of the most popular Christmas songs of all time.

Jim's happiness is soon interrupted when his old partner Ted turns up and steals Linda away from him to be his new dance partner, eventually whisking her off to Hollywood to make a movie about Holiday Inn. With the newspapers announcing Linda's engagement to Ted, the lovelorn Jim is talked into following her west, where he finds that her movie studio has faithfully re-created his Connecticut inn on a soundstage. Art imitates reality when the director within the film tells Linda, "Your Hollywood success was empty. You've lost the one man you loved. You know, the usual hoke," which happens to be exactly the way she feels! She tearfully films a scene in which she sings "White Christmas," only to be pleasantly surprised when Jim joins in. The picture ends with the happy couple back together, and also back in snowy Connecticut, at the real Holiday Inn, reunited for a New Year's show with both Ted and Lila.

CONNECTICUT IN THE MOVIES

47

With *Holiday Inn* and *Christmas in Connecticut*, the holiday romantic comedy was born. Tragically, the director of *Holiday Inn*, Mark Sandrich, died of a heart attack at age forty-four while prepping for *Blue Skies* (1945), a film that would reunite Crosby and Astaire. He was replaced on that project by Stuart Heisler. The success of Sandrich's *Holiday Inn* (1942), however, would seal Connecticut's reputation as *the* place to set your Christmas movie. Thus did many films after *Holiday Inn* feature Connecticut as their central location.

Inspired by his move to Connecticut, Jim Hardy (Bing Crosby) will write the song "White Christmas" in the film, and the world will be forever thankful. Speaking of white Christmases, the "snow" used in *Holiday Inn*, and many other holiday films at the time, was actually made from white chrysotile asbestos. Filmmakers were not aware that it was toxic. (Photofest)

THE FAMILY STONE (2005)

An uptight New York career girl, Meredith Morton (Sarah Jessica Parker), spends Christmas with her boyfriend, Everett Stone (Dermot Mulroney), at his family's (Diane Keaton, Craig T. Nelson, Rachel McAdams) country house in Thayer, Connecticut, where she finds true love—just not with the person she originally thought!

The Family Stone was partially filmed in Connecticut, citing Greenwich and Riverside as locations. They were lucky enough to get real snow, which adds Christmas charm. Most of the action of the film takes place in a beautiful house in Greenwich, built in 1860 (which recently sold for $4,000,000). The interiors were designed to look cluttered and homey. As the weekend progresses, Meredith realizes she and Everett are wrong for each other, but Everett's brother Ben (Luke Wilson) might be a perfect match.

The Family Stone (2005) is one of the best contemporary Christmas comedies. It follows traditional themes of country living comedies, in which sophisticated New Yorkers discover, through the charm of small-town Connecticut living, more authentic versions of themselves. Sarah Jessica Parker described her character as "controlling, rigid, and tightly wound." The Stones are eccentric and fun-loving, and they teach Meredith—similar to the lesson of *Bringing Up Baby*—that life is meant to be lived.

After initially being rejected by Everett's family, Meredith ends up becoming a Stone family

The success of films like *Christmas in Connecticut* made Connecticut a natural place to set Christmas films. *The Family Stone* is a modern-day take on the classic country living theme. Meredith Morton (Sarah Jessica Parker) is the overworked and jaded New Yorker who spends Christmas in Greenwich, Connecticut, with her boyfriend Everett Stone (Dermot Mulroney) and his eccentric family. (Photofest)

Meredith (Sarah Jessica Parker) tries to show the Stone family she's more than a career girl. Her attempt at being a homemaker—similar to *Christmas in Connecticut*—will soon have disastrous results. (Photofest)

The house from *The Family Stone* is in Greenwich.

member herself when she marries Everett's brother, Ben. Her sister, Julie, ends up with Everett, and many happy Christmases continue in Connecticut.

CHRISTMAS CORNUCOPIA OF HALLMARK FILMS

A slew of Hallmark Christmas movies has made Connecticut look like Santa's backyard and a cozy place to spend the holidays—and, yes, still discover who you are. Here are a just a few to keep in mind if you want to binge-watch, have a Connecticut-themed Hallmark movie viewing party, or just visit the locations with some candy canes and hot chocolate.

Broadcasting Christmas (2016) stars Melissa Joan Hart, a Connecticut resident.

Romance at Reindeer Lodge (2017) used a house on Ridge Road near Mount Carmel Avenue in North Haven as its Reindeer Lodge. A scene involving real reindeer was filmed at South Windsor's Dzen Tree Farm—"Where Family Traditions Are Made"—a must around the holidays. Scenes were also shot at Branford's annual holiday "Shop and Stroll" event, where P. S. Fine Stationers at 1028 Main Street was chosen as a location because the production designers admired their Christmas window display.

Christmas on Honeysuckle Lane (2018) was shot in Wethersfield and features that city's Silas W. Robbins House.

Christmas at Pemberley Manor (2018) was shot in Essex and Old Lyme.

A Very Nutty Christmas (2018) was filmed in Mystic, Mystic Village, and Centerbrook.

Holiday for Heroes (2019) was shot in Norwich, Stonington, and New London.

Rediscovering Christmas (2019) was filmed in Old Wethersfield and Hartford.

One Royal Holiday (2021) was made in Putnam.

Christmas in Harlem (2021) was shot on Capitol Avenue in Hartford.

Next Stop Christmas (2021) features the Essex Steam Train.

Ghost of Christmas (2022) was filmed in Hartford.

The Hallmark film *Christmas at Pemberley Manor* (2018) was filmed in Old Lyme (above). It also features the Griswold Inn in Essex. Director Colin Theys, a Connecticut native, has made many holiday-themed films, but his real love is horror movies, as you'll learn in chapter 13, "Creepy Connecticut." (Courtesy Colin Theys)

Filmed in Old Wethersfield and Hartford, *Rediscovering Christmas* stars B. J. Britt and Jessica Lowndes, and was also directed by Colin Theys. (Courtesy Colin Theys)

It's beginning to look a lot like Christmas—even though this scene from *Christmas at Pemberley Manor* was filmed in June. (Courtesy Colin Theys)

Three titans of screwball: Cary Grant, Melvyn Douglas, and Myrna Loy. (Photofest)

CHAPTER 4
THE DREAM OF SUBURBIA

MR. BLANDINGS BUILDS HIS DREAM HOUSE (1948)

You'll recall that in 1914, Sherlock Holmes actor William Gillette designed and built his castle in the hills overlooking the Connecticut River for a cost of over $1,000,000, a staggering amount at that time. In postwar America, though, every man could build his "castle" in Connecticut in an affordable new land called "suburbia." No other film captured the trials and tribulations of home building in quite the excruciatingly funny way that *Mr. Blandings Builds His Dream House* (1948) did, while tapping into a uniquely American postwar ideal. Everyone deserves their dream home. That home just happened to be in Connecticut.

A New York advertising executive, Jim Blandings (Cary Grant), his wife, Muriel (Myrna Loy), and their two daughters, Joan (Sharyn Moffett) and Betsy (Connie Marshall), are living in a cramped New York City apartment. While Muriel is contemplating an expensive apartment renovation, Jim is pining for more space and a better quality of life. While working on the "Wham" ham account—the most difficult account at the agency—he stumbles across a magazine advertisement for a new housing development in fictional Lansdale, Connecticut. (The film references Lansdale as being near Danbury.) The copy reads, "Come to Peaceful Connecticut." Right then and there, he has an epiphany: There is a better way to live. Later he tells his best friend and attorney, Bill Cole (Melvyn Douglas), he isn't just buying a house; he's buying "a lifestyle." What you glean from the exchange is that Blandings wants to acquire a lifestyle of wealth and status by living in a town where only the "right" people would be living.

Fictional Lansdale was based on a very real Connecticut community where many of the "right" people were living. While there were other bedroom communities within reach of New York, like Larchmont and Westchester, none possessed the cachet of a Fairfield, New Milford, or Litchfield County address. Starting in the 1930s, New Milford had become a chic artistic haven boasting residents in the theater and arts such as Leonard Bernstein, Florence Eldridge, Eartha Kitt, Jean Simmons, Lillian Hellman, and Arthur Miller.

This was something that Eric Hodgins, who wrote the best-selling novel *Mr. Blandings Builds His Dream House* in 1946, and its future film producer, Dore Schary, were well aware of, as they were New Milford residents. The film *Mr. Blandings Builds His Dream House* helped to define Connecticut as *the* place to live better than any tourism campaign could ever have done. Not only did it foreshadow Connecticut's post–World War II housing boom, mentioned in *Christmas in Connecticut*, but it also introduced the concept of "superior living" in Connecticut, with its own built-in slogan.

Eric Hodgins's book satirized his own ordeal of moving to the country to renovate an old farmhouse, only to end up building a brand-new, expensive "dream house" instead. At the time, Hodgins was a vice president for Time, Inc., in New York. In 1939 he and his wife bought an old colonial house and property with about thirty acres of land, located in the Merryall section of New Milford. Hodgins ultimately decided to leave the original house intact, building a new house in a colonial style on the property.

Hodgins and his wife designed the new house without ever putting thought into the costs, because—well, it was their dream house. Some of the custom features included relatively new inventions like recessed lighting, central air-conditioning, and one of the first-ever home dishwashers. (Said dishwasher lasted for forty-six years and was later donated to the Smithsonian Institution.) There was a wine cellar, a swimming pool, two wet bars, a spiral staircase that connected the maid's quarters to the butler's pantry, an elaborately painted mural, and an expansive garden. The initial estimate for construction was $11,000. The problem was that nothing went according to plan, the costs rose out of control, and, in the end, Hodgins's "dream house" nearly bankrupted him.

Some of the most memorable scenes in *Mr. Blandings Builds His Dream House* are based on Hodgins's actual experiences. Take, for instance, Muriel's instructions to her painter about the color scheme: "Now, the dining room I'd like yellow. Not just yellow, a very gay yellow." (Hodgins's dining room was indeed a very gay yellow.) "If you send one of your workmen to the grocer for a pound

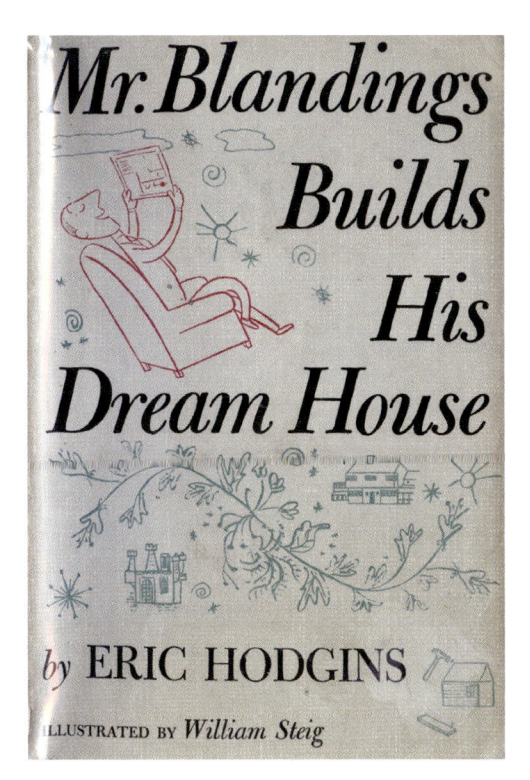

"The book wrote itself," said author and New Milford resident Eric Hodgins about his comedic retelling of home renovation and construction.

of their best butter, and match that exactly, you can't go wrong." It was screenwriters Norman Panama and Melvin Frank who buttoned the scene with the following brilliant aside from the painters. Muriel is confident she'll get the colors she wants, and when she leaves, one painter turns to the other and says, "Got that, Charlie?" and Charlie answers, "Red, green, blue, yellow, white." Charlie is played by actor Don Brodie, who, with just that one line, manages to sum up the workers' point of view about the homeowners' folly.

The final cost of Hodgins's house came to $56,000. This included—as the film depicts—the $1,204 sink for cutting flowers that had a drain in the stone floor.

Hodgins was forced to sell his dream house in 1945, after living there for just two years, taking a loss of $38,000. The book became a bestseller, however, and Hodgins sold the film rights to RKO for $200,000. He tried to purchase his house back, but the new owners refused to sell it to him. After all, it was now *their* dream house. (Hodgins would later write a sequel, *Blandings Way*, published in 1950; although he felt it was a better book, it has never been adapted for the screen.)

Mr. Blandings Builds His Dream House showcases what would become another enduring Connecticut "character," or caricature—the shrewd New Englander who is not above fleecing the pockets of two naive New Yorkers. As Muriel and Jim, accompanied by their realtor, Mr. Smith (Ian Wolfe), drive through the Connecticut countryside, we hear their skeptical lawyer Bill's voice setting the scene. "There they are, two little fish from New York—out in the deep, deep waters of Connecticut real estate. That's Smith, the real estate salesman. Mighty shrewd cookie in a quiet sort of way. Yes, sir, he knows a sucker—I mean customer—when he sees one . . . He sees one!"

Realtor Smith underplays perfectly, getting them emotionally invested. He shares some marvelous but completely fictional historical tidbits, telling them a General Gates stopped there during the Revolutionary War to water his horse. To whet their appetite for the supposed bargain they are about to get, he says, "Now, I'm not trying to sell you anything, y'understand—all I'm saying is that one of these days someone with a little vision and imagination's goin' to come along, and just steal this place—and I mean steal it."

Muriel imagines what a woman's touch could bring to the old house, while Jim imagines what life would be like if he were a country gentleman. He stands in jodhpurs and tweed in front of his Connecticut farmhouse, the picture of contentment. Next thing you know, Mr. Smith has a deal to finally unload his most unloadable property.

Throughout the film there is enjoyment in watching these supposedly shrewd city slickers get taken in by one crafty Yankee after another. Once Smith dupes Mr. and Mrs. Blandings into overpaying for the house, a parade of similar New England characters follows. For instance, there's the well digger, Mr. Zucca (Tito Vuolo), who's dug sixty feet and still can't find water, and the contractor, Mr. Retch (Jason Robards Sr.), who consistently delivers bad news with a maddening, glass-half-full attitude. When Jim Blandings asks where his misplaced windows are, Retch, smiling at the mix-up, replies, "Near as we can find out, they've either been sent to a Mr. Banning in Danbury, or a Mr. Bamburger in Waterbury."

Producer Dore Schary (*I'll Be Seeing You*, 1944; *The Farmer's Daughter*, 1947; *Every Girl Should Be Married*, 1948) was Eric Hodgins's New Milford neighbor. He snapped up the rights for RKO, where he recently had become head of production. Schary himself even makes a brief cameo in one of the early New York scenes, sitting at the counter in a crowded diner. *Mr. Blandings* was his first story acquisition for the studio. Schary had produced the comedy *The Bachelor and the Bobby-Soxer* (1947) with Cary Grant and Myrna Loy, and thought they would be perfect for the two leads.

The script was adapted by Frank and Panama, who had written for Milton Berle and Bob Hope on radio. Their first movie script, *My Favorite Blonde* (1942), was also for Hope, and *Road to Utopia* (1946), with Hope and Bing Crosby, earned them an Academy Award nomination for Best Original Screenplay. Schary envisioned my grandfather Melvyn Douglas as the lawyer, Bill Cole. Schary had been at MGM when he was under contract there, and the two of them shared many liberal political beliefs. Schary had a reputation, as David O. Selznick said, of "being more interested in selling causes than selling pictures." He enticed my grandfather into the role by telling him, "Come on, Mel, we'll make the pictures at RKO we always dreamed about." (Ironically, after convincing my grandfather to sign a three-picture deal with RKO, the studio was purchased by Howard Hughes, and Schary abruptly returned to MGM.) My grandfather had just gotten out of the service and his finances were low, but he was also eager to make a fresh start, and didn't think the character of Bill Cole was "interesting" enough, so he asked Schary if he could be involved in rewriting the part. Meeting with Grant, Schary, and the screenwriters, Frank and Panama, he offered some specific suggestions to beef up the part. He was very happy with the rewrite, and it became what he called "a comedy with comment."

The cast of *Mr. Blandings Builds His Dream House*. Art director Carroll Clark, famous for creating the famed Art Deco look popular at RKO in the 1930s, was also an architect. He designed the Blandings dream house in the colonial style. The white clapboard, two-story house with its green shutters became popular across America. RKO built the original Blandings house in Malibu. As part of the promotion for the film, seventy-three replicas of the Blandings house were sold as kits across the country. There are four Blandings houses in Connecticut. (Photofest)

The film was a happy experience for everyone involved, although my grandfather did mention thel says meekly, "The house just needs someone to love it," and Bill says drily, "Good thing there's two people. One to love it, and one to hold it up." Another scene that shows my grandfather's gift for underplaying is when Bill Cole spends the night after rain has washed out the bridge and he can't get back to the city. In the morning he's enjoying his coffee while wearing pajamas when Muriel's neighbor comes to the door. The nosy New Englander keeps giving him strange looks, and to assure him everything is on the up-and-up, he keeps reintroducing himself, "Bill Cole . . . friend of the family . . . Just came in out of the rain."

Mr. Blandings Builds His Dream House would become director H. C. Potter's most memorable film; *Hellzapoppin'* (1941) and *The Farmer's Daughter* (1947) were also well-received, but *Blandings* has grown in

The crafty Yankee realtor Mr. Smith (Ian Wolfe), who convinces Mr. and Mrs. Blandings with a bit of New England blarney to purchase what becomes their money pit. (Photofest)

popularity over the decades, spawning remakes like *The Money Pit* (1986) and seeping into the cultural landscape. Potter's directing style was pretty straightforward: point the camera at the three leads and let them fly. After all, these three actors, separately or paired opposite each other, were titans of comedy, having starred in some of the greatest screwball comedies of all time. Here are just a few: Cary Grant in *Bringing Up Baby*, *The Awful Truth*, and *His Girl Friday*; Melvyn Douglas in *Theodora Goes Wild*, *Too Many Husbands*, and *Third Finger, Left Hand* (with Loy); Loy in *The Thin Man* series and *The Bachelor and the Bobby-Soxer* (with Grant).

Grant rightly described Myrna Loy as an expert comedienne. She got laughs not so much with jokes but with gestures and attitude. When Muriel does something that irritates Jim, she doesn't get upset; she just shrugs and raises her eyebrows as if to say, "Oh, well, nobody's perfect, dear." Muriel is always one step ahead of her husband and not at all above emotional blackmail. Whether she's cost him extra money on the flower sink or gone overboard with bathrooms for the children,

"Anyone who builds a house is crazy." Mr. Blandings is at his wits' end with his contractor John Retch (Jason Robards Sr.) and architect Henry Simms (Reginald Denny). No film has ever captured the joys and the woes of home ownership in quite the same comedic way as *Mr. Blandings Builds His Dream House*. (Photofest)

The last shot is particularly memorable for breaking the fourth wall. As Cary Grant is reading Eric Hodgins's book, he's joined by the cast, and then he looks up and says, "Drop in and see us sometime." Cinematographer James Wong Howe employed a new technique—a standard lens combined with a zoom lens on a crane-mounted camera—to get the closing shot, which begins with this shot of Grant and then pulls back to reveal the Blandings family, Bill Cole, and the entire house. (Photofest)

when she explains her reasoning behind the added expenses with pursed lips and a little whimper, "It's for the children," it's as if she's suddenly asking for money for the Red Cross, a charity for which Loy was a spokesperson in real life.

Grant had started his career as an acrobat, and he shows off his agility dodging Muriel as she opens the medicine cabinet while he's trying to get a morning shave or juggling hat boxes while trying to get his bathrobe from their overstuffed closet. Often, it's not even that a line is funny, it's Cary Grant's defeated expression, such as when Cole asks him, "What's a Zuz Zuz water softener?" and Grant, who has never even heard of it, just deflates when he sees the bill, as if to say, "It was so expensive, don't even ask." In another scene, Grant drags out, "What's with all the kissing?" when he notices Bill Cole's good-bye kisses to his wife are getting longer and more passionate.

During their first night in the new house, Jim and Muriel have buyers' remorse. They have uprooted their entire lives. Jim realizes he has overpaid for the house. There's no furniture, there's no heat; Muriel is wearing a fur coat and Jim an overcoat. They have a makeshift bed on the floor. No one could play irritation like Grant! We feel for him—especially when he makes a frightening discovery. Jim is setting his alarm for the morning when he realizes Muriel has misread the train schedule. From now on he's going to have to get up at five o'clock in the morning to catch the six o'clock commuter train that arrives at eight o'clock, an hour before he's needed, at nine o'clock, when he never gets there before ten o'clock. He silently calculates how many hours he's going to be traveling, and then sighs. In that quiet moment you may ask yourself, How is it that Cary Grant never won an Academy Award?

Halfway through the renovation, Muriel has made so many changes that their architect, Henry Simms (Reginald Denny), runs away when he sees her. "I was once a happy man," cries Jim. "Anyone who builds a house is crazy!"

At the same time, the couple is imbued with postwar optimism. Bill Cole, once the voice of doom about overspending, sees the completed house and is overcome with emotion. He tells Jim, "Maybe there are some things you should buy with your heart and not your head." This was not only Jim and Muriel's dream; it was the American dream. The themes in *Mr. Blandings Builds His Dream House*—the housing boom, commuter culture, marital discord, city living versus country—became the bedrock of Connecticut's next brand, and would last into the late 1960s, eventually morphing into satire and the suburban sex comedy.

Mr. Blandings Builds His Dream House was one of the first films to have massive cross-promotion and merchandising tie-ins. General Electric, Kellogg's, International Silver, Ford, and others all provided products for the film and were later part of the advertising campaign for the movie. One sequence in the film plays like a future advertisement for Spam. Jim is tasked with coming up with a slogan for the "Wham" ham and is stuck. One night their maid, Gussie (Louise Beavers), is serving Wham to the children and exclaims, "If you ain't eatin' Wham, you ain't eatin' ham!" Jim's eyes light up. Gussie has saved the day. It becomes Wham's slogan, and they use Gussie's picture in the magazine advertisement. Let's hope Gussie got a percentage of that!

This may have been an ingenious way to prime moviegoers for the hundreds of similar-looking ads that cross-promoted the film and various products from silverware to cars to cereal. Although there were no children in Hodgins's book, Panama and Frank gave Blandings two daughters for the film to help make the story relatable to those in the middle class, as men were returning from war and having children. In one scene, Betsy and Joan eat Kellogg's cereal, prominently displayed on the breakfast table. There was paid promotion from Buick and Ford automobiles. Cary Grant drives a 1941 Buick Roadmaster Convertible, and there's also a gorgeous Ford Super Deluxe Station Wagon.

Print ads like this one, for Kellogg's cereal—prominently featured in the movie—meant that consumers could see products that mimicked what had been seen in the film.

Mr. Blandings Builds His Dream House was filled with all sorts of product placements and cross-promotions. Here, Cary Grant and Myrna Loy try out the kitchen set, designed by Carroll Clark for the film. General Electric provided all the appliances, including one of the first home dishwashers. Grant drove a Buick Roadmaster that was also prominently featured in the film. (Photofest)

A publicity trip had my grandfather promoting *Mr. Blandings Builds His Dream House* in Preston Hollow, Texas, outside Dallas, where he recorded several ads on local station KIXL, including: "Program for today. Go to church, eat at Wyatt's, drive out to see the Mr. Blandings' 'Dream House' in Preston Hollow. The pantry shelves in Mr. Blandings' Dream House are stocked with nationally advertised brands of foods . . . from Wyatt Super Markets . . . Mr. Blandings won't mind paying the bill, because at Wyatt's, the prices are really modest. Electrical installation, heating, and air-conditioning of Mr. Blandings' Dallas Dream House are all by Fred Werry Electric Co. When you build *your* dream house, call us for advice."

A kitchen scene featuring General Electric products that the studio cut for length had to be put back because General Electric—which had paid to see its kitchen appliances prominently displayed—didn't see enough of them in the film.

David O. Selznick's publicity man, Paul McNamara, described *Mr. Blandings* as a "promotion man's dream." He came up with a unique publicity gimmick for marketing. RKO and SRO (Selznick's distribution organization) would provide free blueprints to one hundred builders around the country so they could build Blandings dream houses in their own cities. Despite the movie's being about the nightmares of building a house, the campaign went well, and seventy-three dream houses in sixty different cities were built around the country. You may want to check to see if there's one in your town. Along with the original Hodgins house in New Milford, there are four dream houses in

The exterior of author Eric Hodgins's house in New Milford. The "Dream House" has gone through many restorations since it was purchased in the 1940s, but rumor has it that the owners, paying homage to the film, painted the dining room a very gay yellow, just as Muriel had described. Blandings' Way is a private residence.

Connecticut, located in Wethersfield, Trumbull, Hartford, and Bridgeport. In 1948, after the plans were sent out, one builder, the Suez Company in Toledo, Ohio, noticed a problem. Because the blueprints were of the original movie house set, they did not include stairs. Selznick immediately wired Paul McNamara: "Our inexperience in the building business has become apparent." McNamara had publicists take photos of every inch of the set and then had architects redo the blueprints. Builders were known to incorporate their own fixes, as well.

One quirky feature in the film was that all the closets in the house were designed with inside locks. A recurring gag is that Blandings designed his closets with inside locks but keeps getting locked inside, regardless.

J. C. Nichols, a builder in Kansas City, had his own gimmick: He advertised that he could build the same house as seen in *Mr. Blandings*, but for less money than the $30,000 Blandings paid. Nichols not only succeeded as a builder, but he also became well known for his subdivisions, created for people who desired "a better way of life" (although he did come under fire for enforcing covenants to control just who could live in them).

A mark of the Cold War era is that some dream houses had bomb shelters. The promotional dream houses had interiors and furniture from the movie that consumers could admire and later purchase at local department stores. General Electric provided houses with modern gadgets such as garbage disposals, electric garage door openers, and color television sets, all of which had been invented in the previous decade or so. Once the dream houses were built, local businesses in each city would provide everything from furniture to carpeting, paint, wallpaper, curtains, even groceries, to replicate the interior of the movie dream house. Tickets would be sold for 25 cents so people could see the dream houses in their city; proceeds went to local charities. In some cities the studio raffled off the house the same night the film premiered. Four dream houses still exist in Connecticut . . . well, five, counting mine!

A replica of a Blandings house in Trumbull. The home is a private residence.

A replica of a Blandings house in Wethersfield, also a private residence.

CONNECTICUT IN THE MOVIES

Connecticut gets sexy. Joan Collins and Paul Newman in *Rally 'Round the Flag, Boys!* (1958). (Photofest)

CHAPTER 5
SUBURBAN SEX COMEDIES

If *Mr. Blandings Builds His Dream House* lured New Yorkers into moving to Connecticut, there would be a period of adjustment as they adapted to life in suburbia. A crop of films in the late 1950s through the 1960s satirized everything that had once been sacred. Home ownership, love and marriage, even children, were now all fair game. Suburban sex comedies, like *Rally 'Round the Flag, Boys!* (1958), *The Tunnel of Love* (1958), *Wives and Lovers* (1963), *My Six Loves* (1963), and *The Secret Life of an American Wife* (1968), portrayed life in Connecticut in a new way. Good-bye, Currier and Ives. Life in Connecticut was now a well-heeled playground where nonstop cocktail parties and extramarital affairs kept away the boredom. Children no longer fit into these adult-themed activities. They were scarce, for sale, or disposable, and often used as punchlines throughout these films.

Women's roles, too, shifted dramatically. They were portrayed as housebound wives who worried about their weight or attractiveness, slave housewives who chauffeured their commuting husbands, or lecturing mothers who told their children not to bother their father when he came home because he was tired from working hard to give them a better life.

Men's roles, on the other hand, expanded. They gained their freedom, commuting back and forth to their jobs away from their spouses, often drinking to excess, chasing women on the side, living an almost entirely separate life in New York away from their families. Screenwriter George Axelrod (*Breakfast at Tiffany's*, 1961), who worked uncredited on *Rally 'Round the Flag, Boys!* and later wrote and directed *The Secret Life of an American Wife*, summed up the era of suburban sex comedies this way: "I like to see rich people saying witty things and screwing." Why were so many sex comedies set in Connecticut? Was there a loosening up of rigid New England morality as more people from the entertainment industry moved here? Or was the entertainment industry satirizing immorality with its portrayal of the suburban bourgeoisie?

RALLY 'ROUND THE FLAG, BOYS! (1958)

Paul Newman and Joanne Woodward became a married couple the same year they played a married couple in *Rally 'Round the Flag, Boys! (1958)*, a Connecticut suburban sex comedy directed by veteran comedy maestro Leo McCarey (*The Awful Truth*, 1937; *Love Affair*, 1939). The farce was quite a departure for the serious acting duo, who were also members of the Actors Studio. It's not surprising that they never made another comedy together—but the Newmans did relocate to Westport, becoming Connecticut's most famous residents.

Grace Bannerman (Joanne Woodward) is an overly blonde, shrill, clingy housewife who suspects her husband Harry (Paul Newman) is cheating on her with their oversexed neighbor, Angela (Joan Collins). The latter role had been originally written for bombshell Jayne Mansfield, who specialized in playing cartoonish sexpots. *Rally 'Round the Flag, Boys!* is a preview of the kinds of

Husband and wife Paul Newman and Joanne Woodward play husband and wife in *Rally 'Round the Flag, Boys!* (Photofest)

SUBURBAN SEX COMEDIES

one-dimensional roles women were now relegated to, with wincing helpful hints, like don't feed your husband TV dinners, don't join too many committees, don't neglect your husband's "needs," or Joan Collins will come around doing the dance of the suburban seven veils and force him to stray.

The movie was also a preview of a new brand of suburban comedy set in Connecticut. The action takes place in fictional Putnam Landing (although Putnam is a real town in Windham County). When Putnam Landing, Connecticut, discovers the US Army is secretly planning to build a base in their town, Grace is elected head of the Women's Safety Committee for the Protection of Putnam Landing. Hilarity ensues when her husband, Harry, who's been trying to get away for a romantic weekend with her, is recruited by the army to create goodwill in Putnam Landing.

Grace surprises Harry in Washington but discovers her neighbor, Angela (Joan Collins), undressed in his hotel room. Harry comes up with a plan to win back his wife and fulfill the army contract. He and Grace stage a Thanksgiving pageant, where Putnam Landing residents are dressed as American Indians and the army soldiers are dressed as Pilgrims, to reenact the smoking of a peace pipe. *Rally 'Round the Flag, Boys!* has not aged well, with the Thanksgiving pageant probably the most tasteless depiction of Native Americans you will ever see.

The original screenwriter, George Axelrod—who would make his own suburban sex comedy, *The Secret Life of an American Wife*—had a completely different take on the Max Shulman novel, and had his name removed, giving sole screenwriting credit to McCarey and Claude Binyon.

THE TUNNEL OF LOVE (1958)

Director Gene Kelly's *The Tunnel of Love* (1958) is a romantic comedy about a couple, Isolde (Doris Day) and August Poole (Richard Widmark), who move to Westport from Greenwich Village in New York City so Augie can fulfill his dream of becoming an artist. Westport itself appears in the film through stock shots, but the film was made on a soundstage.

Augie and Isolde live in a converted barn on her family's property, surviving on her inheritance from her wealthy grandmother. Isolde wants children, but after failing to conceive they pursue adoption with the Rock-a-Bye Foundation. *The Tunnel of Love* hints that life in suburbia may have caused Augie to lose interest in making love to his wife. Augie's helpful but often tipsy neighbor, Dick Pepper (Gig Young), has some advice for Augie—cheat. With a name like Dick Pepper, that comes as no surprise. Dick is married but has a penchant for chasing women. He has four children and a fifth on the way, which he attributes to his fooling around. "I have to suffer for chasing around . . . at least that's what I say to my analyst," he says.

Dick does have a way with his kids. Here's one of the examples where children are used as punchlines: One of Dad's more endearing quips is when he yells at them over breakfast, "Shut up or

Elisabeth Fraser, Doris Day, Richard Widmark, and Gig Young drink up in *The Tunnel of Love*, which takes place in Westport. *The Tunnel of Love* was originally written by Peter De Vries, first as a novel, and then, with Joseph Fields, as a stage play. De Vries and his wife had moved to Westport, Connecticut, in 1948, where they raised their family. He is buried in Willowbrook Cemetery in Westport. (Photofest)

I'll send you to reform school." Dick—who is either drinking or mixing a drink in every scene he is in—encourages Augie to follow his lead and fool around. He feels this will get the motor running, spice things up in the bedroom, and get his wife pregnant. This is an example of 1960s sex comedy logic. Augie wants to cheat in theory, but he can't. He complains to Dick, "I'm the laughingstock of Westport, I'm so inhibited."

Isolde—played by the perfect image of American beauty, Doris Day—is not considered sexy anymore. This becomes obvious when the Rock-a-Bye adoption agency sends pretty young Miss Novick—played by the sultry Italian actress Gia Scala—to interview Augie and Isolde for an adoption. The plot gets a little wacky here, so hold on. Augie and Dick don't realize Miss Novick is from the adoption agency because she's so unexpectedly attractive. Then Dick gives Augie a tranquilizer, which he downs with scotch so he won't be nervous. Between the drinking and pill taking, this film needs a warning label. Who knew Westport was this exciting?

Dick Pepper—no surprise—starts hitting on Miss Novick, and Augie, who's now high from pills and booze, starts making crazy, drunken statements about raising children. By the time Isolde shows up, Miss Novick has had enough and decides they are not suitable parents. Isolde is fuming and storms off, while Augie goes after Miss Novick to apologize and ask for a second chance. Then, figuring Isolde is angry with him anyway, Augie invites sexy Miss Novick out to dinner. Next thing you know, it's morning in Westport. Augie wakes up alone in a motel on Route 22, and there's a good-bye note from Miss Novick: "Thank you for a lovely evening. You were wonderful."

Nine months later, Rock-a-Bye has a baby for them, and it looks a lot like Augie. Is Augie the father? *The Tunnel of Love* teases us with a possible affair, but he can't remember (always a convenient alibi). Isolde becomes convinced that he cheated on her, that the baby is his, and she packs to leave. Before she can go, though, Miss Novick turns up to see the baby boy she had arranged for them to get. Isolde is incensed at her nerve, but then Miss Novick points out that she, herself, also had a baby—a girl—and that they are now on their way to Australia to rejoin her husband there.

As she goes on her way, all is well again with the Pooles, and apologies are made all around, but then Augie and Isolde realize that she's finally actually pregnant, so we're left to assume that maybe Dick Pepper's logic was correct. Augie has had enough of the suburbs, though, and he tells Isolde, "Let's put this house on the market and move back to the city. The country's no place to bring up kids! Our baby's gonna be born in Manhattan!"

WIVES AND LOVERS (1963)

Like *The Tunnel of Love*, *Wives and Lovers* was also based on a play, this one being Jay Presson Allen's *The First Wife*. Allen, who was married to the famed theater producer Lewis Allen, lived in a country house in Bridgewater. In *Wives and Lovers* (1963), Bill Austin (Van Johnson) is a struggling writer living with his

Five years after making *The Tunnel of Love*, Widmark and his wife, screenwriter Jean Hazlewood, purchased a home in Litchfield County. The 28-acre estate included a 1790s gristmill from its days as a working farm called Heron Mill Farm and a barn they turned into a guesthouse. Widmark thrived as a gentleman farmer and found the home a welcome retreat from Hollywood living. Richard Widmark is buried at Great Oak Cemetery in Roxbury, near his friend Arthur Miller.

Was Connecticut ever this exciting? Janet Leigh, Van Johnson, Ray Walston, Shelley Winters, Jeremy Slate, and Martha Hyer all get very close in *Wives and Lovers*. Janet Leigh has a significant tie to Connecticut: On June 4, 1951, she married Tony Curtis in a private ceremony in Greenwich. Curtis's best man was Jerry Lewis. (Photofest)

wife, Bertie (Janet Leigh), and young daughter, Julie (Claire Wilcox), in—you guessed it—a cramped New York City apartment. He's a stay-at-home dad working on a novel. She's a dental assistant. Bill's literary agent, Lucinda Ford (Martha Hyer), finally gets Bill's novel published and secures a deal for him to adapt the book into a Broadway play. Success means one thing to Bill: "We're moving to Connecticut!"

Bertie reluctantly gives up her job and soon she's a suburban housewife worried about what her toney neighbors think of her. With success, Bill starts to put on airs. He buys a sports car and begins dressing like a country gentleman in tweed and camel hair and spending more nights in the city with his agent, Lucinda. Here is the contrast: In *Mr. Blandings Builds His Dream House*, Jim Blandings fantasized about dressing like a country gentleman. In *Wives and Lovers*, the fantasy is played out, and Bill starts acting more like a playboy than a family man. Bill starts neglecting his wife and flirting with Lucinda, even getting a hotel room at the Algonquin for them so they can "work late." Janet Leigh's blonde American wholesomeness, like Doris Day's in *The Tunnel of Love,* is presented as unsexy.

A bored Bertie meets the "couple" next door. Fran (Shelley Winters), an ex-actress, is a weary divorcée who hangs out and drinks with her "lady's companion," Wylie (Ray Walston). Wylie is effeminate, impeccably dressed, compliments Bertie and Fran on their looks, and refinishes antiques above the garage, all clues to suggest he's gay. Fran and Wylie have time on their hands and drink martinis around the clock. Fran offers Bertie breezy hints about fitting in, such as "Everyone in Connecticut wears what makes them feel good." But when Bertie wants advice about her first party, Fran tells her, "Remember, this is Connecticut," which seems to be code for: Don't screw it up—or if you do, just have lots of booze around and people will forgive you for being déclassé.

Drinking is a major part of the plot of *Wives and Lovers*. As soon as they move to Connecticut, Bill wants Bertie to have a cocktail party to impress the new neighbors. He accuses Bertie of being out of touch because she doesn't have vodka in the bar. "Don't you know that everybody drinks vodka these days? Nobody drinks bourbon." Luckily, Fran has a bottle of vodka she brings over on request to cover Bertie's embarrassment. Even though the bar is stocked with bourbon, rye, and scotch, Bill is convinced that elite people in Connecticut drink only vodka. (And I thought we drank only cider!)

Later, the joke turns out to be on Bill when Lucinda's drink of choice is scotch on the rocks and the lead actor in Bill's play, Gar (Jeremy Slate), prefers bourbon. Bertie requests a vodka martini and Gar insists on mixing it for her in a very theatrical manner. It hits her quickly and she asks for more, and then—flirtatiously calling him "darling"—she asks if he'd mind making it a double. I feel tipsy just writing about their exchange.

Bertie suspects Bill is cheating on her with Lucinda, but, rather than confront him, she tells Fran and then frets about . . . her weight. Janet Leigh looks like a ninety-pound greyhound in this movie, she's so thin. Fran, the wise divorcée, tells Bertie not to "rock the boat," or she'll end up alone, like her, with only a "lady's companion" as a friend. Fran offers Bertie advice: Have an affair with Gar. Again, this is meant to get their marriage back on track.

While Bill is pursuing Lucinda in an Algonquin Hotel room, drinking champagne, Bertie invites Gar back to their Connecticut house where they drink scotch—or should I say, he plies her with scotch? Soon they're making out in the living room—probably not far from the bar. A drunken Bertie admits she's not very good at kissing because she hasn't "necked in years." Suburban sex comedies always use alcohol to justify infidelity.

CONNECTICUT IN THE MOVIES

Bill spends the night at the Algonquin because he's too hungover to go back to Connecticut. Did Lucinda stay with him? Same alibi as Augie in *The Tunnel of Love*: He can't remember. Bertie passed out on the couch, and Gar spent the night upstairs. Did they have sex? She's not sure. The I-can't-remember excuse works. Couples escape any real examination of adultery, yet hint they are not so unhip that they don't think about it.

At this point, you may be wondering, where is their child, Julie? You remember Julie. Well, in this particular scene, Fran had taken her back to her place. Sex comedies were for adults, and the one child in this film—none of the other characters even have kids—becomes a nuisance to the plot. When they were living in New York, Bill was close to Julie. Once they move to Connecticut, she's supposed to understand that, with success, Dad doesn't have time for her. He promises Julie he'll go swimming with her in the morning and then forgets all about the promise. Bertie explains that because Daddy is now in demand, he won't have as much time for either of them, and Julie accepts this. Bertie and Bill maintain a don't-ask-don't-tell attitude about their indiscretions, and the trope that it's an aphrodisiac for their stale marriage continues.

MY SIX LOVES (1963)

My Six Loves (1963) has the least sex of any of the films in the sex comedy genre. Geared as a wholesome comedy, it contains a familiar '60s trope where women must choose love and children over a career. Once again, children are used more as a plot device, and their feelings here are almost never taken into consideration.

In *My Six Loves*, Broadway actress Janice Courtney (Debbie Reynolds), single and overworked, is about to find domestic "bliss" in Connecticut if she puts her career behind her. Her manager, Marty Bliss (David Janssen), who offers a different type of bliss with his name, is against the idea. But after Janice collapses at a reception held in her honor in New York City, her doctor insists the exhausted actress spend six weeks at her country house in Fairmont (which is reminiscent of Fairfield), resting up before her next play starts rehearsals. She, too, is reluctant, telling her best friend and personal assistant, Ethel (Eileen Heckart), "That house in Connecticut was the biggest mistake of my life."

But she follows doctor's orders nonetheless, even though she gets no sleep at all the first night due to the nighttime soundtrack of bugs and frogs and other country delights. The following day, Janice discovers that six homeless children are living in a shed on her property: Leo (Billy Hughes), Brenda (Sally Smith), Amy (Colleen Peters), a set of twins, Sherman (Barry Livingston) and Dulcie (Debbie Price), Sonny (Ted Eccles), and their dog. We're told they left their folks passed out drunk in Torrington, where they had gone to work the tobacco fields.

Her neighbor, the handsome, unmarried Reverend Jim Larkin (Cliff Robertson), helps Janice and Ethel take care of the kids. All goes well until the children's aunt Doreen (Mary McCarty) and uncle B. J. Smith (Max Showalter) arrive unexpectedly, pretending at first to be the kids' parents. As much as they want the brood back in order to keep getting welfare checks, received for their care, they're willing to unload the kids to Janice for a paltry $300 a head. This is all played for laughs, and we never really find out exactly how and why the six children came to be abandoned. As the story progresses, no one—including the judge—bothers to find the children's real parents or really question Janice's suitability as a potential mother. They're simply passed from one adult to another like party favors.

Reverend Larkin wants Janice to end her career as an actress and adopt the kids. She can't possibly be happy, he says. He can't understand why she would want to go back to Broadway to play "a scheming two-headed sexpot" in her new play when a better role would be as a wife and mother. Larkin uses the children to manipulate Janice into giving up her career and marrying him. At first Janice is not interested; "I've worked too hard and too long in my career to wind up as chief cook and bottle washer in Connecticut," she says.

CONNECTICUT IN THE MOVIES

Marty Bliss—quite the city slicker compared to Larkin—wants Janice to dump the kids with the authorities and come back to Broadway. Though Bliss is presented as not right for Janice, unlike Larkin, he never asks Janice to give up her career; her possible friends-with-benefits relationship with Marty seems to be working, but Janice is slowly transformed by the country. She helps Larkin with a white elephant sale—we call them tag sales in Connecticut—for his church, so he can build, as he says, the "swingin'est parish house in the state of Connecticut."

It turns out Janice has to be married if she wants to adopt the kids, which sets the stakes—you guessed it: marriage and motherhood, or career. So, unlike any actress I have ever known, Janice decides to leave Broadway and stardom behind to return to the country with Reverend Larkin. As Bliss says, when he realizes he's lost her for good, "She's gone to seek her euphoria in Connecticut."

My Six Loves is a gentle reminder to women that life in suburbia is complete only once you're a housewife. Once she's stuck in the 'burbs, she may have to find other outlets to relieve her boredom.

THE SECRET LIFE OF AN AMERICAN WIFE (1968)

George Axelrod, who wrote the 1955 sex comedy *The Seven Year Itch,* said, "I make movies about boobs and boobs." As a writer, he was reined in by collaborating with strong directors like Billy Wilder or Blake Edwards, but in his own directing career, Axelrod often pushed the boundaries of good taste—*Lord Love a Duck* (1966), for example.

The cure to marriage blues in most 1960s suburban sex comedies was simple—have an affair. Husbands and wives usually came to their senses just short of consummation, but George Axelrod's *The Secret Life of an American Wife* (1968) went all the way. Taking an avant-garde approach in his directing style, Axelrod has Victoria Layton (Anne Jackson), a neglected housewife in her thirties, speak directly to the camera from her "terribly colonial, terribly Connecticut bedroom" in Westport.

"There was a time when I was pretty groovy," Victoria tells us. *Groovy* had many meanings in the 1960s. Here it hints that, at thirty-four, she worries she may be past her prime. Even Jimmy, the twenty-something grocery delivery boy, pays no attention to her when she greets him nude in her kitchen. Victoria says: "In two years, it'll be all over. Finished. I'll have the Connecticut look . . . People move to the country . . . after a while, something terrible happens to the ladies. They stop having their hair done." She's worried she'll end up like a woman she knows who's gotten "big as a house and now all she can do is raise money for the Democrats."

Victoria's husband, Tom Layton (Patrick O'Neal), is a press agent who spends all his time taking care of his big movie-star client. The couple's children, a boy and a girl, are seen just long enough to know they exist and then are quickly ushered off-camera. As I've written, children are

A bored housewife, Victoria (Anne Jackson), has an extramarital affair with a movie star (Walter Matthau) to spice up her marriage in *The Secret Life of an American Wife*, the most risqué of all Connecticut sex comedies, written and directed by George Axelrod. (Photofest)

superfluous in sex comedies. Here, the young actors don't even get billing.

Axelrod based the character of "the Movie Star," as he's billed in the picture, on Frank Sinatra, whom the writer had worked with when he adapted *The Manchurian Candidate* (1962). Walter Matthau stepped in to play the part.

Victoria chauffeurs Tom back and forth to the train station and doesn't even bother changing out of her nightgown—she just throws a raincoat on over it. But then, when she gets to the station, we see other wives are still in their nightgowns, too. It's a great visual gag: suburbia has turned the women into hausfraus who no longer care about their appearance. Tom tells Victoria he has his work cut out for him in the city. The Movie Star has a proclivity for afternoon trysts with call girls, and he will once again have to find one. With Tom virtually ignoring her, causing her to question her own sexuality, Victoria decides she'll show up as the two o'clock call girl, if only to prove to herself she's still desirable.

The Secret Life of an American Wife stands out as being the only film in the genre to be told from the woman's point of view. Victoria is able to successfully convince the Movie Star that she is a call girl, but then confesses she's not really a prostitute—she's actually Tom's wife. Both are suddenly turned on by the idea that they are cheating on Tom and proceed with their afternoon tryst. Victoria later returns to Westport feeling no guilt about the affair. Tom is none the wiser, and, as a bonus, he suddenly finds her attractive again.

The Secret Life of an American Wife was Axelrod's gender-reversed take on his play *The Seven Year Itch* (1952) (famously made into a 1955 film with Marilyn Monroe), about a husband who contemplates an affair with his upstairs neighbor while his wife is away. While *The Secret Life of An American Wife* is littered with dated sex-comedy tropes—wife-swapping fantasies, a scantily clad sexy neighbor (Edy Williams, who later married Russ Meyer and appeared in his movies), and constant drinking, which seems to make cheating more acceptable—Axelrod's dry observations about Connecticut suburbia produced the most sophisticated fare of the genre.

Axelrod based his character of "the Movie Star" on Frank Sinatra, ironically seen in this advertisement on the same bill. Matthau was a Roxbury resident. One of the stars of *The Secret Life of an American Wife*, Patrick O'Neal, would return to Westport to play a more ruthless kind of husband in *The Stepford Wives* (1974).

The Swimmer takes place in Westport and examines misplaced Connecticut "values"—wealth, money, status— and what happens when the things you once strived so hard to achieve are all taken away.

CHAPTER 6

DARK SUBURBIA

THE MAN IN THE GRAY FLANNEL SUIT (1956)

By the end of the 1960s, the suburban sex comedy was drifting out of style, but in the late 1950s a new brand had already begun to emerge, depicting a darker and more contemplative version of Connecticut suburbia. "We shouldn't be so discontented all the time," says Betsy Rath in *The Man in The Gray Flannel Suit*, Sloan Wilson's 1955 novel about the growing angst in the suburbs. The 1956 film adaptation of that bestseller stars Gregory Peck, Jennifer Jones, Fredric March, Marisa Pavan, Ann Harding, Lee J. Cobb, Arthur O'Connell, and Henry Daniell.

Long before the period drama *Mad Men* (2007–2015) captured the empty lives of Madison Avenue advertising men, *The Man in The Gray Flannel Suit* was exploring themes of

The Man in the Gray Flannel Suit (1956) was based on the novel of the same name by author Sloan Wilson, a native of Norwalk, Connecticut. (Photofest)

disillusionment in the postwar generation. *Mad Men* owes much to Nunnally Johnson's film in both its look and its feel, but it lacks one enormous thing. No one had quite the gravitas, quite the humanity, as the handsome piece of chiseled granite known as Gregory Peck. These days, Peck is rarely classified as one of the greatest movie stars of all time, even though he made over seventy films in a career that spanned more than sixty years. He won an Academy Award for his performance as Atticus Finch in *To Kill a Mockingbird* (1962), a part that became synonymous with the man

To prepare for his role as a Madison Avenue huckster, Peck commuted back and forth on the New Haven Railroad, visited advertising agencies, and spent time at NBC headquarters. (Photofest)

himself. He was at his best playing conflicted men who sought to find their better selves. It was not surprising that when Twentieth Century Fox purchased Sloan Wilson's successful novel, there was only one actor the studio saw playing World War II veteran Tom Rath on-screen, and that was Gregory Peck.

Sloan Wilson was a native of Norwalk, Connecticut, and his novel reads like an alternative version of Eric Hodgins's 1946 comic novel, *Mr. Blandings Builds His Dream House*, which is fascinating, since Sloan Wilson and Eric Hodgins both worked for Time, Inc., and both lived in Connecticut, where both of their books are set. Nine years after the success of *Mr. Blandings*, which told of New Yorkers moving to Connecticut to live a better life, Wilson wrote in *The Man in the Gray Flannel Suit* that the constant striving to achieve—better house in the suburbs, better school, better job—was doing more harm than good. Wilson's novel and Nunnally Johnson's film depict a simmering unrest, a dissatisfaction lurking behind the white picket fences.

For husbands, the endless commuting back and forth to New York meant time alone to reflect, question, brood. The commuter trains were filled with a common anxiety: Where did my life go? For wives, their solitude gave them ample opportunity to worry about their lack of control over their destiny and the fact that they sacrifice their own happiness for the happiness of their husbands and children. There was a feeling that they may have been duped into servitude.

The film begins with this pressure of upward mobility expressed through Tom Rath (Gregory Peck) and his wife, Betsy (Jennifer Jones), who have been married for ten years and have three children.

The greatest thing that's ever happened to swank, arty Westport, Connecticut was the making of "The Man in the Gray Flannel Suit" in their town.

According to this publicity story, Westport was "arty." Below, Peck chats with director Nunnally Johnson.

New York's Rockefeller Center provides the background for these shots of Gregory Peck arriving at his advertising office.

After taking the commuting train back to Westport, Peck talks over day's work with Nunnally Johnson.

FILM LIFE

CONNECTICUT IN THE MOVIES

Their marriage is in a rut, and they blame each other. Betsy sees Tom's lack of ambition as the cause of their problems. Her unhappiness is palpable, and she takes it out on him, becoming shrewish and critical. Tom has become distant, unable to express his feeling that he cannot live up to her expectations. Living in the middle-class suburb of Westport, they are struggling to make ends meet. Betsy calls their house "a graveyard" and wants to move to a better neighborhood, but Tom wants Betsy to "accept things the way they are," refusing any offers of help or advice.

Tom Rath (Gregory Peck), with his wife, Betsy (Jennifer Jones). In flashbacks, this domestic image is mirrored by Tom Rath with his lover, Maria (Marisa Pavan), an Italian girl with whom he fathered a child while stationed in Rome. Rath has been living a dual life with which he will soon have to come to terms. (Photofest)

The fermenting rage between the on-screen couple spilled over into real life. Gregory Peck and Jennifer Jones had worked together previously (and harmoniously) in the torrid love story, *Duel in the Sun* (1946). Here they were cast as the unhappily married husband and wife in *The Man in the Gray Flannel Suit*. Peck began to feel that the anger and resentment in Jones's performance was blurring what had once been a cordial relationship. In a scene in which Betsy discovers Tom's infidelity, the fighting between the two stars was so intense that Jones actually clawed Peck's face with her fingernails. Peck later complained to Johnson, "I don't call that acting, I call it personal." Jones, who was nominated for an Academy Award in four films, winning Best Actress for *The Song of Bernadette* (1943), was married to mercurial producer David O. Selznick.

Tom is given an opportunity for change when his wealthy aunt dies, leaving behind her estate in an even more affluent suburb of Connecticut called South Bay. Tom would have to get a better job for them to afford the move, and he prefers the safer bet of selling her estate and pocketing the money.

Betsy argues that if they sold their house and moved, they could subdivide the property, selling off parcels of land. This way they would not only be able to afford the house but possibly become rich in the process. (Subdividing properties was popular and a common occurrence after the change in zoning laws in Connecticut in the late 1950s.)

As Betsy excitedly makes plans for their future, Tom quells any further discussion, essentially dismissing any of her suggestions. Betsy becomes frustrated; after all, isn't she a partner in this marriage? She has a better aptitude for real estate than Tom, but she finds herself suddenly relegated to the role of supportive wife. In the 1950s, women who had relinquished their jobs in the workplace became dependent on their husband's salaries. If Betsy wants a better life, she has to browbeat Tom into one. She lashes out at him. "What's happened to you?" she cries. "All of a sudden, I'm ashamed of you."

Betsy eventually gets what she wants, but she discovers that material things—bigger house, better neighborhood—do not always guarantee happiness. Tom has been remote since he came home from the war. Betsy can't identify why he seems like a stranger to her. Tom doesn't want to relive his wartime experiences, so he keeps from Betsy the fact that he is suffering from what we know today as PTSD. One of the incidents that continues to trouble him is his accidental killing of his best friend with a grenade. Another secret he keeps from Betsy is the affair he had with an Italian girl named Maria (Marisa Pavan), whom he met while stationed in Rome, a liaison that may have produced a child. His guilt about the affair is another wedge between them.

Still, Tom wants to make Betsy happy. He hears about a job opportunity as a public relations man at United Broadcasting Network; he applies and accepts their job offer because the higher salary means they can move to South Bay. Life in the corporate world is not what he bargained for, though, and Tom has a hard time finding his way. He cringes at the cutthroat office politics, telling Betsy, "There are a lot of tricky angles." The head of the network and Tom's boss, Ralph Hopkins (Fredric March), takes an immediate liking to Tom, who reminds him of his only son, whom he lost in the war.

Ralph takes a chance, assigning Tom, along with two senior colleagues, Gordon Walker (Arthur O'Connell) and Bill Ogden (Henry Daniell), a new project: to come up with an ad campaign they can show doctors, on how to better promote and establish mental health services. It's an idea ahead of its time, and Tom is enthusiastic, and eager to please the boss.

But Walker and Ogden are old hands at maneuvering the corporate ladder, and they undermine Tom, thwarting his ability to succeed with the project. Ogden gives Tom withering critiques about his writing and demotes him to the sidelines. Workplace anxiety begins to get to Tom, and he stops giving insights on the campaign for fear of being fired, deciding it's better to be a yes man to Ogden, even though he strongly disapproves of the creative ideas being presented. Betsy pushes Tom to be truthful when Hopkins asks for Tom's opinion on his speech, which has been ghostwritten by Ogden. Tom decides he will, informing Hopkins that he thinks it's "phony." Hopkins is at first taken aback by his honesty, but it leads to a more personal and revealing conversation between the men, one that neither man can share with his spouse.

The male bonding scene is well written by Nunnally Johnson, who began his career as a journalist and became a screenwriter in the 1930s. He was nominated for an Academy Award for his adapted screenplay for *The Grapes of Wrath* (1940). He began writing and directing, and had worked with Peck previously on *Night People* (1954).

Having lost his only son, all Hopkins now has is his work. He describes how his life has been shaped by the war. Tom opens up about trying to readjust to civilian life, confessing, "One day a man's catching the 8:26, and then suddenly he's killing people. Then a few weeks later he's catching the 8:26 again."

Hopkins is successful, living in the most prestigious part of South Bay, where Tom has just moved. But he's also divorced and has a strained relationship with his daughter, who elopes without telling him. He wants to return to his wife, Helen (Ann Harding), but she tells him it's too late. After a few drinks and hearing about Hopkins's life, Tom admits he is probably better suited to be a nine-to-fiver than an executive. It's the one time that Hopkins scolds him like a disappointed parent. "Big successful businesses are not built by men like you, nine to five and home and family," he says, and then he lays it out. A man must choose—success or happiness?

Tom runs into his old army buddy Caesar (Keenan Wynn), who's working at UBC as an elevator operator. It seems Caesar is in contact with Tom's Italian girlfriend, Maria, and he lets Tom know that she survived the war and is raising Tom's child, a boy. Tom wants to provide for the child but realizes he must tell Betsy everything.

Betsy, who is happily ensconced in her new home in South Bay, settles down in bed as if she's about to hear a bedtime story from Tom. Tom begins to talk about the war, killing seventeen men, stabbing one in the chest just to obtain his coat, accidentally killing his best friend, the affair with Maria, and the child. For Tom, the confession is cathartic. He gains a kind of spiritual awakening. But Betsy's world has been smashed to bits. "I believed that love meant faithfulness," she wails. The irony is that Betsy has been pushing Tom to be honest, but when he finally bares his soul—which truly takes guts—she doesn't want to hear it; she realizes that the man she has been living with, and has put her faith in, is a stranger.

Betsy runs outside their beautiful house in South Bay and collapses on the lawn. She weeps and clings to the earth, trying to hold on to something solid. Is this Betsy's punishment for wanting a better life, a subtle warning to women that you really can't have it all? Tom tries to comfort her, but Betsy's rage and confusion cannot be contained. What's interesting about this scene (my favorite in the film) is that, for Tom, confessing the affair and the child has restored his identity, but now Betsy's identity has been completely ripped from her. What might be subversive on Jennifer Jones's part—and goes along with Peck's feeling that for Jones, the acting had become too "personal"—is that even though Betsy pulls herself together and comes back to Tom, for the rest of the film she is shell-shocked. Her uncombed hair and her tear-streaked cheeks are a reminder not only of her breakdown, but signify that she is a woman scorned. Betsy stays in the marriage, but it's unclear if she'll find her way back as Tom did. She has become a casualty of suburbia and upward mobility.

After they meet with Judge Bernstein (Lee J. Cobb) to set up a trust for Maria's child, Tom and Betsy get in their car. There's a moment of quiet before they drive away. Tom asks, "Would you mind if I tell you I worship you?" Betsy doesn't respond; she is barely able to form a smile

THE SWIMMER (1968)

Michael Kearney and Burt Lancaster in *The Swimmer*. One thing critics agreed on: It was weird. Vincent Canby wrote, "It has the shape of an open-ended hallucination." Geoff Andrew wrote, "A large looney allegory." Burt Lancaster, who ultimately described the film as one of his favorites, but acknowledged its flaws, said, "The whole film was a disaster." It's a beautiful disaster, though—the best example of Connecticut's Dark Suburbia genre. (Photofest)

CONNECTICUT IN THE MOVIES

Burt Lancaster jokingly referred to *The Swimmer* as *Death of a Salesman* in swim trunks, but the part of nowhere man Ned Merrill was a part he desperately wanted, and he convinced director Frank Perry that he could handle it. Lancaster was well into his fifties, and although he was athletic, he was not a swimmer, and had to train for months to get into shape. He was also going through a divorce when he came to Connecticut to shoot *The Swimmer*. His personal life reflected his own reality as an aging movie star, and his stripped-down performance—visible scars and all—plays like a deconstruction of his own larger-than-life persona.

As Ned Merrill—the man who gamely proclaims, "Here's to sugar on our strawberries" as he tries to hang on to some form of reality—Burt spends the entire movie in a wet bathing suit, looking like a fading Adonis, completely confused and out of place, and trying to figure out what the hell went wrong with his life. It's never far from your mind that a once-young and virile Burt Lancaster wore a version of those exact same swimming trunks fifteen years earlier in *From Here to Eternity* (1953).

The Swimmer is a great film that is filled with imperfections. It's difficult to designate either praise or criticism. The adapted screenplay and direction were by the then-married team of Frank and Eleanor Perry (*David and Lisa*, 1962; *Last Summer*, 1969; *Diary of a Mad Housewife*, 1970). For years, devotees like me had to pass around VHS recordings of these movies, some of which I obtained from Perry himself. But two different directors were at times shooting two different films, first Perry, and then an uncredited Sydney Pollack (*Tootsie*, 1982; *Out of Africa*, 1985), whom Lancaster handpicked to replace Perry. Additional scenes of *The Swimmer* were reshot and directed by Pollack.

Perry and Lancaster had clashed about interpretation and performance—not just *his* performance, but everyone's performance. Joan Rivers (in her first screen appearance) recalled in her autobiography, *Still Talking* (1995), the difficulties on set. Lancaster, she wrote, "redirected every line. . . . Frank [Perry] wanted a happy girl who then got hurt. Lancaster was going to be Mr. Wonderful who came up against a mean bitch and was right not to go off with her."

Actress Barbara Loden, cast as Ned's ex-lover Shirley Abbott, was replaced by Janice Rule after Lancaster showed rushes to Loden's then husband, director Elia Kazan. Loden was so upset about being fired that she decided to make her own film, *Wanda* (1970), which she wrote, produced, directed, and starred in. (*Wanda* was shot partly in Connecticut; see chapter 9.) With Sydney Pollack, the pivotal scene between Rule and Lancaster was reshot in California. It lacks the finesse of Perry's work and feels over-rehearsed. Rule's theatrical manner clashes with Lancaster's primitive bull-in-a-china-shop acting style.

The Swimmer opens with that beautiful Connecticut landscape. It feels safe and recognizable. Deer look up from their grazing; rabbits scurry in the brush. A middle-aged man—Ned Merrill—

The Swimmer was based on a 1964 John Cheever short story of the same name. Cheever was sometimes called "the Chekhov of the suburbs." Director Frank Perry with Burt Lancaster and Michael Kearney in Westport. (Photofest)

wearing nothing but blue bathing trunks, emerges from the woods and dives into a crystal-blue pool. When he comes up, an icy drink enters into the frame. A couple of minutes later, Donald Westerhazy, the owner of the pool, moans, "I drank too much last night." It's practically the first line of the movie and somehow, we know right away that we are in Connecticut. He asks Ned where he's been keeping himself, and the reply is, "Oh, here and there, here and there."

The Westerhazys are hungover, but they're already discussing plans for a midday party at the Grahams' estate. Everyone in *The Swimmer* is either having a party or hungover from one the night before. Helen Westerhazy (Diana Van der Vlis) fills Ned in on some gossip, telling him with a bit of envy that the Grahams put in a pool last June. Ned is surprised he didn't know about that. All the WASP-y names let us know immediately we are in an affluent community. That community is Westport, although it's never mentioned.

Helen prattles on about the Bunkers, the Lears, the Grahams—until Ned asks about the Biswangers. She purses her lips and refers to them as "those awful people on Red Coat Road? They're always talking about their Caribbean cruises or their electric toothbrushes." "Those awful people," she calls them, with an implied "They don't belong in our neighborhood." Helen tries to get Ned to go with them to the Grahams' house. Right in front of her husband she says, "We've all known each other so long, there's not even anyone to flirt with," as if Ned is some jocular stud all the housewives

CONNECTICUT IN THE MOVIES

91

Filming *The Swimmer*. (Photofest)

lust after. Ned tells her he would have flirted with her.

As Ned looks out across the lush valley and takes in the magnificent morning, he comes to a revelation. With the knowledge that the Grahams have a pool, Ned realizes he could swim the chain of pools as if it were a river, all the way back to his own home. "This is the day Ned Merrill swims across the county," he announces. Ned names his odyssey "the Lucinda River," in honor of his wife, whom he says is waiting for him at home with their two young daughters. Immediately, he jumps in their pool, climbs out on the other side, and runs off. Helen murmurs, "Swim to his house? Why would he want to do that?"

The first pool Ned Merrill encounters after that is at the Grahams' home, where he is welcomed as an old friend, but at the next one, Mrs. Hammer angrily throws him off her property after he swims a lap without permission, and he doesn't seem to understand why.

After racing a horse along a fence, Ned arrives at a backyard where Muffie Lear (Alva Celauro) is swimming in her parents' pool with her friend, Julie Ann Hooper (Janet Landgard). Seeing Julie Ann reminds Ned that she was once his children's babysitter. Looking at her grown-up body, now covered only by a gingham bikini, he begins to court his young princess, inviting her to join him in his swim across the county. She accepts. As they walk in the woods toward the Bunkers' pool, Julie Ann tells Ned she used to have a crush on him and would pretend when he drove her home that they were "desperately in love." Mia Farrow was originally offered the part of Julie Ann, and Landgard

Ned Merrill (Burt Lancaster) is living in the well-heeled suburb of Westport when he loses everything, including his identity. Above is Joan Rivers in her first screen acting role. (Photofest)

shares her doe-eyed sincerity, which is needed as the conversation veers into creepy.

The Bunker house is next, and there's yet another midday cocktail party going on. A man approaches Ned, telling him about a job opening. Ned becomes agitated. It's the first direct sign that what is happening in Ned's mind is out of sync with how his neighbors view him. He quickly pulls Julie Ann away from the party and they're off again.

Soon, alone in a secluded barn, Ned tries to make love to Julie Ann. His clumsy pass breaks the romantic mood. Julie sees her courting prince, her handsome childhood hero, revealed to be just an old letch. For Ned, obscene reality has entered his fantasy world. Neither can face it. Julie runs off and Ned ignores it all, continuing his journey.

The Hallorans' Black chauffeur recognizes Ned and stops to offer him a ride to the house. (Original casting notes had Billy Dee Williams as the chauffeur, but it's actor Bernie Hamilton who filmed this small but important scene with Lancaster.) Ned calls the chauffeur "Steve," but he corrects Ned, explaining that Steve was the previous chauffeur. "I don't know why I thought you were Steve," Ned says, laughing nervously." Of course, *we* do, and so does the chauffeur, who never offers his own name. After the exchange, both ride along in awkward silence, two displaced men sitting side by side in a car that neither one of them owns.

Ned approaches the next driveway and meets a small boy named Kevin Gilmartin (Michael

Kearney), sitting by himself on one of those great ancient stone walls so typical of Connecticut. It's a curious sight, seeing a boy without his parents, and Ned asks him if his mother is home. "She's in Europe," Kevin tells him. The boy goes on to explain matter-of-factly that his father, who also appears to be absent, is—according to his mother—in love with a manicurist. Ned listens to Kevin's story with what appears to be great empathy, then asks if he can use the pool.

Another grand house in Fairfield featured in *The Swimmer*. This is a private residence.

He and Kevin walk on to the house and the pool, only to find it completely drained. Kevin explains that they took the water out of the pool because he had never been a good swimmer. Ned again lapses into his fantasy world, telling Kevin, "If you make believe hard enough that something is true, then it is true for you." Ned and Kevin then "pretend" to swim the length of the pool. For Ned this is a valuable coping lesson. Just pretend, and all the bad things, unhappiness—even reality itself—will disappear. The only relief Ned finds is by plunging into the next pool, and the next, submerging himself in the cool water, pretending that with every pool he dives into, there is hope that when he emerges, he will finally be absolved of his sins.

Ned arrives next at the Biswangers' home, "those awful people," who spot him crashing their late-afternoon pool party. Ned is trying to digest what is happening to him, telling a party guest (Joan Rivers) with as much dignity as he can muster, "They're not even on our Christmas card list." She had been chatting him up, thinking he was a rich, available bachelor, but a man comes up and whispers something in her ear and she and other guests start to back away from Ned. After he swims a lap in the pool and then makes a scene, Mr. Biswanger confronts him. "You crashed in, now crash the hell out!" The Biswangers—"those awful people," the people Ned didn't think were worthy of a Christmas card—have shunned him.

That morning, Ned had looked like a muscled wet stallion. By the time he ends up at the home of his former lover, Shirley Abbott (Janice Rule), he is broken and limping, looking like an animal that needs to be shot and put out of his misery. Shirley Abbott will provide that service. Trying

REAL ESTATE

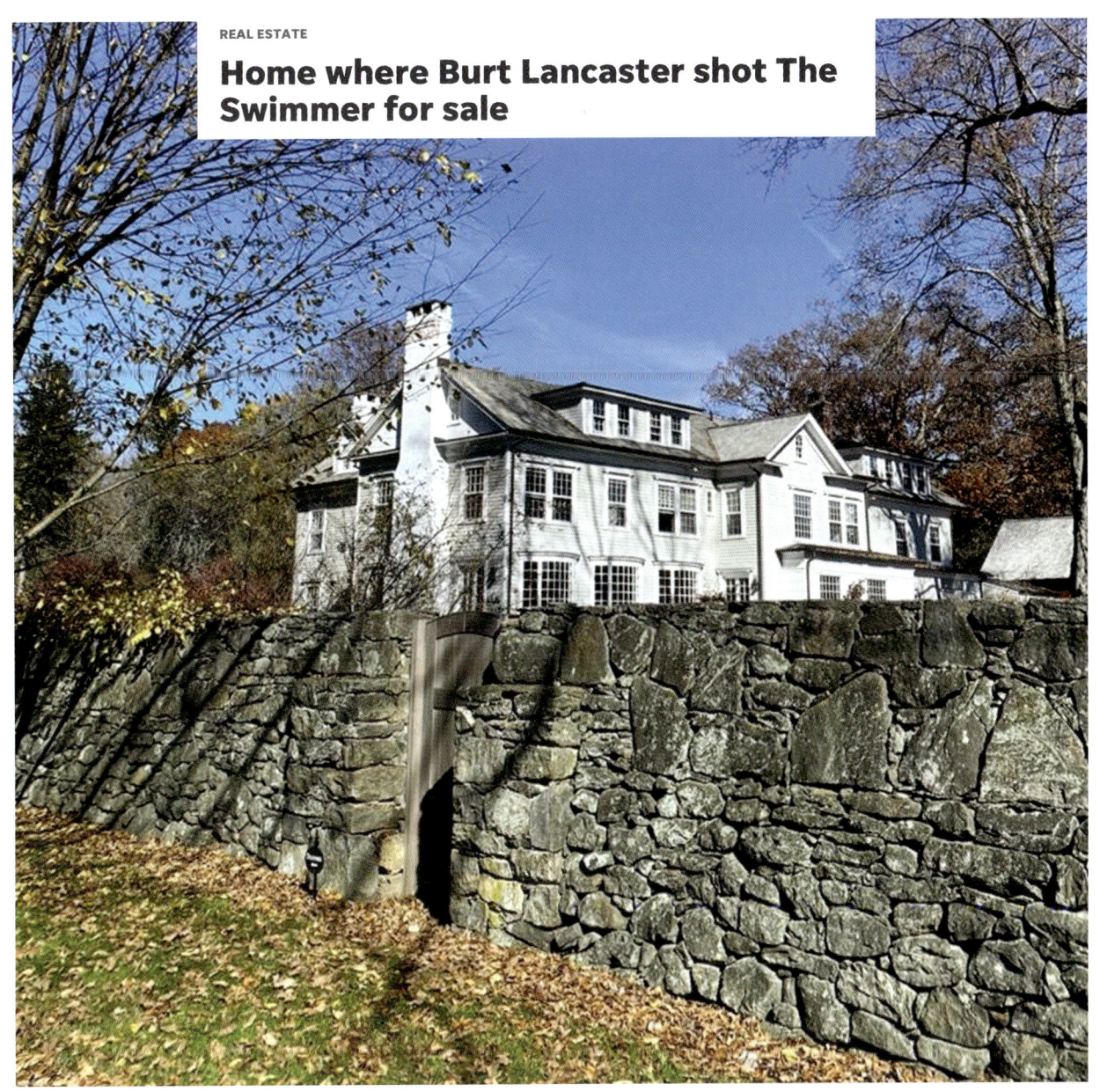

Home where Burt Lancaster shot The Swimmer for sale

A few houses and their swimming pools were featured in *The Swimmer*. This one, located in Fairfield, is a private residence. In the film, the modern pool house, with its natural bluestone patio, was meant to show the nouveau riche lifestyle of Westport in the 1960s. When the house went on the market, one of the selling points was that the pool and pool house had been featured in the Burt Lancaster film, *The Swimmer*. Splashy advertising for sure!

to regain a sense of his pride, Ned reminds Shirley of their lovemaking, but Shirley laughs at him, telling him it sickened her. "You loved it," Ned screams, as Shirley stomps back into her house, leaving Ned alone in her pool. He sinks to the bottom, the weight of his own life drowning him. When he rises, he is barely able to pull himself out of the water.

"This is the day Ned Merrill swims across the county," he'd initially proclaimed optimistically, but "the Lucinda River" was not quite the romantic expedition we were promised. Along the way, we've learned that Ned is a man who cheated on his wife, alienated his children, let down his friends, and lost himself. "The Lucinda River" has become a reflection both of who he was and who he has now become: a ghost.

Ned has one final pool to swim in order to get home, and that's the dreaded "community pool," where former acquaintances, merchants he used to deal with, greet him with barbed comments, like "How do you like our water, Mr. Merrill?" and "Stings your eyes a little, huh?," referring to the heavily chlorinated waters on the wrong side of town. Another beer-bellied local calls Ned a deadbeat who owes money all over town. The grocer's wife shares a tidbit about Ned's wife with smug superiority: "Plain mustard ain't good enough for Mrs. Merrill. She had to have Dijon mustard!" (The ultimate '60s status symbol!)

Ned finally does make it home. The camera peeks through a broken window of his empty, decaying mansion, and we see the wreckage of his life. A price tag hangs from an unsold chandelier left over from a white elephant sale. Confronted by his terrible reality, Ned Merrill huddles in a fetal position, hanging on to the ornate locked door to what was once his Connecticut dream house as a torrential rain pours down . . . The End.

Pretty bleak. "When You Talk about '*The Swimmer*,' Will You Talk About Yourself?" read the promotional poster. It was like a threat. In 1968, people in Connecticut—or probably anywhere—didn't want to see this dark of a depiction of suburbia. Because if Ned Merrill was a sham, then maybe the whole mythology of "Come to Peaceful Connecticut" and superior living in suburbia that had begun with *Mr. Blandings Builds His Dream House* was a sham.

Frank Perry would go on to make many films, including *Play It as It Lays* (1972), *Man on a Swing* (1974), and *Mommie Dearest* (1981). Perry died in 1995 of pancreatic cancer, before an interest in his work could take hold. Many of his films, including *Diary of a Mad Housewife* (1970), are now considered masterworks. One of Perry's final films was a 1987 Shelley Long comedy vehicle called *Hello Again,* which marked the first brief onscreen appearance from yours truly and led to a lasting friendship with its director. Back in the 1980s, I worked for film publicist Peggy Siegal; we shared our offices with Perry, which is how I ended up being cast in *Hello Again*. At the time, I wasn't aware of Perry's films beyond his then-latest ones, *Mommie Dearest* and *Compromising Positions*. A huge three sheet poster of *Mommie Dearest* hung in Perry's office, but he came to have mixed feelings about the success of that film, as it narrowed the kind of films he was being allowed to make—hence his accepting a directing gig on the rather slight comedy, *Hello Again*. When I expressed my interest in filmmaking, Perry gave me copies of all his films to watch. It was *The Swimmer* that affected me the most, provoking my own memories of growing up in an affluent community in Connecticut and feeling like I didn't "belong." In *The Swimmer* Ned Merrill's fall from grace is greeted with a stinging puritanical judgment that he no longer belongs. (Photofest)

CONNECTICUT IN THE MOVIES

Hard to imagine with scenes like this, one advertisement of *Loving* boasted that it was, "A love story . . . Westport style." *Loving* was based on the novel *Brooks Wilson Ltd.* (1967) by Westport author and illustrator John McDermott, written under the pen name J. M. Ryan, but McDermott was so unhappy with the film that he wore a T-shirt to the Westport premiere that read in large letters, "They Changed It." (Photofest)

Eva Marie Saint plays Selma Wilson and George Segal plays her husband, Brooks, in *Loving* (1970). A comedy-drama released by Columbia, *Loving* is a frank examination of marriage and infidelity set in Westport. (Photofest)

LOVING (1970)

By the late 1960s, the veneer of the suburban sex "comedy" was gone, revealing a deep angst and very little to laugh about. Movies like *Loving*—I call it *Anti-Loving*—took a hammer to the American dream and smashed it to bits. It plays like the alt version of *Mr. Blandings Builds His Dream House*, if Blandings had started to booze and cheat on his wife. Here was another examination of upper-middle-class life and marriage, also set in Westport, but *Loving* is a shade darker and even more graphic than *The Swimmer* (1968). Though marketed and reviewed as a comedy about social mores in suburbia, *Loving* is more like a male primal scream about breaking free from the responsibilities of being a good husband, father, and breadwinner.

Loving has curious parallels to *Mr. Blandings Builds His Dream House*. Both men are in advertising. Brooks West (George Segal) is a successful commercial artist and illustrator. Both men moved to Connecticut and commute to their New York offices by train. Brooks lives in Westport

Locations for *Loving* include the Saugatuck train station, Green Farms Elementary School, and Main Street in Westport. (Photofest)

and is about to purchase an even bigger home. Both men are married with two little girls. Brooks has a beautiful wife, Selma (Eva Marie Saint), who dotes on him, as do his two girls, Lizzie and Hanna (Lorraine Cullen, Cheryl Bucher). Where they differ is that though Blandings may have been comically on the verge of a nervous breakdown from the pressures of work and building a new house, he loved his family and would never want to hurt them. Brooks West is determined to remove one by one the underpinnings of what appears to be a happy and successful life and career.

Selma is similar to the wife Jennifer Jones played in *The Man in the Gray Flannel Suit*, trapped in the traditional role of a long-suffering 1950s housewife. Though she has a mind of her own, she never gets the opportunity to share her feelings with Brooks; she just copes with his. She plays the understanding nursemaid, hoping that one day Brooks will explain what it is he's so depressed about, or believing that once they purchase that bigger, better house, things will improve between them. Selma senses Brooks is pulling away from her (they are no longer intimate; they dress in silence; they sit across from each other at the breakfast table in silence); she suspects his infidelity

The wild party scene in *Loving* is said to have been filmed in Westport. Local residents Paul Newman and Joanne Woodward are even rumored to have appeared as extras.

but never questions him about it, as if there is quiet dignity in her patient and loving attitude.

Part of Brooks's midlife crisis is that he no longer knows what he wants, and everything he thought he wanted no longer excites him. As if moving to suburbia dulled his senses. After boarding the train from Westport, Brooks shifts into his alternative life in New York as an aging hipster, spending time with his younger mistress, Grace (Janis Young), who sees right through him, while struggling to still be relevant at the office. Grace wants him to commit to her, but he's ambivalent. He's also ambivalent about having an affair with Nelly Parks (Nancie Phillips), the oversexed wife of his associate, Will Parks (David Doyle). He's ambivalent about making love to his wife or even purchasing a new home. When Selma shows him around what will be their new home, he can't wait to get out of there, he feels so trapped. The one thing Brooks thinks he cares about is landing the Lepridon account, hoping that will boost his self-esteem, but Mr. Lepridon (Sterling Hayden) sees through him, too, and even dislikes his work, which causes Brooks to doubt himself and to drink more. Brooks's final act of self-destruction occurs while attending a party with Selma at a neighbor's house in Westport.

The party is swinging and Selma drifts off to another room. Brooks gets blindly drunk and decides to take Nelly up on her offer. They consummate their affair in a sloppy, uncontrolled way in

CONNECTICUT IN THE MOVIES

a children's playhouse, unaware they are being watched by everyone at the party—including Selma—on a closed-circuit television. Here is the suburban sex comedy, without any comedy, just straight-up depravity. Not only are the partygoers not bothered by Brooks fornicating with one of their wives, but they gather around the screen to watch and hoot.

Selma has been so publicly humiliated it's hard to imagine that she will ever recover. She runs out of the party in tears, a half-dressed Brooks chasing after her, looking once again for forgiveness. Inexplicably, he sheepishly tells her he has landed the Lepridon account. Why he chooses that moment to tell her is left unexplained, but Selma begins beating him, her pent-up anger finally released. Brooks withstands the blows, feeling he deserves them. The film ends in a standoff: Selma stands literally and metaphorically at a fork in the road with Brooks, and we are left to wonder if the fractured marriage, so damaged by infidelity and booze, will survive.

Director Irvin Kershner began his career in features making relatively small personal films, such as *A Fine Madness* (1966). He went on to direct *Up the Sandbox* (1972) and, in 1980, the film with which he is most associated—*The Empire Strikes Back*. The conundrum of *Loving*—and maybe that's the point—is how Brooks, even in the midst of a midlife crisis, could ever cheat on Selma, his gorgeous, idealistic wife, played so sympathetically by Eva Marie Saint. There is a self-justification to Brooks's actions that makes the film difficult to embrace. *Loving* came out in an era when couples were experimenting with affairs outside marriage; the film was likened to Paul Mazursky's *Bob and Carol and Ted and Alice* (1969). But while we watch Brooks satisfy his every carnal desire, the film forgets that the route to recovery might be learning to be loving, not just to have a wife who loves you unconditionally.

THE STEPFORD WIVES (1975)

Ira Levin's original intention with his novel *The Stepford Wives* (1972) may have been to decry robotic conformity in suburban Connecticut, but the 1975 film version stands out more for its conflicting stance about the emerging women's rights movement of the 1970s. Did men really want women to be equal partners in work and marriage? Or, given the option, would they prefer a malleable female programmed to care only about shopping, housework, and sex? The '60s sex comedies set in Connecticut had all been veering in this direction, and now here was a sly take on the same subject. *The Stepford Wives* was billed as satire, or "science fiction," but maybe the underlying message was closer to the truth. Did men secretly harbor a fantasy to kill their wives and replace them with robots programmed to service their needs?

British director Bryan Forbes was chosen specifically for the material; producers hoped that, as a foreigner, he might have a unique take on American culture. Forbes's wife and frequent collaborator, Nanette Newman, was cast as one of the Stepford wives. She has a memorable turn as Carol, an ex-alcoholic

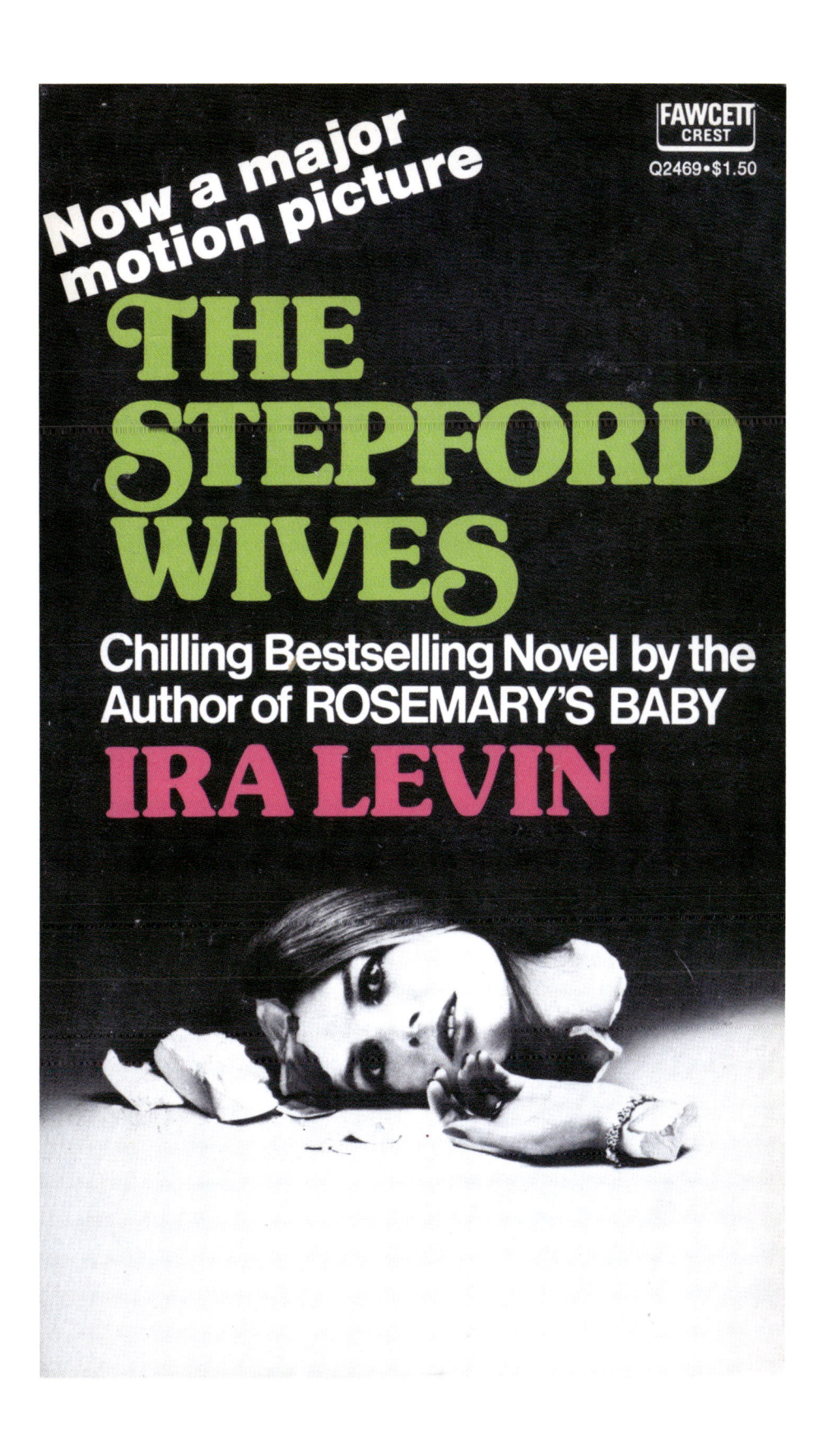

CONNECTICUT IN THE MOVIES

Of course, if you want the perfect wife, you might just have to build one, as they did in the darkest film about suburbia yet, *The Stepford Wives*. (Photofest)

who short-circuits after a car accident, goes back to drinking, and starts endlessly repeating "I'll just die if I don't get this recipe" at a pool party, before she's led away to get some mechanical work done under her hood.

Forbes said he thought he was making a satire that women would embrace and relate to, and was genuinely shocked by the negative response the film received from women's rights groups. At a New York prerelease screening for female "opinion makers," which included screenwriter Eleanor Perry (*Diary of a Mad Housewife*, 1970; *The Swimmer*, 1968), director Joan Silver (*Hester Street*, 1975), author Betty Friedan (*The Feminine Mystique*, 1963), and the former president of the National Organization for Women (NOW), there were audible groans, guffaws, and hisses.

After the film, an "awareness session" was held at which the women could voice their opinions. The filmmakers, of course, hoped positive responses would help sell the film, but instead they received harsh critiques. Writer Linda Arkin said, "It dumps on everyone—women, men, suburbia." Friedan got emotional, calling the film "a rip-off of the women's movement," and stormed out of the screening room.

It was Friedan who had opened the door for the feminist movement in America when she wrote about the dissatisfaction and malaise of being a suburban housewife in her landmark book, *The Feminine Mystique*. In 1966 she helped form NOW, its principal mission being to bring women into equal participation in all areas of society. Here she was being asked to promote a film that seemed to mock everything she stood for.

What may have also struck a nerve is that by the time *The Stepford Wives* came out, infighting within the women's lib movement was causing it to implode. Friedan's branch of the movement was competing with another so-called women's liberation movement. Younger civil rights and antiwar activists were organizing, formulating theory, and grabbing headlines with events like a demonstration protesting the Miss America beauty pageant, and burning items in trash cans that they considered symbols of female oppression. (In fact, although they never really burned bras, they were nicknamed "bra burners" nonetheless, and any woman interested in the women's liberation movement was tagged with this divisive term. This is captured in a scene in *The Stepford Wives*.) The very idea of female bonding or consciousness-raising was made to look silly, and the women's lib movement at the time was denigrated by . . . other women. It did not go unnoticed by the women assembled to watch the film.

Joanna (Katharine Ross) says she wants to start a female consciousness-raising group in Stepford, but she assures her one close friend, Bobby (Paula Prentiss), "I messed a little bit with women's lib in New York, [but] I'm not contemplating any Maidenform bonfires." Eleanor Perry was appalled, and responded to the scene, wryly saying, "Men made this movie, right? It's just something no woman would have put in as a line." William Goldman, who wrote the buddy film *Butch Cassidy and the Sundance Kid* (1969), costarring Katharine Ross, originally envisioned the women of Stepford dressed like Playboy bunnies—maybe the ultimate male fantasy—in hot pants and halter tops (but presumably no bunny ears). It was Nanette Newman, the director's wife, who vetoed that idea. That's how *The Stepford Wives*' antebellum look—long skirts, wide hats, and ruffled blouses, reflecting southern gentility—came about.

Forbes was in denial that *The Stepford Wives* might be seen as insensitive to the women's rights movement; he recalled, "I remember saying to this particular savagely disturbed woman, 'You've missed the whole point; a) it's fantasy; b) if anybody looks stupid, it's the men. It's not an attack on women, it's an attack on women being exploited by men.' " Forbes didn't understand that *The Stepford Wives* might represent a woman's very real fear of losing her identity. Betty Friedan was reacting to the ease with which Joanna's freedom is taken from her, how she is dragged back into servitude like a 1950s housewife—the very thing she had written about escaping from in *The Feminine Mystique*. There is no equality in *The Stepford Wives*; there is only slave and master. The antebellum outfits serve as a reminder of the culture it represented.

The movie opens on a New York City housewife, Joanna Eberhart (Katharine Ross), staring pensively at her own reflection in the mirror of her Upper West Side apartment. Downstairs, a

Identity and loss of one's identity runs through *The Stepford Wives*. From a man carrying an unclothed plastic mannequin across a crowded New York City street, to everyone driving the same Ford station wagon in Stepford, to the ending when a vacant-eyed Stepford wife kills her living, breathing counterpart. In the years since *The Stepford Wives* came out, the word "Stepford" has become synonymous with a certain type of uptight Connecticut mentality. In March 2007, Ira Levin, author of *The Stepford Wives,* seemed to broaden the term when he denounced the town of Wilton, Connecticut, in a letter to the *New York Times*. Levin was responding to a story about a Wilton High School principal who halted production of a high school play called *Voices in Conflict*, about the war in Iraq, for fear it was inflammatory. He called out the principal for being a "Stepford principal," and went on to write, "Wilton, Conn., where I lived in the 1960s, was the inspiration for Stepford, the fictional town I later wrote about in *The Stepford Wives*." Ross began her career in television, and received a Supporting Actress Oscar nomination for playing Elaine in *The Graduate* (1967). She was at the height of her career when she made *Butch Cassidy and the Sundance Kid* (1969) and *Tell Them Willie Boy Is Here* (1969). Ross met and married the cinematographer of these films, Conrad Hall, but they divorced in 1973. After *The Stepford Wives*, she appeared in the disaster film *The Swarm*, *The Betsy*, and *The Legacy* (all 1978); while working on the latter, she met her future husband, actor Sam Elliott, to whom she is still married. (Photofest)

The men of Stepford are cooking up more than a barbecue. (Photofest)

packed station wagon is waiting to take her to suburbia. Joanna's lack of enthusiasm for the journey foreshadows her own eventual doom at the hands of her loving husband. As Charlie the doorman (Tom Spratley) helps the children, Kim (Mary Stuart Masterson) and Amy (Ronny Sullivan), into the car, along with the dog, he says brightly to Joanna, "Take care! Be happy," and she can only respond glumly that she'll try, as her husband, Walter (Peter Masterson), quickly drives them away.

As they ride toward Connecticut on the Merritt Parkway, Joanna looks like a dog heading to a kill shelter. Every instinct she has to escape will be thwarted by her domineering husband. She's not as strong as him. She's not as smart as him. He makes all the decisions. We learn it was Walter's idea to move to Stepford, and when Joanna expresses her apprehension, Walter immediately shuts her down, saying, "It's perfect. How could you not like it?"

The Stepford Wives weaves sexism like this throughout the film. Why does Joanna agree to leave behind her budding career as a photographer, her social network of female friends, her former groovy boyfriend in the biotech industry, whom she will later reveal she still has feelings for? Why? To please her husband? Did Walter really need to turn her into a robot? She already does everything he tells her to do.

When they arrive in Stepford—the actual location is Fairfield County—Joanna finds the many corporations that dot the landscape of Stepford strange, but Walter mansplains that they are a representation of wealth and status, and she accepts that. Walter keeps gaslighting her, telling her to give the town a chance even after their daughter Kim (Peter Masterson's real-life daughter) tells her mom she is so creeped out, she is afraid to ride the bus or attend school—although she tells her mother it's not her, it's her teddy bear that is unhappy.

CONNECTICUT IN THE MOVIES

The Stepford Wives spawned several TV movies—*Revenge of the Stepford Wives* (1980), *The Stepford Children* (1987), and *The Stepford Husbands* (1996), as well as a remake, *The Stepford Wives* (2004), also shot in Connecticut. (Photofest)

Walter, a successful attorney, hears about the very elite Men's Association, and he's invited to join. Another little sexist note here: The men can have an "old boys' club," but the women wanting to start a consciousness-raising group is somehow crazy. Speaking of crazy, you have to wonder if Walter knew all about the activities of the association, and that is what led to his desire to move to Stepford in the first place.

Joanna goes along with Walter's wish to join the men's club, and when Walter has the other men over, she even dutifully serves them drinks, staying in the background. It's yet another sexist touch. I mean, we all know about women's intuition; did Joanna's take the night off? She doesn't seem suspicious when one man casually sketches her portrait, or another man asks her personal questions and records her voice—a hobby, he says. Both will later be used as a template to make her robot.

The Stepford Wives suggests again and again that if only women weren't so bothersome, if only they didn't argue or question things, if only their minds, their bodies, and their opinions could be controlled, they (and, more importantly, their husbands) would be much happier.

The Stepford Wives' director Bryan Forbes with his cast in Westport, Connecticut (along with a visiting Bette Davis, who lived on Crooked Mile Road). Forbes's wife, Nanette Newman—who plays Carol—is sitting left of center. Screenwriter William Goldman was displeased that Forbes had cast his wife as Carol, as Goldman had imagined a much younger and sexier actress. "A sex bomb she isn't," he said. (Photofest)

Joanna decides once again to accept the will of her husband and try to fit in with their new community. She and Bobby go ahead and create their women's support group and encourage the other wives to talk about their feelings. It starts out well—Charmaine (Tina Louise) shares her fears that she's a trophy wife, that her husband married her only for her looks. The meeting changes course when other Stepford wives start discussing their favorite brand of spray starch. After the meeting, Charmaine suddenly goes away, and when she returns from a "spa weekend," she has stopped playing tennis, her favorite activity—she even has her courts torn out—and is now a Stepford wife, too.

Little by little, Joanna and Bobby piece together an unlikely theory as to what the Men's Association is really all about: turning women into submissive "Stepford wives." Something in the water, they think at first.

Joanna is shocked when she discovers outspoken Bobby in full housewife mode in her kitchen, dressed in a frilly maxi dress, hair done up, and making coffee. In the film's most memorable scene, Bobby mindlessly drops coffee cups and repeats to Joanna, "I thought you were my friend," after Joanna stabs her in the stomach to see if she'll bleed. Spoiler: She doesn't. To Joanna's horror, Bobby has been "Stepfordized."

Later, in a scene reminiscent of Ira Levin's novel-to-screen adaptation, *Rosemary's Baby* (1969), Walter has second thoughts. He breaks down in tears and tells Joanna that he really loves her, but when Joanna insists that they move out of Stepford to Eastbridge, he changes his mind and goes ahead with his original plan.

In a sinister move, Walter lures Joanna to the Association's headquarters by supposedly taking their children there, knowing her maternal instincts will make her go to retrieve them. We then get to the crux of the film as she questions the group's leader, Dale (Patrick O'Neal), as to why he is doing this to all the

CONNECTICUT IN THE MOVIES

women, and he opines that if their roles were reversed—if women had thought of this—they would do the same thing. This seems to imply there really was a battle of the sexes going on in 1975—that men's fear of women having power over them was so great that the only way to stop them was to lobotomize them. In another "Men made this movie, right?" moment, Dale says, "Wouldn't you like some perfect stud waiting on you around the house? Praising you? Servicing you?" Joanna is never allowed to answer, but if she had been, she might have responded that her "perfect mate" might be someone who shared her hopes and dreams, career goals, and responsibilities for caring for the house and children: basically, equality.

The final scene of *The Stepford Wives* contains a warning. The robotized women of Stepford glide past each other in the supermarket in a sea of pastels, exchanging beatific smiles, seemingly happy. But if you look closely, you'll notice Joanna has more of a Mona Lisa–type smile, her eyes revealing a deep well of sadness. If Joanna has been correctly programmed to smile, she has also been correctly programmed to suffer in silence.

The deconstruction of Connecticut suburbia that began with *The Man in the Gray Flannel Suit* was complete. I was reminded of the happiness that Mr. and Mrs. Blandings felt when they moved their family to Connecticut in the 1940s so they could have a better quality of life. In the 1950s, Tom and Betsy Rath in *The Man in the Gray Flannel Suit* also moved to Connecticut in search of upward mobility, but the film reflected the separateness that had crept between men and women in marriage. By the time we get to *The Stepford Wives* in 1975, we have a married couple, the Eberharts, purchasing a classic two-story, white, colonial house—very much like the Blandings house—but here Connecticut is a little too perfect, as if to say that something this perfect is not perfect at all. Suburbia is a prison of conformity. Cinematographer Owen Roizman, who had shot *The French Connection* (1971) and, later, *Network* (1976), reimagined the Connecticut countryside and suburbia in *The Stepford Wives*. The hyper-real look became synonymous with a new brand of films about Connecticut—Dark Suburbia. After *The Stepford Wives*, by merely setting a story "in Connecticut," you were signaling to the audience that something very bad was going to happen.

Scenes from the original *The Stepford Wives* and its remake were shot at the Lockwood-Mathews Mansion at 295 West Avenue in Norwalk, built in 1864 in the Second Empire style by the railroad magnate LeGrand Lockwood. Additional scenes were shot in Weston, Darien, Fairfield, and Redding.

CONNECTICUT IN THE MOVIES

It Happened to Jane (1959). (Photofest)

CHAPTER 7
LOCATION, LOCATION, LOCATION: THE TOWN IS THE STAR

IT HAPPENED TO JANE (1959)

Don't get between a woman and her lobsters. Jane Osgood (Doris Day) is a widow with two children running a lobster business in "Cape Anne," Maine. When changes implemented by the Eastern and Portland Railroad's new president, Harry Foster Malone (Ernie Kovacs), cause three hundred of Jane's lobsters to perish (I think any New Englander would agree that three hundred lobsters going uneaten is indeed sacrilege), Jane sues Malone and the E&P for the loss of income, recruiting her friend, local lawyer George Denham (Jack Lemmon)—who is conveniently smitten with her—to help.

The Old 97. You can ride a train like the one in *It Happened to Jane*. The Essex Steam Train is located at 1 Railroad Avenue in Essex.

Jane's lawsuit becomes a PR nightmare for Malone, and he retaliates by shutting down train service to the town. Jane hatches a plan to get the Old 97 steam train out of retirement to get her lobsters to market. Jane's fight with Malone catches on with the media, and a handsome reporter from the *New York Mirror*, Larry Clay (Steve Forrest), starts writing a David-and-Goliath story about her. A romance develops, and now Jane has to decide if she'll marry the New York lawyer Larry or stay in Cape Anne and marry George—if George can ever get up the courage to ask her.

It was a complete fluke that Columbia made *It Happened to Jane* in Chester, Connecticut. As of this writing, the town looks pretty much the same as when they made the movie there back in the summer of 1958. There really is no "Cape Anne," Maine, with Chester doubling for the fictional town all the way through the picture. In one scene at Chester Junction, a news reporter, Gene Rayburn, comes to town. Rayburn—playing himself—is a reporter for WTIC, which is a local Connecticut television network. He would go on to become the emcee for the popular game show *Match Game* on CBS.

Columbia had sent Richard Quine location pictures of small towns all over New England

Director Richard Quine's spirited comedy *It Happened to Jane* from Columbia Pictures, starring Doris Day, Jack Lemmon, and Ernie Kovacs, is a salute to Connecticut's "stick-to-itiveness" as well as a celebration of small-town New England Americana. A perk of watching the film and then visiting Chester is that many of the locations in *It Happened to Jane* are still there. The waterfront scenes were filmed on and around Jennings Pond, off Spring Street. The Chester Meeting House, which became the "Cape Anne" Town Hall, still hosts all of Chester's town meetings, and voters line up to vote there for elections. The "Cape Anne," Maine, Telephone Exchange was above what is now a Century 21 real estate office. Bill Breslin's package store (in the Villager building) became the marine supply store. Jack Lemmon's law office was above the old Robbie's store on Main Street. Carmine Grote's Appliance Store became Aaron Caldwell's Fine Foods General Store. You can also see the United Church of Chester, on Route 148, and Chester Depot, where Doris Day drives up in a woody wagon to unload her lobsters. The director of photography was Charles Lawton Jr. Lawton's prolific career at Columbia including shooting *The Lady from Shanghai* (1947). Lawton had previously worked with Quine on *Drive a Crooked Road* (1954) and *My Sister Eileen* (1955). *It Happened to Jane* was not without controversy. Art director Cary Odell needed to install parking meters on Main Street for a gag in the script about First Selectman Aaron Caldwell's (John Cecil Holm) penchant for collecting from expired meters outside his store. Chester didn't have any parking meters in 1958, but the production unit convinced Chester officials it might be a good source of income, so actual working parking meters were installed. Local townspeople were incensed. Columbia was forced to remove all the meters after filming was completed. Ahem. There are currently no parking meters in downtown Chester.

that were better suited to filming, but he didn't feel any of the towns had the right "atmosphere" he was looking for. Quine decided to drive up the coastline from New York and search himself. He was on Route 9 when he saw the sign for Chester and told his chauffeur to make a right. Quine later said, "Somebody must have been tugging at my elbow, because it's the only time I said it the entire trip." In 1958, Chester was a town of just two thousand people. After walking around, Quine called screenwriter Norman Katkov and excitedly told him, "I've got it! Chester, Connecticut." Not surprisingly, Katkov said he'd never heard of Chester. What started out as a fluke became a mutual love affair between Hollywood and the town, with one cast member actually relocating to Chester.

Quine, who had recently separated from his second wife, rented a sprawling, six-bedroom colonial

It Happened to Jane. In "A Town in the Grip of Glamour: Hollywood Descends on Connecticut," written for the *Hartford Courant* in June 1958, Robert Ramaker wrote that Jack Lemmon described Chester as "the most restful place he'd seen." (Photo by Peggy Breslin, Courtesy Chester Historical Society) Here on River Road in Deep River (below) is the house where Doris Day and her husband, producer Martin Melcher, stayed while making *It Happened to Jane*. Somehow I like to picture Doris Day singing "Que Sera, Sera" in the shower.

house on Liberty Street in Chester that he shared with his son, as well as Jack Lemmon, Norman Kratkov, music director Fred Karger, and, later, actors Ernie Kovacs and Casey Adams (aka, Max

116   LOCATION, LOCATION, LOCATION: THE TOWN IS THE STAR

Lemmon and Day with the Cub Scouts in Chester. (Courtesy Chester Historical Society) Local Cub Scouts spent all night filming with Doris Day and Jack Lemmon at Jennings Pond in Chester. Lemmon and Day sing "Be Prepared," which was cowritten by director Richard Quine. (Photofest)

Showalter). Jack Lemmon recalled that on his second night in town, a neighbor, Mrs. Curtis Bishop, came by the house with a large bunch of white irises from her garden and a jar of her homemade tomato preserves. She welcomed Lemmon to town and reminded him if he needed anything, anything at all, to just ask. Lemmon, touched by the generosity of his new neighbor, later recounted the story to local reporters visiting the set. Columbia's production unit head, Burt Astor, was tasked with finding the residents of the Liberty Street house the best cook in Chester. Her name was Mrs. Dorothy McNutt. Halfway through shooting, Quine complained that he and Lemmon were putting on too much weight and she needed to stop bringing them treats.

One thing that makes *It Happened to Jane* so enjoyable is that the plot of the film—a small town pitching in to rally around a neighbor who needs their help—mirrors the actual environment of the making of the film. Quine found the "atmosphere" he was looking for. He discovered a way to showcase the folksy charm of Chester, making it a character but never a caricature. Every scene in *It Happened to Jane* is filled with Chester residents; children, Cub Scouts, and even a local basset hound named Clarence are prominently seen (although you can catch a lot of them holding back laughter or accidentally looking into the camera in many of the crowd scenes). *It Happened to Jane* looks like a movie travelogue made by the Chester Chamber of Commerce in which they somehow got movie stars like Doris Day and Jack Lemmon to show up.

The meetinghouse scene with Jane and George, in which the town votes for the first select-

CONNECTICUT IN THE MOVIES

Doris Day said, "I like to have fun on set." She and Lemmon demonstrated how game they were for physical comedy. In a scene shot on the train, George shovels coal to keep Old 97 going while Jane, dressed in white, tells him that Larry (Steve Forrest) wants to marry her. George stops to talk, but Uncle Otis (Russ Brown) yells, "More steam!" to keep him shoveling. George finally tells Jane he loves her and she shouldn't marry Larry. Jane yells, "Oh, George, I love you." George yells back, "I love you!" Uncle Otis yells, "More steam," as the lovebirds kiss, with Day still smiling. (Courtesty Chester Historical Society)

man, is filled with Chester residents. Another scene has residents collecting coal to run the Old 97 steam train. The Chester Fife and Drum Corps (founded in 1868) appears in the final parade scene. The Chester Cub Scouts are featured, singing a song with Doris Day and Jack Lemmon appropriately called "Be Prepared." Quine cuts to close-ups of the Scouts, making sure every boy gets on camera. One of those boys, John Divas, who was a second-grader at the time, later recalled, "It was a fun experience because we were with all the people we knew from our Scout troop." The nighttime shooting went past midnight, but the Scouts received "a small compensation." Not a bad way to spend the summer—getting paid to stay up all night singing with Doris Day and Jack Lemmon!

It was a boon for Chester to have a Hollywood movie made in the town. First Selectman William Johnson, a Democrat, acted as the go-between, negotiating the needs of the town and the filmmakers. Johnson was offered a salary of $25 a day but declined, saying that as a public official it

Jennings Pond today, in Chester.

might not look right. He does make a cameo in the film (as does the screenwriter Norman Kratkov, playing the bailiff in the town hall).

The film company paid the town's police budget for a month to ensure that constables were on hand to maintain order during filming. Local carpenters were tasked with building a large wooden locomotive—a replica of the Old 97 steam train, which is prominently seen at the end of the film. They also built a complete replica of "Cape Anne Station." They even devised a way to create authentic sag to the roof by attaching heavy cables and pulling it just enough to make it look dilapidated. The newly painted yellow-and-brown station was doctored by covering it in soot to give it some age.

Sam the Lobster was also made in Chester. "Sam No. 1" was made in Hollywood. He arrived weighing thirty pounds and proved to be too challenging to operate, so the production hired a local taxidermist to make "Sam No. 2," from an actual lobster. Because he was supposed to be the family's pet, wires were inserted to make Sam functional. Quine was thrilled—until he realized that because of certain gags in the script, Sam the Lobster had to be left-handed, and his crusher claw was on the right. He was afraid the audience would spot the error, so they found a lobster with its crusher claw on the left. (I never knew lobsters were left- or right-handed until I wrote this!)

It Happened to Jane is a comedy, but it touches on a serious topic, foreshadowing the end of train service in the Connecticut River Valley, and depicting greedy businessmen "running roughshod

CONNECTICUT IN THE MOVIES

over the consumer," taking away local train routes and giving way to the age of the freeway. The very steam trains used in the film, which once ran through Chester up to Middletown and on to Hartford, were put out of service by railroad executives. Railroads like the fictional E&P in the film eliminated routes to small towns, thereby leaving commuters and businesses stranded. By the late 1960s, thriving mill towns like Chester faced deterioration from lack of businesses. As kids we would walk the abandoned railroad tracks from town to town. It was a convenient, off-road way to get around—little did we know of their former glory.

There is a nostalgic scene in which George's uncle Otis (Russ Brown) reminisces about his days as a train engineer with Jane's son Billy (Teddy Rooney, son of Mickey Rooney). As he tells him what it was like driving Old 97, "The Battle Hymn of the Republic" plays softly in the background. Quine brought just the right note of sentiment to bring a tear to your eye. When it came to filming these scenes, a New Haven 2-8-2 train was pulled from storage to re-create the freight and passenger train called the Old 97. This was the last time the New Haven steam-powered J-1 2-8-2 no. 3016 engine was ever used. It was scrapped after filming. Today train enthusiasts who want to journey to the past can take a ride on the Essex Steam Train, still in operation now as a tourist attraction, and close to the Chester location along the river.

Jack Lemmon later said, "*It Happened to Jane* was a charming film at a time when 'charming films' were still being made." There are a lot of great characters, including Matilda Runyan (Mary Wickes), for example, who provides the right amount of New England quirk as Cape Anne's lone newspaperwoman on the hunt for a good story. Wickes costarred with Day in *On Moonlight Bay* (1951) and *By the Light of the Silvery Moon* (1953). She later guest-starred on a 1969 episode of *The Doris Day Show*.

Ernie Kovacs took a risk in basing his character of Harry Foster Malone, "the meanest man in the world," on the former head of Columbia Pictures, Harry Cohn. Cohn had recently died; otherwise, I doubt that Kovacs's dead-on impression of a gruff loudmouth, complete with cigar and bald pate, would have gone over well. Malone the railroad tycoon turns out to be a benevolent villain, however, with shades of W. C. Fields. He grumbles, "That miserable broad," every time someone brings up Jane's name, but in the end, he helps save the day.

Kovacs began his career in television. His inventive TV comedy shows in the 1950s were an inspiration to later comedians like David Letterman. Kovacs balanced careers on both the small screen and the big screen, and found success in both. His larger-than-life personality translated well to films, and he stood out in supporting roles in the few movies he made. His first film was Richard Quine's *Operation Mad Ball* (1957), with Jack Lemmon. He and Lemmon became close friends and costarred again in *Bell, Book and Candle* (1958) before working on *It Happened to Jane*. He worked with Quine a third time in *Strangers When We Meet* (1960). Ernie Kovacs died in a tragic car accident in 1962. He was only forty-two. His wife, Edie Adams, was so distraught that she enlisted his dearest friend, Jack Lemmon, to go to the morgue to identify her husband.

Casey Adams (aka, Max Showalter) played Harry Foster Malone's lawyer, Selwyn Harris. Showalter (who later went back to using his real name) is the actor who fell in love with the area while filming *It Happened to Jane* and later moved there. Describing the eighteenth-century farmhouse that became his home, he said, "I went up the driveway and said, 'My God, this looks like Brigadoon. I'm taking it.'" While living in Chester, he often visited his neighbor Katharine Hepburn (a Connecticut native), who lived in the Fenwick section of Old Saybrook.

Showalter became a beloved resident of Chester. He produced an annual film festival that brought luminaries like Debbie Reynolds and Dana Andrews to town. He got his friend Mary Martin to participate in a fund-raising event for the National Theatre of the Deaf (based in Chester from 1983 to 2000). He performed in local theater at the Ivoryton Playhouse, and donated his collection of memorabilia, films, and theater manuscripts to the Goodspeed Opera House in East Haddam. He even participated in annual screenings of *It Happened to Jane* at the Meeting House, sharing his recollections with residents. When Showalter passed away in July 2000, his memorial was held in a tent on the Chester Meeting House Green. Doris Day sent a condolence letter thanking the people of Chester for taking Showalter into their hearts.

It Happened to Jane holds up as a wholesome family comedy and harkens back to a bygone era. There's a scene where Jane is showing reporter Larry Clay around and they stop at the Chester town green to talk. You can hear the whistle of a steam train passing. It's not a sound effect. During filming, the local headed toward Hartford was still running. Larry looks around and says, "I envy you. It must have been fun growing up here." It's my favorite line in the movie. And of course, it's true.

The 1960s brought a changing attitude toward Connecticut on-screen and this is reflected in Delmer Daves's sweeping melodrama, *Parrish* (1961), shot in Windsor, Old Saybrook, Essex, Hadlyme, and Groton, Connecticut, in 1959 and 1960. (Photofest)

PARRISH (1961)

"Does one generation ever completely understand the next?" asks Ellen McLean (Claudette Colbert) in *Parrish*. Colbert and Donahue, two stars from two vastly different eras, both saw their screen careers end as Hollywood changed direction in the 1960s. (Photofest)

The film adaptation of New London native Mildred Savage's novel *Parrish* (1958) was a far cry from the wholesome movies of the 1930s and 1940s about life in Connecticut. The film, billed as a story about love, lust, and ambition in Connecticut's Tobacco Valley, exposed the lives of Connecticut's nouveau riche and country club elite. It was also a generation-gap movie, pitting a mother's need for conformity against a son's battle for independence.

Parrish depicted a culture, on-screen and off-, on the cusp of radical change. By the mid-1960s, Warner Bros.—the studio that made *Parrish*—had begun to disintegrate. Glossy melodramas like *Parrish* went out of favor as films like *Bonnie and Clyde* (1967), with their emphasis on realism and violence, represented the new movement in cinema. *Parrish*—shot in glorious Technicolor by the great Harry Stradling Sr.—marks the end of an era in studio filmmaking, the last gasp of Eisenhower-era glamour: elegant women dressed in gowns by Howard Shoup, shot in close-ups with lenses smeared with Vaseline, clean-cut young men in collegiate sweater vests faux-rebelling against the constraints of society—a timeless romance set to a tender Max Steiner score.

Mildred Savage went on to write *In Vivo* (1964), *Cirie* (2002), and a true crime book called *A Great Fall* (1970), based on a 1965 murder of a housewife in Litchfield, Connecticut. But nothing came close to the stir that *Parrish* caused in Connecticut, especially when it was announced that

The cast and crew of *Parrish*. You can see a picture of the state capital in the photograph.

Troy Donahue—hot off Delmer Daves's *A Summer Place* (1959)—was cast in the title role. *Parrish* was originally slated to go to director Josh Logan (*Picnic*, 1955), but a disagreement about casting— he had wanted Warren Beatty to play Parrish—led him to leave the project. Daves saw *Parrish* as a follow-up to *A Summer Place* and wanted to expand on the same themes of a generational divide between parents and children, "to show the need for a young man to establish his individual liberty in the world's increasing push toward conformity."

Although Troy Donahue had become an overnight star with *A Summer Place*, he was insecure about his acting. Daves said, "To this point his youth and looks and sex appeal are carrying him, but I'm going to make an actor out of him for the long haul. There's a lot there—a hell of a lot more than meets the eye."

The casting of Claudette Colbert—after a five-year screen absence—was a headline-grabber. What better way to convey a generation gap than by casting an old movie star like Claudette Colbert opposite a recent movie star like Troy Donahue? That gap would be apparent off-screen as well;

Troy Donahue once said about himself, "The person does not reflect the image." The same might be said of moviegoers' ever-changing perceptions of on-screen Connecticut. (Photofest)

Karl Malden and Claudette Colbert at First Congregational Church in Essex. *Parrish* was Colbert's last film. She was in her mid-fifties. In keeping with her movie-star status, she was driven to the filming location every day from Manhattan while the rest of the cast stayed at the Statler Hilton Hotel in Hartford.

different methods of work caused friction between the old pros and young Warner Bros. contract players. Colbert said in 1960: "I didn't intend on making another picture. I'm a mature woman, but I can't put on gray hair and play character roles, and mother roles are too Pollyannaish for me. I took this one because I felt it had a point of view. The mother wants to break the silver cord and lead a normal sex life of her own."

Colbert was famously controlling about her image, refusing to have the right side of her face photographed. She was not thrilled the movie was shot in color, preferring black and white, which she felt was more forgiving. She also hated outdoor scenes, favoring the control offered by studio lighting. The overly lit close-ups of her, filmed through nylon, will make you think there is something wrong with your eyesight, as it cuts back and forth to Troy Donahue, who is perfectly in focus.

Diane McBain (cast as Alison Post) said she was so nervous working with Claudette Colbert that in their first scene, she just froze, recalling that Colbert looked at her with disdain from that point on. In her book *Famous Enough: A Hollywood Memoir* (2014), which she co-wrote with Michael Gregg Michaud, McBain wrote: "Colbert was a total mystery to me. She was treated like

First Congregational Church in Essex, where scenes from *Parrish* were filmed.

royalty by the studio. There was a sturdiness to her that seemed unbending. Sometimes she spoke in a stentorian tone that caused everyone to drop what they were doing and accommodate her."

A telling interview may explain Colbert's frustration. Daves said, "To get the best out of Troy I go over a scene more often, and shoot it six or seven times, whereas Colbert can wring out a role in an average of two takes." In an on-set interview, Donahue said, "It means so much to have someone kindly yet authoritative, strong yet helpful, in scenes with me. The look in her eyes compels one's best response. And Karl [Malden] is great. I can feel the sympathy and concern emanating from both of them. I really try to generate something extra out of myself so as not to let them down."

The feeling was not mutual. In his memoir, *When Do I Start?*, Malden had some criticism for his costar, Donahue. He wrote: "What was fascinating to me was having the chance to watch two different schools of acting in action. Claudette was the consummate pro. One or two rehearsals and she was ready for a take. The younger actors—Donahue, Connie Stevens—had a completely different style. They were often unprepared and relied on blocking time to learn their lines." (A frustrated Malden often appears to be yelling at Troy Donahue rather than his character, Parrish—but the dynamic works for the strained stepfather–stepson relationship.)

Connie Stevens, who plays Lucy, told me: "I had no idea until I shot *Parrish* that Connecti-

CONNECTICUT IN THE MOVIES

127

Postcard of Connecticut tobacco workers around the time *Parrish* was filmed. Native Americans growing and harvesting tobacco in the Connecticut River Valley shared their farming process with settlers in the 1600s. The settlers soon discovered what the natives already knew—that the rich Windsor soil was perfectly suited to growing tobacco. In the 1800s, with pipe and cigar smoking on the rise, commercial tobacco farming took off. What set Connecticut's tobacco crop apart was the invention of shade tobacco in the 1900s.

cut even grew tobacco. I found the entire process fascinating." Yes, amid the steamy love story of Parrish and the four women who lust after him, you'll get a plethora of on-screen archival footage of the planting and harvesting of tobacco in the Connecticut River Valley.

Shade tobacco farming was the process of covering tobacco fields with enormous white cloth tents and cutting off direct sunlight to increase the humidity. The green fields covered in white tents were a part of the landscape. Shade tobacco was a major crop in Connecticut for over a century. People came from all over the country to work in the tobacco fields.

In the 1940s, Martin Luther King Jr. worked on a tobacco farm in Simsbury, Connecticut, to earn money for college. In an excerpt from *The Autobiography of Martin Luther King, Jr.* (ed. Clayborne Carson, IPM, Time Warner, 1998), King wrote his parents, "We are having a fine time here and the work is easy. We get up every day at 6:00. We have very good food. And I am working kitchen, so you see, I get better food. On Sunday we went to Church in Simsbury. It was a white church. The white people here are very nice. We go anyplace we want to and sit anywhere we want to." King

Connie Stevens and Madeleine Sherwood alongside actual workers at Thrall Farm in Windsor. Director Delmer Daves used the workers for key scenes showing how tobacco is cultivated. (Photofest)

Sharon Hugueny and Dean Jagger at Thrall Farm. Hey, is that a Connecticut license plate? (Photofest)

Today Thrall Farm in Windsor no longer grows tobacco but remains in operation, growing barley and wheat used for craft brewing.

goes on to write, "After that summer in Connecticut, it was a bitter feeling going back to segregation . . . I could never adjust to the separate waiting rooms, separate eating places, separate rest rooms, partly because the separate was always unequal, and partly because the very idea of separation did something to my sense of dignity and self-respect."

Delmer Daves gives the viewer a top-to-bottom, behind-the-scenes tutorial. You'll see how shade tobacco was grown and how the tents were laid. You'll learn about "wire worms" and "blue mold" and "suckering," about how "fleck" causes spots on the leaves, and what the Bemis Transplanter does. You'll even learn the dangers of tobacco poison on the skin and how it can be cured with calamine lotion, as Connie Stevens demonstrates when she rubs it on Troy Donahue's back in a circular motion after he's been exposed to the stuff.

Daves wrote the screenplay for *Parrish* in 1959 while staying at the Bee and Thistle Inn at 100 Lyme Street in Old

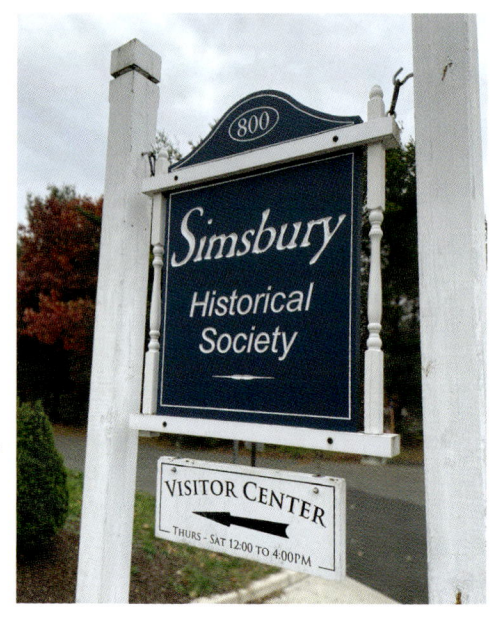

For more information about the history of Connecticut's tobacco industry and Martin Luther King's experience working on a tobacco farm on Hoskins Road and Firetown in Simsbury, visit the Windsor Historical Society at 96 Palisado Avenue in Windsor, and Simsbury Historical Society at 800 Hopmeadow Street in Simsbury.

Lyme, Connecticut. He said, "They gave me the peace and quiet I so much needed to complete the 130 pages of screenplay." While staying there, Daves discovered Terra Mar in Old Saybrook. Terra Mar was known as a toney "boatel," where guests like Frank Sinatra could arrive by yacht from Long Island Sound, drink cocktails by one of its three pools, and dance till midnight. Daves used Terra Mar for a number of key scenes, including a drunken showdown between Alison and her husband, Wiley (David Knapp), and a reunion between Parrish and Paige Raike (Sharon Hugueny).

Parrish opens on a beautiful location shot of the Hadlyme Ferry in Chester, Connecticut (in operation since 1769). Forget the geography; it's supposed to be Boston. Ellen McLean (Claudette Colbert) and her handsome son, Parrish (Troy Donahue), leave Boston for the greener tobacco pastures of Windsor, Connecticut. Ellen is a mature woman of great breeding, but apparently very little money, who is hired by the tobacco baron Sala Post (Dean Jagger) to groom his wayward daughter Alison for her debut.

After crossing the Connecticut River (they're actually heading to Hadlyme), they arrive at Boston's Logan Airport (actually, Bradley Airport in Windsor Locks) and board a Mohawk Airlines flight bound for Connecticut. (If you are a fan of AMC's *Mad Men*, you might remember that Mohawk Airlines was featured in a storyline over multiple seasons.) Mohawk was a regional airline, the first to hire a Black flight attendant, in 1958. Mohawk went out of business in 1972.

Ellen and Parrish take up residence on the Post farm. Ellen gets a room in the house, but Parrish is sent to live with the farmhands because Sala Post doesn't want Parrish around his daughter. Teet (Dub Taylor)—yes, that's really the character's name—has a very pretty niece, Lucy (Connie Stevens), who is immediately taken with her new coworker, Parrish. Max Steiner wrote the iconic score for *A Summer Place*. As Lucy shows Parrish around their ramshackle house, you'll hear some familiar opening chords. Connie Stevens told me Steiner spent time with each actress to create a unique theme for each of them. "Lucy's Theme," written for Stevens, became a hit.

Chester–Hadlyme Ferry, where scenes from *Parrish* were shot.

CONNECTICUT IN THE MOVIES

Terra Mar, Old Saybrook, Conn.

(Courtesy Old Saybrook Historical Society)

Parrish tries to keep to himself and learn the art of tobacco growing, but it's hard when Lucy keeps coming around in her low-cut blouses, inviting him to kiss her in the hay barn. Lucy and Parrish start sleeping together, but Parrish finds out Lucy has a secret boyfriend, Edgar Raike (Hampton Fancher), and things cool between them. Up at the house, Ellen has her hands full with the willful Alison. She's a spoiled country-club debutante, and she doesn't mind a drink or three. While Ellen prattles on to her about her debut, Alison drinks scotch, adjusts her stockings, and informs her she's going out for the evening. When she comes back from her date with Wiley Raike, she meets Parrish for the first time and he immediately piques her interest. After apologizing for almost running him over with her sports car, she offers him champagne, and soon they are kissing in the moonlight. "Sorry to kiss and run," she says before heading back to the house. (It might be my favorite line in the movie.)

While Parrish battles his inner urges, two local tobacco barons, Sala Post and Judd Raike (Karl Malden), battle each other. Raike wants to own all the tobacco farms in the valley and will do anything, even forcing his sons, Edgar and Wiley, whom he calls idiots, to do his dirty work for him. This includes making Edgar set fire to a rival's farm to put him out of business. The drama continues. We soon learn that Edgar, although married, is Lucy's secret boyfriend and the father of her child. Connie Stevens revealed to me that Hampton Fancher was her secret amour off-screen. Fancher—

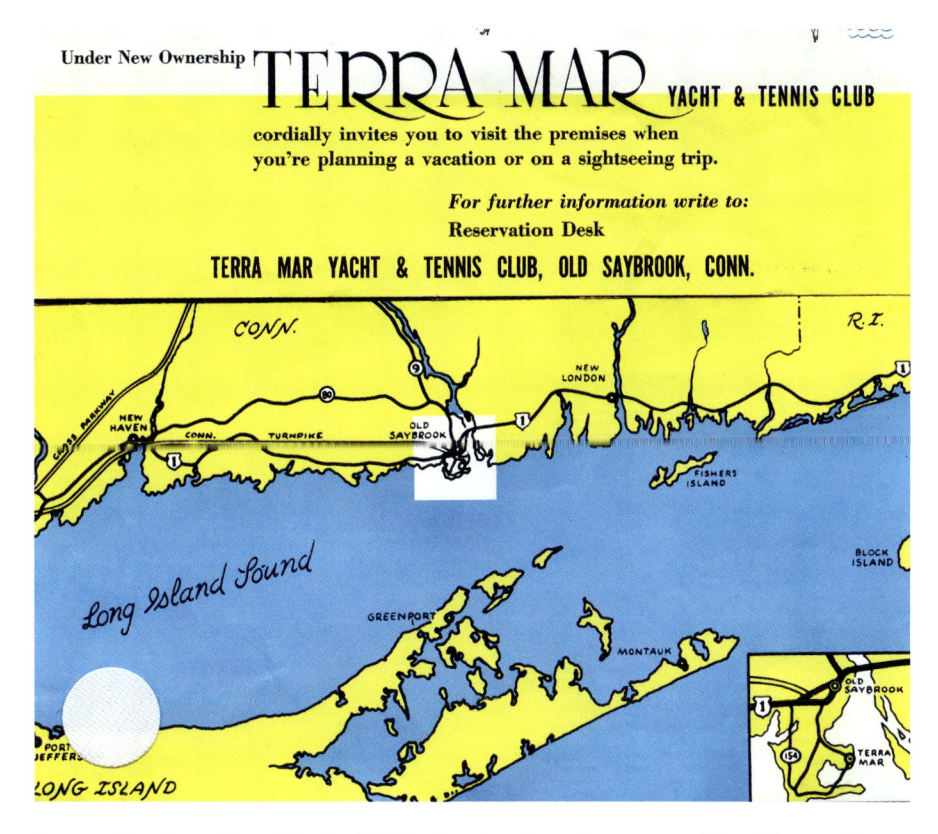

A pamphlet from Terra Mar in Old Saybrook, where key scenes of *Parrish* were filmed. (Courtesy Old Saybrook Historical Society)

The Saybrook Point Resort & Marina replaced the storied Terra Mar. Its glory days far behind it, Terra Mar became the scene of a notorious police raid in the 1980s, then was shuttered for good. When I went to the Old Saybrook Historical Society to ask for information about Terra Mar, one of the women raised her eyebrows, leaned in, and whispered, "You mean the notorious Terra Mar?" Another woman told me she was a teenager when they filmed *Parrish* at Terra Mar. She told me, "We skipped school so we could see the movie stars. I saw Troy Donahue get out of a black limousine. My car was in the parking lot, and you can see it in the movie." (Courtesy Old Saybrook Historical Society)

who was many years later screenwriter of *Blade Runner* (1982) and *Blade Runner 2049* (2017)—is still close friends with Stevens today.

Up at the Post farm, Ellen meets Judd Raike, who comes there to intimidate his neighbor. Raike may be a ruthless bastard trying to put Ellen's employer out of business, but he's worth $20,000,000, so Ellen sets her sights on marrying him. Ellen decides it's time to have a "talk" with Parrish to break the news. Having a facts-of-life discussion at Connecticut's number-one tourist destination—Mystic Seaport—certainly adds a "salty" flavor to the discussion. Ellen wants Parrish to stop seeing Lucy because she is not the right "kind" of girl. Parrish accuses his mother of having "narrow-minded conventions," and says he wants his "freedom." Ellen is frustrated with Parrish. "Nobody is free," she says. What she means is, first, you don't marry for love, you marry for money or social position; and second, you do what your parents tell you to do. This was the generational divide that Daves sought to capture. Children are trying to break free from their parents, but their parents refuse to let them.

The women in *Parrish* seem to be caught between two eras. Lucy has Edgar Raike's baby out of wedlock, but keeps it secret because he provides her family with new furniture. Alison loves Parrish, but when she discovers he's not interested in making money, she marries the wealthy but aimless Wiley Raike. Soon she is taking lovers on the side. Ellen pursues a marriage with Judd Raike, even though she does not love him, because it will cement their social position.

After an intimate dinner at Terra Mar, Raike takes Ellen back to his boat—which he calls his "floating office." (This takes place in the Old Saybrook Marina.) She puts him off, holding out for a wedding. Judd Raike agrees to marry her, to prevent "gossip." (The nuptials are held at the First Congregational Church in Essex.) Ellen's unhappiness once she marries is upsetting to Parrish, but she accepts it as the bargain she had to make. Her new stepsons refer to her as "that servant." Even when Judd Raike browbeats Parrish, Ellen justifies his display of temper by saying, "That's how powerful men act."

Finally, after one shouting session, Ellen tells Raike, "I've had enough of your cruelty," but then storms upstairs and changes into another fabulous Howard Shoup dinner dress. The only control she has is deciding which dress she will wear. (By the way, I'm not sure if it was in her contract, but Colbert has a different outfit in almost every scene.) Alison and Ellen are beautifully coiffed, girdled, shiny, and glamourous, but their inner lives are empty. Daves chooses to have Lucy, who is blue-collar, and Paige, the young college student, both in blue jeans to represent a new type of female, independent and free-spirited.

Delmer Daves wrote, produced, and directed under his production umbrella, Double-D Productions at Warner Bros. As a screenwriter, he gave the world such classics as *The Petrified Forest*

(1936), *Dark Passage* (1947), and *Broken Arrow* (1950); as a director, he oversaw the likes of *Destination Tokyo* (1943), *Demetrius and the Gladiators* (1954), and *3:10 to Yuma* (1957).

After suffering a heart attack in 1958, Daves was advised by doctors to avoid shooting any more strenuous action films. That's when he transitioned to an entirely new genre—teen romance. The romance niche fit in nicely with Warner Bros.' roster of fresh, young faces. Daves knew how to coax performances out of young actors, and worked with Troy Donahue on three successive films. The director often dressed Donahue in red, believing the color favored him. While it's tempting to dismiss these films as "fun camp," as critic Andrew Sarris wrote, it's important to remember that they were very successful. Warner Bros. gave Daves complete autonomy over scripts, casting, locations, music, and costuming, as well as producing and directing. Exercising a degree of control few other directors had, he captured the teen angst of the early 1960s in the way John Hughes's films would capture it in the 1980s. He also used landscapes like the tobacco fields in *Parrish* to envelop his lovers, creating an us-against-the-world motif. Daves took couples on a journey of innocence and loss of innocence, often showing how circumstances, or people, taint love and make it dirty. Couples undergo some sort of profound change—usually brought about by the experience of love.

One critic called Daves's films "garishly sex-scented." And it's true; people spend a lot of time kissing and making love. I happen to think that's what makes them appealing. For instance, Connie Stevens told me Daves spent time making sure her peasant blouse was positioned just enough off her shoulder to catch a glimpse of her breast when she's applying the cooling calamine lotion to Parrish's naked back after he gets tobacco poisoning. Parrish is embarrassed to take off his shirt to show Lucy. When he does, Daves leaves the camera on Lucy, and we see a smile of interest on her face as he exposes his bare chest to her.

In Delmer Daves's films there is always a code of "decency" between men. There are decent men, and there are vile, ruthless men who need to be exposed as such. What Daves found in Troy Donahue was an actor who could portray decency, but who was also sensitive, idealistic, maybe a little more interested in peace and love than work. He embodied the spirit and ideals and youthful optimism of the generation that came of age during the Camelot years. "You think I'm tough," Judd Raike tells Parrish. Daves was indicating that the pendulum was swinging away from the kind of hypermasculinity of the 1950s. What was emerging was a new kind of movie hero in whom sensitivity indicated not weakness but decency. At the end of *Parrish*, Judd Raike watches from his limousine—his ivory tower—as Parrish plants his first crop of tobacco on what will be his own little piece of land.

Daves hand-picked the three young Warner Bros. contract players who made their screen debuts in *Parrish*: Sharon Hugueny, Hampton Fancher, and David Knapp. Connie Stevens, who was

Diane McBain and Troy Donahue filming at the Groton submarine base. (Photofest)

twenty-one when she was cast as Lucy, told me: "Del was a father figure to all of us. Well-read. He would take us out to dinner." In fact, when I asked her how she enjoyed working in Connecticut, the first thing she exclaimed was, "Indian pudding! Del took us out to dinner at a fancy restaurant in Hartford and we had Indian pudding. I'd never had it before, so I asked the restaurant for the recipe, and I still make it." When I asked Stevens if she had auditioned for the role, she said, "No, I never auditioned. Del told me I was going to be in the film. He said, 'I'll be with you the whole way.' He was a director that instilled confidence in you. He believed in me more than I did. Once, after playing a scene, he said, 'You don't know how good you are.' " Stevens would go on to star in Daves's next film, *Susan Slade*—again, with Donahue—in what might be her best performance.

In her memoir, *Famous Enough*, Diane McBain wrote, "Daves wanted me to 'know' Troy 'like you would know a man who has changed your whole life . . . Then when you look at Troy in a scene, your face will show an understanding of him, and reflect past your feelings discovered in the rehearsal immediately before.' His direction of me was simple—dream and daydream about Troy Donahue."

Daves seemed to be able to capitalize on the stiffness in Donahue's acting to convey an awkward shyness with women, a lack of life experience. When women were the aggressors, it made him more appealing. Donahue was not particularly athletic—as the fight scene in the movie reveals—and

136   LOCATION, LOCATION, LOCATION: THE TOWN IS THE STAR

yet even his not being able to throw a decent punch is kind of adorable. He's a lover, not a fighter. Daves molded Donahue into the "perfect man." He was sensitive, needed love, mothering, a tender hand. Donahue later reflected on the trap of playing "the perfect guy," saying, "I didn't realize that I didn't have to be perfect and that I didn't have to live up to all those things written about me."

As the studio system collapsed, so did Donahue's career. He let his hair grow long, cultivated a beard and mustache, and tried to play bad guys. No one wanted him to be a bad guy. He fell into a life of drugs and alcohol. At one point he was living homeless in Central Park, relying on the kindness of strangers for his next meal. His old schoolmate Francis Ford Coppola gave him a bit part in *The Godfather: Part II* (1974), but it failed to reignite his career. His friend and costar Connie Stevens told me she sat by his bedside one day before he died, in 2001. They had grown up together, and now he was leaving this world behind. He had once been a teen sensation, his face gracing thousands of magazine covers, but now he was unrecognizable. Just another guy who lay dying in a hospital. Donahue said to Stevens jokingly, "Tell them who you are so I'll get better treatment."

Daves was not above exploiting Donahue's teen appeal. In the scene where Paige (Sharon Hugueny) gets the "Girls' League of Valley High" to help Parrish plant his tobacco field, students of nearby Loomis Chaffee School in Windsor served as extras. Donahue spent time meeting all the girls, and they left with autographed pictures as keepsakes. The pictures can be found in the lobby of the Plaza Theatre in Windsor.

CONNECTICUT IN THE MOVIES 137

MYSTIC PIZZA (1988)

Made in the era of "the feel-good movie," *Mystic Pizza* is without a doubt the best-known film associated with Connecticut—I mean, it has Mystic right there in the title. There's even been a jukebox musical of the same name inspired by the film. Since the film's release, fans and tourists from all over the country have lined up to take a photo at the site where a young Julia Roberts "slung" pizza and sampled the "slice of heaven" at the world-famous Mystic Pizza Restaurant at 56 West Main Street in Mystic. (There is a second location in Stonington, and the restaurant now offers a frozen version in stores.)

The movie that earned Connecticut's niche in cinematic and gastronomic history was almost not filmed here, though, and how the story idea came about is even more happenstance. When Amy Holden Jones's *Mystic Pizza* script was being shopped around, Universal Studios agreed to make it, but only if the women's roles were changed to men's. Samuel Goldwyn Jr. optioned the property but wanted to relocate the story to Palm Beach. Somehow, the idea of Palm Beach Pizza—three girls in skimpy bikinis serving pizza beachside—does not sound like a movie that would later become a classic. Goldwyn relented; the story stayed in Mystic, but he did make two significant changes. Jones's original script was conceived as "a female *Diner*," inspired by Barry Levinson's film *Diner* (1982). Her script had four female friends. Goldwyn—whose father had made *A Letter to Three Wives* (1949)—

Mystic Pizza (1988), a romantic comedy about three working-class girls who grow up in the seaside community of Mystic—Lilli Taylor, Julia Roberts, and Annabeth Gish. (Photofest)

Amy Holden Jones, screenwriter of *Mystic Pizza*, at Mystic Pizza. She saw the sign, wrote the film, and a legacy began. (Courtesy Amy Holden Jones)

was convinced that three was a magic number, so he asked that one character be removed. The other significant change was that Goldwyn would not allow Jones the opportunity to direct the film. This was particularly sad, since it was on a day trip to Mystic that Jones had conceived of the entire idea for the movie.

The mythic history of *Mystic Pizza* actually begins with fried clams. Jones's husband, world-class cinematographer Michael Chapman (*Jaws*, 1975; *Taxi Driver*, 1976; *Raging Bull*, 1980), happens to be from Maine. The couple was driving up the coast from New York to Maine and Chapman was looking for a good place to stop and have fried clams. Amy told me they were using one of their favorite books, *Roadfood*, by Jane and Michael Stern, to find out-of-the-way joints. He came across a recommendation for a place called the Sea Swirl at 30 Williams Avenue in Mystic. They stopped for clams—Jones tells me they were great—and while walking around the town, Jones strolled by Mystic Pizza, looked up at the sign, and thought, "That would be a great title. What's the movie?"

Memories of the town stayed with them . . . or was it the clams? Anyway, not long after their visit, Jones called a realtor. They ended up purchasing a house on High Street overlooking the Mystic

Mystic Pizza celebrates Portuguese culture—something not seen before in a film set in Connecticut. The Portuguese began settling in Stonington in the 1850s. Their knowledge of fishing allowed them to adapt well to Mystic. The first of three pairings for D'Onofrio and Taylor, they went on to make *Household Saints* (1993) and *Brooklyn's Finest* (2009). (Photofest)

River. It was there that Jones penned *Mystic Pizza*. So, cheers to the Sea Swirl!

I loved *Mystic Pizza* when it first came out, and I still love it. It retains a 1980s innocence, and even today, it's rare to see a movie that so accurately depicts female friendship and sisterhood. It also showcases the location and the cultural fabric of the borough of Mystic. *Mystic Pizza* captures the feeling of what it was like to live in a resort town that was both exclusive to the rich and excluding to the poor. The rich dialogue is filled with accurate vernacular of the time, such as calling people "townies" and "preppies," something I had not previously heard in a movie about Connecticut. *Mystic Pizza* was also Connecticut's first comedy devoted to depicting a culture—the Portuguese—that we had not yet seen on-screen, but that populated much of the coastal part of the state.

Before the seeming overnight success of *Mystic Pizza*, Amy Holden Jones already had an interesting backstory. After graduating from AFI Film School, she worked as an assistant to Martin Scorsese on *Taxi Driver*. It was there she met her future husband. Jones began working with the low-budget guru Roger Corman, editing several films for him and working with directors like Joe Dante and Hal Ashby.

Julia Roberts and Annabeth Gish shooting at Mystic Pizza. What is the secret ingredient—do you remember? (Photofest)

It was from Corman she learned the concept of writing a movie around a great title—a trick that served her well that fateful day when she spotted the *Mystic Pizza* sign. Jones transitioned to writing and directing, first for Corman, with *The Slumber Party Massacre* (1982), one of the few female-directed slasher films. Next came *Love Letters* (1983) and *Maid to Order* (1987). Though both of those films did pretty well, they did not lead to further directing gigs, so Jones wrote *Mystic Pizza*, believing that, like Barry Levinson's *Diner*, it would be her breakout movie.

This was an era when female directors were rare. Even though Jones had made three films, Goldwyn hired Donald Petrie, someone who had never made a film before, to direct *Mystic Pizza*. Jones says, "That was what life was like for a woman trying to direct her own material in the 1980s. It was a long, uphill fight." Not to take anything away from Petrie, because he did an admirable job—I mean, the film is a classic—but after speaking to Jones at length, I was conflicted about the outcome. Jones, who was inspired to write the script because of her chance discovery of Mystic Pizza, and who later mined the world of Mystic while she lived there, was not able to complete her vision of the film.

Dreams are big in small towns. Young Daisy Araujo (Julia Roberts) couldn't possibly have known she was destined for bigger things when she resignedly told her boss, Leona (Conchata Fer-

CONNECTICUT IN THE MOVIES 141

Director Donald Petrie on location in Mystic for *Mystic Pizza*. (Photofest)

rell), "I'm gonna be slinging pizza for the rest of my life." She was wrong, of course, but *Mystic Pizza* is memorable for many things other than being Julia Roberts's breakout film. (It's also the first screen appearance for Matt Damon, as Charlie's brother.)

What's the secret to its longevity? Yes, it's a story about love and heartache and friendship, and, yes, there's the chemistry and youthful enthusiasm of the cast—especially the three lead actresses—but what makes their performances feel so authentic is incorporating Mystic into almost every scene. Kat motors wistfully around the city on her Vespa, dropping off pizza for her mom, Mrs. Araujo (Joanna Merlin), at Ferriera Lobsters. We understand Daisy's despair watching Charles inside the Mystic Harbor Yacht Club while she is outside looking in. We get Jojo's frustration as she shouts at Bill from the Mystic Bridge while his lobster boat pulls away from the dock.

The film examines deep-rooted class systems. Here are three girls who have just graduated from high school, but their choices are limited because of their financial circumstances. They have emotional dilemmas that are also tied to their Mystic roots. Jojo (Lili Taylor) comes from a working-class family, and she works for a living because she can't afford to go to college. She wants to run Mystic Pizza, if she could ever get the "secret recipe" out of the owner, Leona. Jojo is a traditional girl but doesn't want to marry her longtime boyfriend, Bill (Vincent D'Onofrio), who works as a

If you visit Mystic, there are reminders of *Mystic Pizza* everywhere. wherever you look. Memorabilia is on display at Mystic Pizza Restaurant on 56 West Main Street. A replica set of the restaurant is in Stonington, at what is now the location of the Stonington Harbor Yacht Club Sailing Foundation. It was close to Skipper's Dock, the "Mystic Harbor Yacht Club" location at 66 Water Street, where Charlie and Daisy go on their date, which subsequently closed in 2013. The "Peg Leg Pub," where Daisy and the girls play pool, and where Daisy first meets Charlie, is Zack's Bar and Grill, located at 201 North Main Street in Stonington. Charlie's family's large colonial mansion, to which he takes Daisy, is located near Cannon Square at Church Street in Stonington. Daisy and Kat Araujo's and Jojo Barboza's houses are both in Pawcatuck. The opening scene takes place in St. Peter and Paul Polish National Catholic Church in New London, at 730 State Pier Road. Ferriera Lobsters, the lobster-processing plant where Kat and Daisy's mom (Joanna Merlin) works, was really Ford's Lobsters, located at 15 Riverview Avenue in Noank. The scene of the restaurant reviewer, the "Fireside Gourmet," was shot at a restaurant then called the Seamen's Inne, located at Mystic Seaport and Museum at 105 Greenmanville Avenue. Later named Latitude 41, it closed in 2022, to be replaced by a hotel. (Courtesy Amy Holden Jones)

CONNECTICUT IN THE MOVIES

lobster fisherman, because she'd lose her independence—but she still wants to have sex with him. It's Bill who thinks sex without marriage is a sin. "I think that when people love each other, they should make a commitment!" he tells her. When her strict Portuguese parents catch them in the act in their living room, Bill gives Jojo an ultimatum: marriage, or they break up. Initially she chooses her independence, but it's her best friends, Kat and Daisy, who remind Jojo that the love she shares with Bill is one of a kind, and the two eventually do marry.

Daisy hopes her looks and easy availability will land her a rich guy. She will marry up. Her mother lecturing "All I want is for you to make something of yourself!" only causes her to be more rebellious. Daisy knows there are a lot of rich guys in Mystic, but they don't usually hang out on her side of town. Then, one night, the wealthy Charles Gordon Windsor (Adam Storke) is slumming at the local pub and pool joint, the Peg Leg Pub, and he spots Daisy. Daisy thinks he's a poseur, and though she accepts his invitation to a date, says cynically, "This a habit with you, picking up townies and luring them to your big fancy house?" She does splurge on a $160 dress, but with the intention of returning it after she's worn it. (Get ready for some 1980s high fashion here!) Even though Charles invites her to his family's mansion on the waterfront after a nice dinner, Daisy has a chip on her shoulder and thinks it's a stunt to make his parents angry, because she's a low-class Portuguese "townie."

Later, when Daisy sees Charles at the exclusive Mystic Harbor Yacht Club with a girl (it's his sister), she thinks he's cheating on her and angrily pours barrels of fish guts into his Porsche convertible. He forgives her—why not? She's Julia Roberts—and Daisy gets her Prince Charming.

Daisy's sister, Kat (Annabeth Gish)—whom Daisy dubs Saint Katherine—gets into a more complex situation. She's working at Mystic Pizza, saving up for college to study astronomy at Yale in New Haven. Kat has always done the "right" thing and been the "good" girl, whereas Daisy has been seen as the family failure. That dynamic changes when Kat takes on another part-time job, babysitting the daughter of a handsome and charming architect, Tim (William R. Moses), who also attended Yale. Though he's married, his wife is briefly away in England. Tim begins a flirtation that Kat believes is leading to something deeper. Daisy warns her sister that she's being naive, but Kat thinks she knows better, and is hoping for a proposal of marriage. One rainy night she and Tim make love, only to find later that evening that Tim's wife has unexpectedly returned. Kat realizes he was never going to leave his wife, and she is shattered. Afterward, Daisy is finally able to offer her sister comfort and a shoulder to cry on, which brings them closer.

After Jojo finally takes the plunge and marries Bill (they have a traditional Portuguese wedding at the restaurant), the three girls meet outside. Without saying a word about it aloud, they realize (and the film's closing theme, "These Are the Times to Remember," echoes it), that they will always be in each other's lives, no matter what. Each woman will follow her own unique path, but they will be bound in spirit by the town where they all grew up—Mystic.

JACKNIFE (1989)

Jacknife (1989) was one of the first big studio films made in Connecticut since the 1970s. Producer Bob Schaffel said that after searching "from the Deep South to Maine," Meriden was chosen for its "gritty location" and because it "fit the words" of the script by Cheshire native Stephen Metcalfe,

Robert De Niro and Ed Harris filming in Meriden. *Jacknife* featured a lot of Meriden. The Victorian house where siblings Martha (Kathy Baker) and Dave (Ed Harris) live is on Linsley Avenue. Megs's (Robert De Niro) house was on the corner of Maple and West Streets, but was torn down. The uptown garage where Megs works is now a Texaco station. (Photofest)

adapted from his play, *Strange Snow*. Metcalfe had strong feelings about Meriden, which abuts his hometown. *Jacknife* brought a significant economic boost to the area, and producers later rewarded the city by holding an exclusive premiere in the town where much of the film was shot.

In *Jacknife*, two Vietnam vets, Joseph "Megs" Megessey (Robert De Niro) and Dave (Ed Har-

David Jones rehearses with Robert De Niro and Kathy Baker at the Olympia Diner in Newington. (Photofest)

ris), had made a pact during the war that if they made it out alive, they would go fishing together on opening day of the season in the town where they grew up. On the battlefield, there is one absolute: A soldier never leaves another soldier behind. Both survived the war, but their emotional scars have kept them from a full recovery.

The Vietnam flashbacks were filmed in an industrial park in Cromwell. The diner was located in Wethersfield. The vets' support group scenes were filmed at the former East Main Street Polish Legion of American Veterans Hall. A local veteran, Richard S. Tomczuk, appeared in the scene. Tomczuk served as a paratrooper with the Screaming Eagles of the 101st Airborne Division, participated in the Battle of Hamburger Hill, and was a recipient of the Bronze Star, as well as a Purple Heart.

There was tremendous excitement from locals who pitched in, at times providing props for the movie. Meriden resident Richard Trombley supplied his own 1967 Chevelle SS for De Niro's character to drive. Trombley said, "My car is like the character. If it had a name, it would be Robert De Niro." Though hundreds showed up to be cast as extras, one bar owner turned down the oppor-

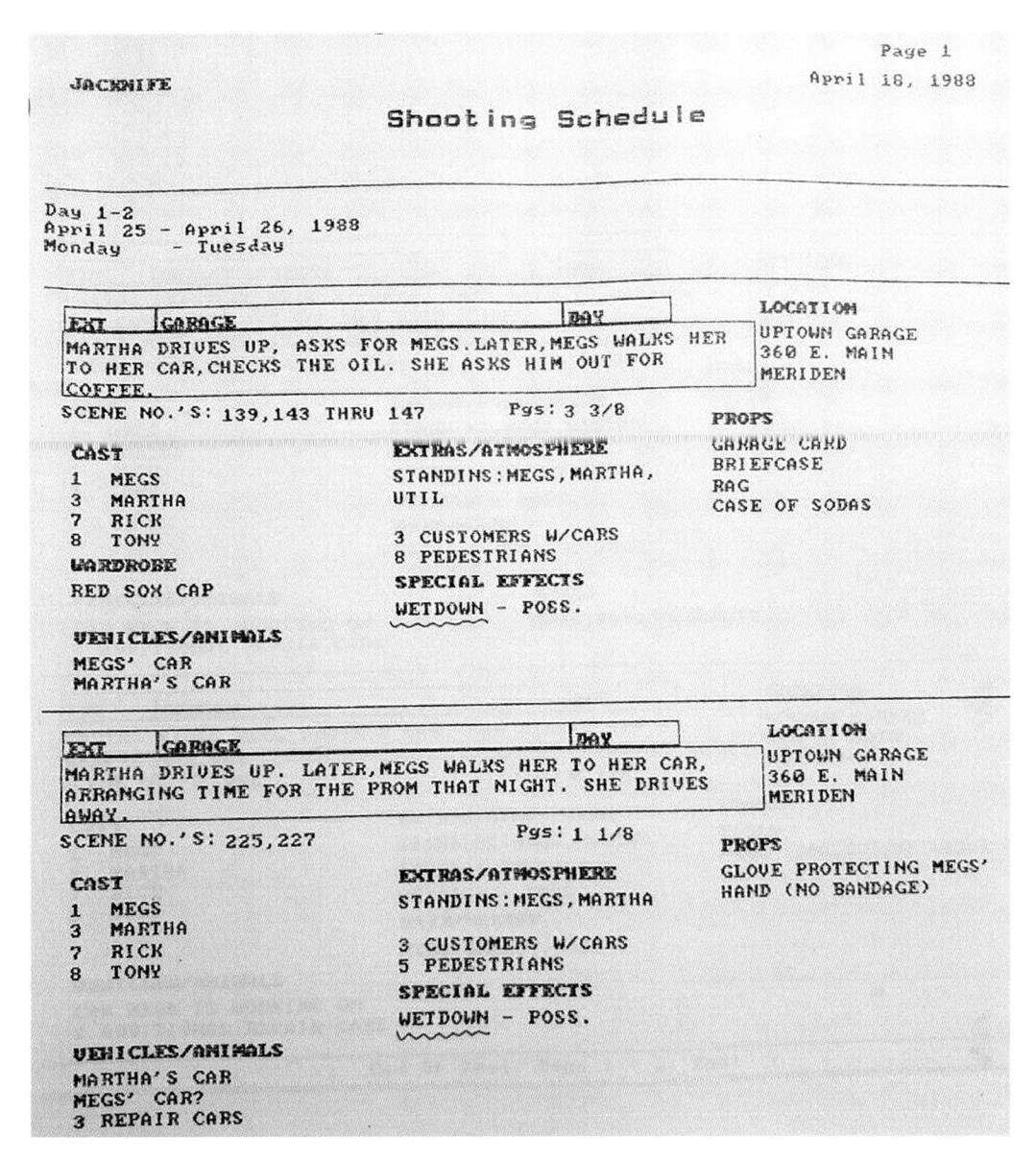

```
                                                              Page 1
JACKNIFE                                                 April 18, 1988
                         Shooting Schedule

Day 1-2
April 25 - April 26, 1988
Monday     - Tuesday

EXT   GARAGE                                 DAY      LOCATION
MARTHA DRIVES UP. ASKS FOR MEGS. LATER, MEGS WALKS HER UPTOWN GARAGE
TO HER CAR, CHECKS THE OIL. SHE ASKS HIM OUT FOR      360 E. MAIN
COFFEE.                                               MERIDEN
SCENE NO.'S: 139,143 THRU 147    Pgs: 3 3/8
                                                      PROPS
CAST                    EXTRAS/ATMOSPHERE             GARAGE CARD
  1  MEGS               STANDINS: MEGS, MARTHA,       BRIEFCASE
  3  MARTHA             UTIL                          RAG
  7  RICK                                             CASE OF SODAS
  8  TONY               3 CUSTOMERS W/CARS
WARDROBE                8 PEDESTRIANS
RED SOX CAP             SPECIAL EFFECTS
                        WETDOWN - POSS.
VEHICLES/ANIMALS
MEGS' CAR
MARTHA'S CAR

EXT   GARAGE                                 DAY      LOCATION
MARTHA DRIVES UP. LATER, MEGS WALKS HER TO HER CAR,   UPTOWN GARAGE
ARRANGING TIME FOR THE PROM THAT NIGHT. SHE DRIVES    360 E. MAIN
AWAY.                                                 MERIDEN
SCENE NO.'S: 225,227             Pgs: 1 1/8
                                                      PROPS
CAST                    EXTRAS/ATMOSPHERE             GLOVE PROTECTING MEGS'
  1  MEGS               STANDINS: MEGS, MARTHA        HAND (NO BANDAGE)
  3  MARTHA
  7  RICK               3 CUSTOMERS W/CARS
  8  TONY               5 PEDESTRIANS
                        SPECIAL EFFECTS
                        WETDOWN - POSS.
VEHICLES/ANIMALS
MARTHA'S CAR
MEGS' CAR?
3 REPAIR CARS
```

This shooting schedule shows the Meriden location for *Jacknife*.

tunity to act with De Niro. While on a location scouting expedition in Meriden, the producers had walked into the Sportsman's Café to inquire about shooting a scene there. After deciding the bar was too small, they asked the owner if he knew of any good fishermen in the area. The bar owner happened to be an avid fly fisherman, so the producers asked him if he would be interested in teaching Robert De Niro, Ed Harris, and Kathy Baker how to fish. He agreed, setting up several fishing lessons for the actors on the Salmon River in East Haddam. Though the three actors couldn't have been nicer—Kathy Baker even sent him a thank-you note—he declined an opportunity to be in the film alongside De Niro, telling them he was more interested in spending his off-time fishing, not acting.

Jacknife hit home with many veterans coping with alcoholism, depression, and trauma in the aftermath of the Vietnam War. It brought awareness and offered hope and understanding to men who did not feel their voices and struggles were being heard. *Jacknife* shed light on a difficult topic, one that still did not have an actual name in movies, beyond being called battle fatigue or shell shock. The diagnosis of what is now called PTSD—post-traumatic stress disorder—was recognized in 1980 when the American Psychiatric Association added PTSD to its *Diagnostic and Statistical Manual of Mental Disorders*, the *DSM*.

Joseph Megessey, "Megs" for short, is a Vietnam vet who has learned to cope with his anger and mood swings by talking with a veterans group leader named Jake (Charles S. Dutton), who tells him, "It makes me feel good to know I'm not alone." It is by sharing their feelings that they keep each other in check.

Robert De Niro's tuxedo from *Jacknife* at Modern Formals.

Megs wants to help his friend Dave, a fellow vet he served with, who has become an isolated alcoholic. Having found some stability—Megs lives modestly in the uppermost level of a triplex Victorian house in Meriden, and is working as a mechanic—he wants to see if he can get his old war buddy back on track, but Jake warns Megs, "Don't let him pull you down, man." This small but important role was one of the first screen appearances by the great character actor Charles S. Dutton, a graduate of the Yale School of Drama in New Haven.

Megs decides to search for Dave and eventually finds him living at his late parents' house—a dilapidated Victorian with a wraparound porch—with his sister, Martha (Kathy Baker), a schoolteacher who has put her emotional life on hold to care for her brother. When Megs comes to pick up Dave so they can go fishing, he's so hungover he can hardly walk, so Megs and Martha join forces to get him dressed. His angry outbursts show Megs that Dave's in very bad shape. We learn that Dave is haunted by a third buddy, Bobby, who didn't make it out alive, and that he blames Megs for Bobby's death.

Martha thinks she is helping Dave. She feeds him, does his laundry, takes his abuse, even lets him drink, but Megs recognizes that she's just enabling him. Megs senses Martha's role as a full-time

Modern Formals on Washington Street in Middletown is where you'll find the tuxedo De Niro wore in *Jacknife*. I had a lovely time talking to Sal and John Dominello about how their father ended up not only providing a tuxedo for Robert De Niro, but also acting alongside him in *Jacknife*. They recalled that two producers had scouted Sal's shop for a scene in the film where De Niro's character Megs gets fitted for a tuxedo. Sal agreed to let them film in the shop, but on the day they filmed the scene, De Niro and the producers were not convinced by the actor they had hired to play the tailor, so they asked Sal to step in and play the part instead. He and De Niro had an unexpected chemistry. Sal's son told me, "They got along like long-lost cousins." They remember being invited to the set with their father, and even having lunch with De Niro in his trailer. Filming ended, but a lifelong friendship came of it. De Niro had relatives in Plainville, and whenever he came to town Sal would get a call from one of them to come have dinner with "Bobby." Sal received two tuxedos worn by De Niro in *Jacknife*. He donated one from the scene he acted in to be auctioned off for charity. The white tuxedo with silver cummerbund that De Niro wears in the prom scenes is in the store. Though many have asked to try it on, it's not allowed. Hey, it was tailored for one man and one man alone: the great Robert De Niro.

CONNECTICUT IN THE MOVIES

"caregiver" is a convenient excuse for her not to get involved in a real relationship with a man. Megs's sympathy turns to love, and he and Martha begin a tentative romance. On one of their dates they go to Castle Craig, Meriden's most famous local landmark, a stone observation tower on East Peak where you can get panoramic views of the city.

Try as he might, Dave cannot put the pieces of his life back together. He disapproves of Megs, and, fearing Martha will abandon him, wants her to leave him. Now, Martha must decide between the love she has for her brother and the love she has found with Megs. When Martha invites Megs on a special date—chaperoning the high school prom—Dave shows up at the school drunk and spoils their evening, destroying the glass cases holding awards and trophies he had won in high school. The outburst is, of course, a metaphor showing how broken and shattered Dave has become. Megs confronts him, telling him things he doesn't want to hear about Bobby, and Dave runs.

Even with all the destruction Dave has caused, Megs refuses to give up on his buddy. Later, Martha and Megs are back at the house, planning to go out looking for Dave, when he shows up bloody and hurt, but calmer. It is in that moment, at his lowest point, that Dave finally recognizes that he is not alone. Megs has redeemed himself by refusing to leave another soldier on the battlefield. We then see Dave attending the veterans' support group for help, and Megs returning to Martha, as both men finally begin to heal.

Jacknife marked the beginning of a long film association for De Niro and Connecticut. His next movie, then titled *Union Street*, would be shot in Waterbury in the summer of 1988. That film was later retitled *Stanley & Iris*. Since then, Robert De Niro has made more films in Connecticut than any other screen actor. These include the Barry Levinson–directed comedy *What Just Happened* (2008), based on producer Art Linson's book of the same name (De Niro plays a struggling Hollywood producer, but nearly the entire film was shot in Connecticut); *Everybody's Fine* (2009), a family dramedy that brought De Niro to Stamford to film; and *The Big Wedding* (2013), filmed in Greenwich.

What Just Happened (2008). (Photofest)

Everybody's Fine (2009). Director Kirk Jones with Robert De Niro at Union Station in New Haven. (Photofest)

CONNECTICUT IN THE MOVIES

Jane Fonda and Robert De Niro filming a scene from *Stanley & Iris* in Waterbury. (Photofest)

STANLEY & IRIS (1990)

In Arthur Miller's play *Death of a Salesman*, the glad-handing traveling salesman Willy Loman reminisces about a trip he took to Waterbury, Connecticut: "Waterbury is a fine city. Big clock city, the famous Waterbury clock. Sold a nice bill there." Miller would have known Waterbury to be a bustling industrial town when *Death of a Salesman* was written in 1949, its large clock tower a symbol of its prosperity. The Waterbury Union Station, designed by the illustrious New York firm of McKim, Mead & White, was handling sixty-six passenger trains a day, taking commuters in and out of the city. It was nicknamed "The Brass City." Brass stamp and rolling mills were making brass gears for the Waterbury, Thomaston, and Terryville clock-making enterprises. By the 1920s, more than one-third of the brass manufactured in the United States was being made in Waterbury.

During World War II, more than fifty thousand brass workers were employed in the Naugatuck Valley. The Waterbury Clock Company also numbered workers in the thousands, at one point manufacturing twenty thousand clocks per day. Its fabled history has included inventing the "Jumbo" pocket watch in 1892, named for P. T. Barnum's elephant; the mass-produced one-dollar "Yankee" pocket watch, which saved the company eventually called Timex from bankruptcy; and the first Mickey Mouse watch for Disney, in 1933.

The Waterbury Button Company had been making stamped-metal buttons going back to 1812. As the company grew, it expanded to making everything from metal toys to bomb fuses, plastic lenses for gas masks, vinyl records, laundry tubs, and bread boxes. In 1939, the company provided authentic brass buttons for Union and Confederate uniforms for the film *Gone with the Wind* (1939). Now the abandoned building itself would be the setting for a movie.

The storied history of Waterbury's industrial past is precisely what drew me to *Stanley & Iris* (1990), shot on location in the summer and fall of 1988. Setting the film in Waterbury was not accidental. Production designer Joel Schiller said, "We wanted a town that depicted the hardships and the dignity of the American working class."

The workers in these Waterbury factories had come from successive waves of German, French, Irish, Polish, and Italian immigrants. By 1930 half of the population of Waterbury was foreign-born. Many of their homes—three-story structures known as "triple-deckers"—were within walking distance of the mills. Like many mill towns, Waterbury began to experience an economic decline after World War II. The hum of factories grew faint, manufacturing jobs ceased to exist, and the histories of centuries of working-class people were forgotten. With its overcast skies and rust overtones, *Stanley & Iris* captures a tarnished "brass city" a half a century past its heyday. There are mentions of crime and unemployment—not something you usually hear about in a love story. Even Robert De Niro's scenic bike rides along the Mad River lack any kind of joy, devoid of people doing

Postcard of Waterbury Clock Company in the 1930s. In the PBS series *The War: The Four Towns*, Waterbury native Tom Cairo describes the city of Waterbury: "You could compare it to a miniature Times Square. It was never quiet because there were so many factories, and each factory had different shifts. There was always something going on. The restaurants downtown were booming. Theaters were always full. It was really wonderful."

Did you know that the brass buttons on Ashley Wilkes's military costume in *Gone with the Wind* came from Waterbury? (Photofest) Postcard (below) depicting Waterbury's industrial past.

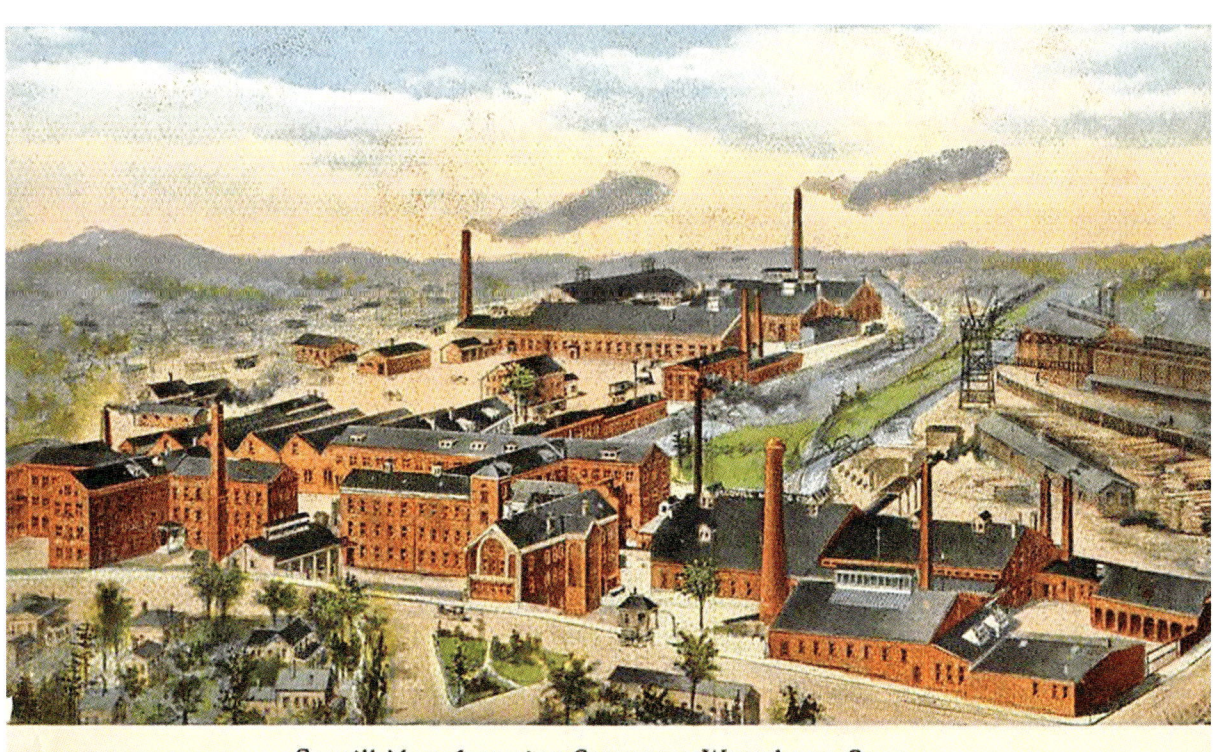

Scovill Manufacturing Company, Waterbury, Conn.

Director Martin Ritt, Robert De Niro, and Jane Fonda shooting *Stanley & Iris* in Waterbury, Connecticut. (Photofest)

anything fun or social. Sadness permeates *Stanley & Iris*, giving it a secondary meaning.

Stanley & Iris opens with a significantly long, wide panning shot of Waterbury that features many of the brick factory buildings and sawtooth roofs, popular at the turn of the twentieth century, and reflective of this once-thriving mill town. You can see the Waterbury Mixmaster, a series of intersecting bridges connecting Interstate 84, Route 8, Waterbury Hospital, the Clock Tower, Union Station, and Holy Land USA, a religious theme park inspired by sections of the Bible. This roadside attraction is also featured in *Wanda* (see chapter 9). The shot ends with factory workers exiting what was once the Waterbury Button Company—now the fictional Nevins and Davis Bakery. It's not hard to imagine the thousands of immigrant workers who walked these same paths. What were their hopes and dreams as they moved here? How did they feel when the factories began to close down, and jobs became scarce in the very city that they had helped to build? *Stanley & Iris* is a tribute to the workers of Waterbury whose stories have never been told.

Director Martin Ritt was not only looking for an abandoned town with abandoned factories; he also wanted an abandoned feeling. "You have to look beneath the surface," he said,. He was interested in characters who found themselves at a crossroads, and he often made "socially conscious" films. His left-leaning political bent got him in trouble in the 1950s, and he was blacklisted. Refusing to name names, he found work by teaching acting at the Actors Studio. It may be because he faced injustice in his own life that he incorporated these themes into his films. He was a man of principle, known to be patient and sensitive with actors, having once been one himself.

In 1957, Ritt secured work on *No Down Payment*, starring Joanne Woodward. This led to his long association with Woodward and her husband, Paul Newman, directing them in *The Long, Hot Summer* (1958) and *Paris Blues* (1961). In 1963, he directed Paul Newman in the blockbuster hit *Hud*. It garnered seven Oscar nominations and three wins for actress Patricia Neal, my grandfather Melvyn Douglas, and cinematographer James Wong Howe. In the 1970s, at the top of his game, Ritt directed *The Great White Hope* (1970), *Sounder* (1972), and *Conrack* (1974), all films depicting the Black experience. He ended the decade with his best-known film, the multi-nominated and award-winning *Norma Rae* (1979), which dealt with exploitation of factory workers in their attempts to unionize. He was credited with crafting the performance that won Sally Field an Oscar. What he brought to all his films—something that is deeply felt in *Stanley & Iris*—is his depiction of, and respect for, the workingman.

Stanley & Iris is based in part on a British novel by Pat Barker called *Union Street*, loosely adapted for the screen by the husband-and-wife team of Harriet Frank Jr. and Irving Ravetch. They collaborated with Ritt on eight films, going back to *The Long, Hot Summer*. Like the director, they often focused on social issues, and the inspiration for their screenplay came when they read a study that found one out of every four people in America could not read. Fearing a movie about a man who learns to read would lack "inherent drama," they added a love story.

A movie about literacy was not for everyone. One critic wrote, "After it makes its point, *Stanley & Iris* gets dull." Harriet Frank was frustrated by the reviews, which dwelled on the miscasting of Jane Fonda as a "plain" bakery worker. One reviewer wrote, "I simply can't get beyond her California tan and golden locks." Harriet Frank felt the importance of the subject matter got lost with the carping. More serious issues arose with the casting of Jane Fonda. Some veterans' groups, upset at her upcoming presence in Waterbury, organized against her.

A story in the *New York Times* on August 4, 1988, entitled "Jane Fonda Finds Peace in Her Time," covered the controversy:

Frank Fabbri, World War II veteran and American Legionnaire, couldn't figure it out. This used to be a tough town, a "Better Dead than Red" kind of town. Why were all those people rushing up to Jane Fonda for an autograph? Didn't they remember Vietnam? Hanoi Jane? . . . Mr. Fabbri [is] one of a half-dozen demonstrators standing outside the brick warehouse-turned-movie-set where the actress was mobbed by 200 starry-eyed extras last Friday . . . Mr. Fabbri . . . was part of a small but widely publicized effort bent on stopping Ms. Fonda from filming a love story, Stanley & Iris, *in Waterbury. The group, mostly veterans, sold 6,000 "We're Not Fond'a Hanoi Jane" bumper stickers.*

Downtown Waterbury, with a glimpse of Holy Land USA.

The mayor was vocal too. Although the film brought $5,000,000 in revenue to the city, he said through a spokesperson, "Waterbury is and always has been a very patriotic town. We honor Flag Day, we honor Veterans Day, we're out there in the rain, the snow, the sleet, marching. Everyone has their flags out in front of their businesses. This is a salt-of-the-earth, blue-collar, patriotic American town."

In her 2006 autobiography, *My Life So Far*, Jane Fonda wrote: "When it was announced that I would be filming *Stanley & Iris* in Waterbury, Connecticut, a furor was unleashed that raged for months and was reported widely in the press. Local veteran Gaetano Russo—a World War II veteran and former chair of the local Republican party committee—formed the American Coalition Against Hanoi Jane and tried to pass a resolution to bar me from Waterbury. He was joined in his efforts by local Republican congressman John G. Rowland, who later became governor of Connecticut." A local minister arranged for a meeting between Fonda and twenty-five vets from the area to defuse the tension.

In her book, Fonda writes, "We went around the room telling our story. It was raw, angry,

Waterbury train station.

and emotional. Many tears were shed . . . I had not realized how many families in that part of Connecticut were first generation Americans. For these young men, serving their country in Vietnam was a rite of passage to true citizenship." (Fonda and Robert De Niro worked with Vets Who Care, a Connecticut Vietnam Vets group who held a fund-raising event at Lake Quassapaug.)

The empathy gained from the emotional meeting with the vets may have colored her performance. Just as Jane really listened to the concerns of the vets, Iris really listens to Stanley. Helping him will change his life and, in turn, her own. *Stanley & Iris* is a small film with an enormous message. By facing what we fear most, we can find help, find our true purpose, and even find ourselves.

Robert De Niro is Stanley Cox, a man in his forties who is functionally illiterate. He lives with his elderly father (Feodor Chaliapin), who, like Willy Loman, was once a traveling salesman.

Because his father's job necessitated moving from town to town, Stanley was taken in and out of school and never learned to read or write. It's a secret he has managed to hide his entire life, and it would have stayed a secret had he not met his coworker, Iris King (Fonda), while working as a cook at the Nevins and Davis Bakery.

When we meet Iris, she's a woman who has kind of given up on any real chance of happiness. She's a recent widow whose long days at work are filled with anxiety about her financial future. In addition to her two kids, she supports her unemployed sister and brother-in-law who live with her (Swoosie Kurtz and Jamey Sheridan). There's a pointed message that as former factory workers, they are having a hard time finding work. Iris's teenage daughter (Martha Plimpton) gets pregnant and ends up working alongside Iris. It's a fate Iris had hoped she would avoid. Iris tells her, "Don't you know this line doesn't go anywhere?"

Iris and Stanley meet after Iris is robbed of her purse and her much-needed paycheck on her bus ride home. Stanley happens to be riding the bus because his bike was stolen. (There are a lot of mentions of crime in *Stanley & Iris*.) A few days later Stanley sees Iris again outside the factory, waiting for the bus—which is out of order. He offers her a ride home on his recently purchased secondhand bicycle. This scene, set against John Williams's score, harks back to a bygone era. There's something very sweet about two grown people riding a bicycle as they get to know each other.

As their friendship grows, it becomes harder for Stanley to mask his disability. He covers his fear with remoteness. Stanley meets Iris again at the local Laundromat, where they are both doing laundry after work. Stanley invites Iris to join him for Chinese food while they wait for their laundry. They sit outside under the stars. Everything is going great; you get the feeling it's been a while since either one has been on a date. But things go awry when Iris breaks open her fortune cookie. She reads, "Make new friends and trust them," joking, "Hey, did you write this?," almost flirting with Stanley.

Iris is waiting for Stanley to read his fortune, but he doesn't. Iris says, "Why don't you open it?" Stanley just shrugs, "Nah, no point in opening mine. I'm not lucky." The conversation, the intimacy, all the fun they were having, just stops. Iris says nothing, knowing somehow it's best to leave it alone, even though his actions clearly signal that something is off. Stanley's secret is wrapped in shame. Jane Fonda said in an interview, "It says to anyone who is illiterate, don't hide it. Don't fake it, don't pass. You can get help: it's never too late."

At the bakery, Iris has a headache and asks Stanley if he has a Tylenol behind the lunch counter. He produces one bottle after another—none of them Tylenol. As Stanley gets more and more frustrated, everything adds up for Iris. His boss comes out and starts complaining about a purchase order that he thinks Stanley signed. While Stanley tries to tell him he didn't sign the paperwork, Iris blurts out Stanley's secret, as if it all makes sense now: "He can't read, and he can't write."

Iris's revelation has consequences. Once Stanley's boss discovers he can't read, he is fired. His inability to read means he can only find menial work. He can no longer afford to care for his father and has to commit him to a state-run facility, where he shares a room with three other men. When Iris tracks down Stanley so she can apologize, he is now living in a garage. Stanley shows her an invention he is tinkering with—a cake-cooling device. She is impressed that he could build this without knowing how to read or write. The scene is meant to convey that although Stanley can't read, he's intelligent.

Stanley opens up about how his disability has isolated him. "I make inventions," he says. "This is what I made in my prison." The invention works. (For this scene, production designer Joel Schiller designed a fully functional cake-cooling device that Schiller later patented after several bakeries expressed interest in the machine.) A visit to the nursing home a few weeks later reveals that Stanley's father has died. At this point, Stanley is now at one of Ritt's crossroads, and though he is upset with Iris, she also becomes a catalyst for change.

Some of my favorite De Niro performances—for example, in *Bang the Drum Slowly* (1973) and *Awakenings* (1990)—use his own inability to communicate easily. With the rain pouring down, Stanley goes to the factory to ask Iris for help, but his embarrassment holds him back. Finally, as Iris gets on the bus, Stanley runs after her, and manages to get out "Teach me to read" as the bus doors shut. Stanley is looking up toward the camera, up toward Iris, which gives the scene an added spiritual overtone.

Teaching Stanley to read is not an easy process for either of them. Encouraged by the strides he is making, Iris wants to test Stanley, so she walks him to a nearby neighborhood and gives him a written map to find his way back. Stanley gets confused and soon finds himself lost. He can't read the signs, and he eventually gives up in frustration. When he finally meets up with Iris much later, his frustration turns to anger. They both come to the realization that perhaps learning something new at this time in their lives may be out of reach. *Stanley & Iris* is a movie about how handicaps, both visible and invisible, hold us back. If Stanley can't read, Iris can't see.

The two begin to develop feelings for each other, but the thought of intimacy scares Iris. Having been with only one man, she can't imagine that she could love again, so their first time in bed is a disaster: Iris is in tears, and Stanley feels inadequate. One of the things I love about their relationship is their struggle to trust each other. You're not sure until the very end of the film if they are even going to make it as a couple. Iris says, "Why do they call it a good cry? It makes you look like hell." Stanley tells Iris, "I like you, Iris, just about as much as I love you." Over time, Stanley learns to read, and Iris learns to trust.

In the film's original ending, Stanley goes to Detroit to sell his invention while Iris awaits his return in Waterbury. She asks him to write letters to her while he is away. We hear the beautiful words Stanley has written to her while Iris walks through the bakery. Iris is filled with pride that words, letters, brought them together, but she's also anxious, wondering if now that Stanley can read, he will no longer need her and won't return. She picks up her frosting tube and spells out Stanley's name in red letters. It's a hopeful—not happy—ending.

The studio wanted a definitively happy ending, which is what they got: Stanley returns from Detroit long enough to propose to Iris, with the intention of gathering her and the kids and driving off, leaving Waterbury behind.

For me the movie will always end with Iris in the bakery. It showcases the singular theme of Martin Ritt's films—respect for the dignity of working men and women. I'd like to imagine the former workers of Waterbury Button Factory would have preferred that ending too.

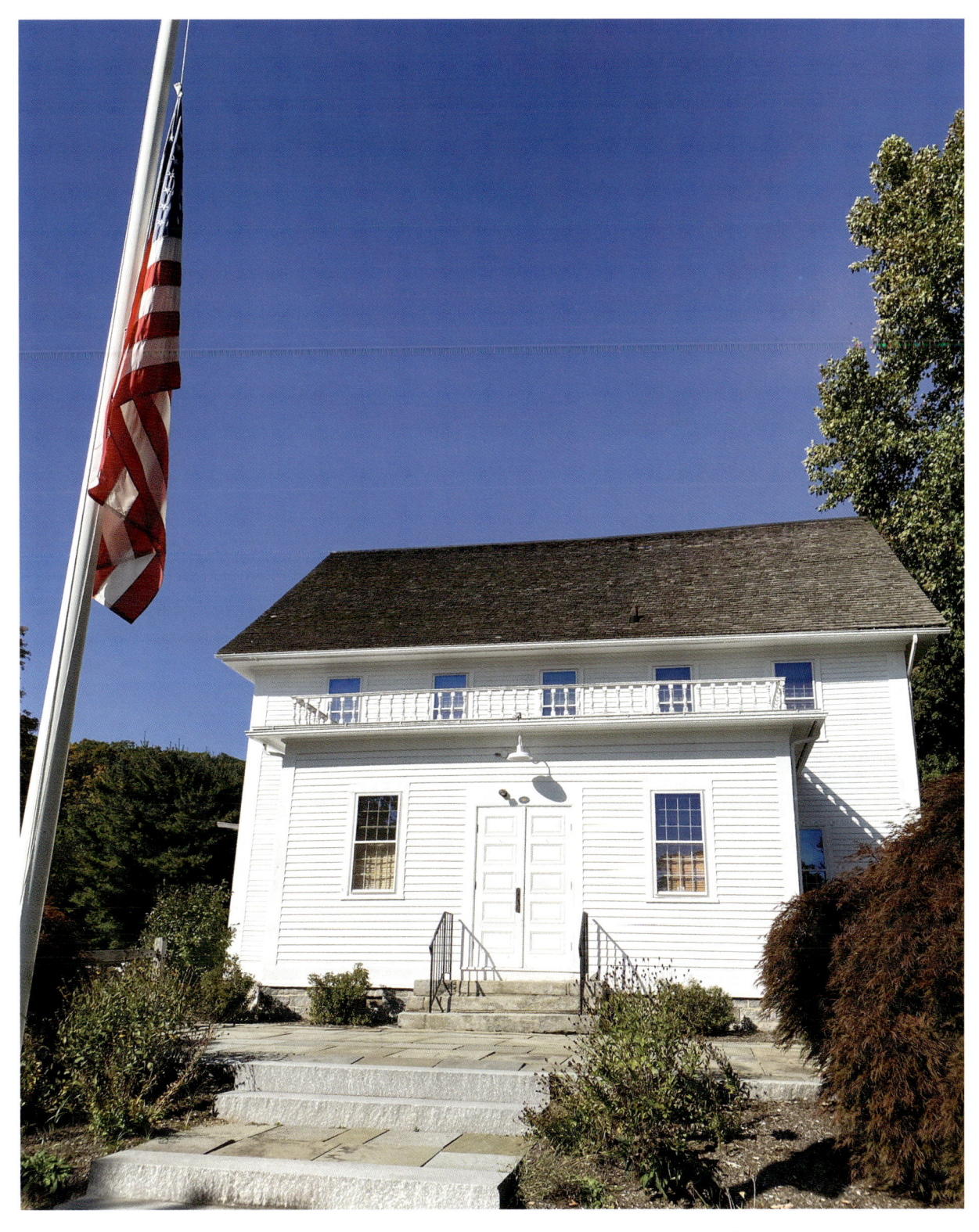

One last look at one of my favorite locations, the old town hall in Chester, where scenes from *It Happened to Jane* were filmed. Today it is a theater.

CONNECTICUT IN THE MOVIES 163

After screening *Gentleman's Agreement* for the first time, Darryl Zanuck congratulated Kazan, writing, "It's the most important film to come out of this town." (Photofest)

CHAPTER 8
CRIMES AND MISDEMEANORS

GENTLEMAN'S AGREEMENT (1947)

Laura Z. Hobson's novel *Gentleman's Agreement*, published in 1947, brought to light hidden prejudices Jews were experiencing in postwar America. Set partially in exclusive Darien, Connecticut, it examined the existence of restrictive covenants, or unspoken "gentleman's agreements," designed to preserve the racial homogeneity of upper-class suburbia. Though *Gentleman's Agreement* was well received, becoming the third-best-selling novel of 1947, the topic of anti-Semitism was still so sensitive that it took the courage of a non-Jewish producer—the maverick Darryl Zanuck at Twentieth Century Fox—to purchase and adapt the novel for the screen.

When Zanuck sent the script to Gregory Peck (a Roman Catholic), offering him the starring role of Phil Green—a journalist who assumes the name Greenberg so he can go undercover to write a story about anti-Semitism—Peck's agent urged him to turn it down for fear it would ruin his career. Gregory Peck was no stranger to liberal politics and social activism. He was vehemently opposed to the House Un-American Activities Committee (HUAC) and its ongoing investigations, rooting out supposed communists in Hollywood.

Dorothy Malone, Gregory Peck, and John Garfield in *Gentleman's Agreement* (1947). One line from Moss Hart's screenplay (based on Laura Hobson's novel) that directly mentioned Darien was not in the movie. While reading Kazan's script in the Wesleyan Cinema archives, I noticed that the line "And that's the Jew of it—you can tell the type a mile away in this section of Darien," must have been cut from the final film. (Photofest)

One actor in particular the committee would later target was John Garfield, who was cast in the pivotal role of Dave Goldman in *Gentleman's Agreement*, a Jewish army veteran being discriminated against. Garfield had rocketed to stardom in *Four Daughters* (1938), receiving an Academy Award nomination for Best Supporting Actor. Garfield had also been a member of the Group Theatre, learning his craft alongside director Elia Kazan at the Group's rehearsal space at Pinebrook Campgrounds in Trumbull. While Kazan made the controversial decision to name names before HUAC's committee, Garfield refused, and in 1951, four years after his acclaimed performance in *Gentleman's Agreement*, he was blacklisted and died tragically young—some say from a heart attack brought on by the stress.

Peck's decision to accept the role shaped much of his future career and how he was perceived. His sensitive portrayal would garner him his second Academy Award nomination as Best Actor, which established him as one of the top ten box-office draws in America. In a career that would span sixty years, Peck continued to be cast to play noble characters like Phil Green—men with a strict moral compass and code of honor. He eventually won an Academy Award for the role with which he would become most closely associated, that of Atticus Finch in *To Kill a Mockingbird* (1962).

Elia Kazan, Gregory Peck, and Dorothy McGuire. Gregory Peck reportedly received more fan mail than any other male star at that time. One letter from an ardent female read, "Let me spend the night with you. It would make my dreams come true." Peck's secretary was instructed to write back, "I'm all booked up!" (Photofest)

In *Gentleman's Agreement*, the magazine writer Phil Green is a widower with a young son, Tommy (Dean Stockwell), working on a story about anti-Semitism with his editor, John Minify (Albert Dekker). In the course of his assignment, Phil meets and begins a romantic relationship with Kathy Lacy (Dorothy McGuire). Kathy and her sister Jane (Jane Wyatt) live in an exclusive and restricted neighborhood in Darien. ("Restricted" in this context refers to an unwritten covenant prohibiting real estate sales to Jews in order to keep the neighborhood Anglo-Saxon.) Kathy is aware that Darien is restricted, but since it hasn't affected her, she's never really thought about it.

After the war, Darien became a popular destination for wealthy New Yorkers, which transformed it into a residential suburb of New York that was not only restricted but had rules—gentleman's agreements—that made the practice acceptable. In her novel, author Hobson (née Zametkin), herself the daughter of Russian Jewish immigrants, described this kind of ingrained discrimination when she wrote, "And New Canaan's even stricter about Jews than Darien."

Phil lets Kathy know he's adopted a Jewish persona, Phil Greenberg, to explore anti-Semitism, and he makes her promise that she will keep his real identity a secret while he's writing the story. Kathy starts out believing she is liberal and open-minded, and agrees with the principles of Phil's story; however, she insists that Phil allow her to reveal the truth to her sister. Since Jane lives in restricted Darien, Kathy asks Phil not to go by the name Phil Greenberg when they attend Jane's cocktail party. Kathy is afraid it will upset her sister's neighbors if she brings someone who is Jewish, but she has a hard time admitting that, even to herself, so she covers by telling Phil that it will just "confuse things."

Phil is appalled, and begins to understand that the roots of anti-Semitism may be much deeper and more complicated than he first thought. He learns his secretary, Elaine Wales (June Havoc), formerly Estelle Wilovsky, changed her name in order to get hired by the magazine, yet still confides to Phil that its new anti-discrimination policy might allow "the wrong kind of Jews" there. When Greenberg tries to rent a room at a hotel and is turned away after he tells the clerk he is Jewish, he is incensed. The hotel clerk scolds him, "Don't you raise your voice with me!"

Phil begins to personalize these incidents, and takes it out on Kathy. Their relationship is further undermined when Phil's friend Dave Goldman (John Garfield) is unable to obtain housing after returning home from the army, because he's Jewish. Phil is aware that Kathy's cottage in Darien is empty, but she won't rent it to Dave because of her fear of breaking the "gentleman's agreement," which ultimately leads to their breakup.

Phil begins to see that it's "nice" people like Kathy that are part of the problem. Not only does he feel that her not taking a stance against restrictive practices is wrong, but Kathy's defensiveness about not wanting to rock the boat reveals her own hidden prejudice. After talking to Dave and revealing her own conflicted feelings, she has a crisis of conscience. Kathy begins to understand that being silent is the same as being complicit, and agrees to rent the cottage to Dave. Kathy's willingness to change her behavior leads to a reunion with Phil.

After screening *Gentleman's Agreement* for the first time, Darryl Zanuck congratulated Kazan in a telegram, writing, "It's the most important film to come out of this town." Anne Revere, who played Peck's mother in the film, wrote Zanuck a personal note telling him how proud she was to be associated with it. Darryl Zanuck's bet on a "message picture" (a film that is socially conscious or points out society's ills) paid off. *Gentleman's Agreement* (1947) was nominated for eight Academy Awards, winning three, including Best Picture for Zanuck and Fox, Best Director for Elia Kazan, and Best Supporting Actress for Celeste Holm, who portrayed fashion editor Anne Dettrey, Phil's friend and confidante. Holm, who I was lucky enough to work with in a movie called *Alchemy* (2005), said of *Gentleman's Agreement*, "I think the reason the picture made such an impression was because the writers had a real sense of responsibility to the audience. They had a point. That seems to have gone out of style."

Though *Gentleman's Agreement* garnered many awards and shined a light on discrimination, in 1948, one year after the film came out, in a case known as *Shelley v. Kraemer*, restrictive covenants were deemed unenforceable by law under the Fourteenth Amendment. The ruling did not find that the covenants themselves were illegal, and property deeds continued to include clauses meant to exclude Jews and Blacks from purchasing property in many wealthy and exclusive towns in Connecticut. It was not until the Fair Housing Act of 1968 that the writing of these covenants came to an end. These days, "message pictures" are considered about as old-fashioned as a rocking chair, but the most important "message" of *Gentleman's Agreement*—that deep-seated bigotry might be born from ignorance—remains as relevant today as it was in 1947. The film serves as a reminder: If you see prejudice, fight it, but when you see it in yourself, fight it even harder. We can all learn, and we can all change.

BOOMERANG! (1947)

Boomerang! (1947) came out before Kazan's triumph with *Gentleman's Agreement* (1947), but I find myself partial to the underseen *Boomerang!* because it had more of an impact on Kazan's artistic career, and also, how Connecticut may have played a part in that.

It was while on location in Stamford, far from the confines of studio filmmaking, that Kazan was able to experiment with a more economic style of film production. While both films contain subject matter about Connecticut and were filmed in Connecticut, *Boomerang!* is more significant in Kazan's directing career because it represents a new approach—shooting in real locations, casting locals and nonprofessionals—a style Kazan adopted in follow-up films like *Panic in the Streets* (1950), *Viva Zapata!* (1952), and *On the Waterfront* (1955).

After the success of his first feature, *A Tree Grows in Brooklyn* (1945), Kazan began shooting his second film, a big-budget MGM vehicle for Katharine Hepburn and Spencer Tracy called *Sea of Grass* (1947) (in which my grandfather, Melvyn Douglas, costars). Traditional costume dramas like *Sea of Grass* were going out of fashion, but Kazan was excited about the idea of getting to shoot the film on the Great Plains of Nebraska. He was in the middle of scouting locations when MGM scrapped the idea in favor of shooting *Sea of Grass* on the lot, with a rear-screen projection of Nebraska instead. Although *Sea of Grass* made money, Kazan called it "terrible picture" because of his lack of artistic control.

If Kazan had been happier with *Sea of Grass* he might well have stayed in Hollywood, continuing to make studio pictures. Instead, he decided to go back to his theater roots in New York. He helped start the Actors Studio, creating a new approach to acting called "the Method." He also began

The State of Connecticut v. Harold Israel has been cited as an example of both the shortcomings of the criminal justice system and the responsibilities of a prosecutor. Connecticut state's attorney Homer Cummings's actions in the 1924 murder trial in Bridgeport, Connecticut, made him a standard-bearer to prosecutors, launched his political career, and inspired a film based on events of the case, directed by Elia Kazan, *Boomerang!* (1947). (Photofest)

to make more personal films, the first of which was *Boomerang!*

The Method had come out of his days as a member of the Group Theatre, along with Harold Clurman, Stella Adler, Sanford Meisner, Lee Strasberg, and others. In 1930s and '40s, the Group had spent summers in Connecticut, first in Brookfield, and then Pine Brook Country Club in Nichols (see chapter 2). In this camp-like atmosphere, acting workshops were held and plays dedicated to social issues, like Clifford Odets's *Waiting for Lefty*, were developed for Broadway. The relationships Kazan made in the Group Theatre were shattered in 1952, when Kazan claimed the Communist Party was trying to take over their membership. He became a cooperative witness for the House Un-American Activities Committee, naming fellow Group Theatre members such as Odets, Morris Carnovsky, Tony Kraber, and Paula Miller (who later married Lee Strasberg) as communists. Since

Dana Andrews had a turbulent and somewhat tragic off-screen life. Known for his underplaying, the star of such classic films as *Laura* (1944) and *The Best Years of our Lives* (1946) brought a soulfulness to all of his performances. Andrews battled alcoholism his entire career, finally giving it up in the 1970s, after which he appeared in several public service commercials about the subject. Andrews's own inner turmoil translated well on-screen as the fictionalized version of state's attorney Homer Cummings, a man who must consider convicting an innocent man or risk ruining his career. (Photofest) Arthur Kennedy as "John Waldron," based on Harold Israel, and Dana Andrews as "Henry L. Harvey," based on Homer Cummings. A telegram to Elia Kazan from Darryl Zanuck during filming read, "Rushes continue to be excellent, and Dana Andrews is giving an outstanding performance, particularly in the courtroom." (Photofest)

Kazan directing *Boomerang!* in Stamford, Connecticut. Cinematographer Norbert Brodine also shot producer Louis de Rochemont's cinema verité film, *The House on 92nd Street* (1945). Elia Kazan (who left his papers, known as the Elia Kazan Collection, to Wesleyan University), had ties to Connecticut long before he shot *Boomerang!* and *Gentleman's Agreement*, working with the Group Theatre and Harold Clurman, first in Brookfield and then in Trumbull (see chapter 2). In the 1930s, Kazan moved to the Sandy Hook section of Newtown, living on Old Mill Road. Over the years he expanded his property, purchasing additional land from the estate of his neighbor, sculptor John Angel. Kazan's property eventually encompassed 200 acres. After his death, the Department of Environmental Protection purchased 153 acres to be set aside as open space. (Courtesy Wesleyan University's Reid Cinema Archives)

Kazan was the most successful member, his actions were seen as mercenary.

Just one day after giving the names to the committee, Kazan signed a contract for $500,000 with Spyros Skouras and was able to continue working, while members of the Group Theatre whom he had named were blacklisted. Arthur Miller, whose Pulitzer Prize–winning play *Death of a Salesman* (1949) had catapulted Kazan's career, initially stopped speaking to him. Just a few years earlier, Miller had made a cameo appearance as a murder suspect in *Boomerang!* Inside Kazan's personal *Boomerang!* script, I had spotted the name "Art Miller" scrawled in pencil, along with his telephone

172   CRIMES AND MISDEMEANORS

number, a symbol of the trusted working relationship they must have had. Kazan and Miller would eventually reconcile, brought together by the intervention of Marilyn Monroe, who Miller later married.

Boomerang! is a hybrid of studio filmmaking technique and Kazan's emerging naturalistic style. Unlike his experience filming *Sea of Grass*, he said, "I want to be able to do this picture the way I think pictures should be made . . . It was our neo-realism." (Italian films like *Bicycle Thieves*, 1948, came to be called neorealist, as they were shot on location, often with non-actors.) Kazan had free rein on selection of locations and actors, many of whom came from Broadway or his newly formed Actors Studio.

The impressive acting roster represents the greatest hits of twentieth-century theater and film. Alongside its stars, Dana Andrews (*Laura*, 1944; *Best Years of Our Lives*, 1946) as Henry Harvey and Jane Wyatt (*Gentleman's Agreement*) as Madge Harvey, *Boomerang!* marks the first credited appearance of Ed Begley (as Paul Harris, a corrupt politician). Begley was a Connecticut native born in Hartford in 1901. He would go on to win an Oscar for *12 Angry Men* (1957). It was also Karl Malden's first significant film role, although he is not credited. Malden would work with Kazan in both the stage and film versions of *A Streetcar Named Desire* (1947 and 1951, respectively), winning an Oscar for the role of Mitch. Sam Levene, best known for playing Nathan Detroit on Broadway in *Guys and Dolls* (1950), plays the Bridgeport reporter who leads police to the murder suspect, John Waldron (Arthur Kennedy). Lee J. Cobb (who plays Police Chief Harold "Robby" Robinson) and Kennedy would star in Kazan's original production of Miller's *Death of a Salesman*. Ironically, Kennedy later starred in Arthur Miller's requiem for the blacklist, *The Crucible* (1953), playing a character based on Kazan. Rounding out the cast was a young member of the Actors Studio, Cara Williams. She would go on to be nominated for a Best Supporting Actress Oscar for *The Defiant Ones* (1958).

Part of the realistic docudrama look of *Boomerang!* must be attributed to producer Louis de Rochemont, whose newsreel series, *The March of Time*, inspired the opening shots of *Citizen Kane* (1941). He is credited with introducing a semi-documentary style called docu-noir into Twentieth Century Fox films such as *The House on 92nd Street* (1945). It was de Rochemont who had come across a *Reader's Digest* article called "The Perfect Case," by Fulton Oursler, published in 1945 and based on the unsolved murder of a Bridgeport priest, Father Hubert Dahme, in 1924.

Father Dahme had been taking his daily constitutional near the Lyric Theatre in downtown Bridgeport. People were outside the theater waiting for the curtain to rise on *The Laughing Lady*, starring Ethel Barrymore. Father Dahme was about to cross the street when a man came up behind him, shooting him once in the back of the head with a .32 caliber revolver and running off. Patrons standing in line at the Lyric rushed to his side, but in all the confusion, no one called for a doctor

Boomerang! night shooting in Stamford. Arthur Kennedy is wearing the leather bomber jacket. Kazan stayed at the Taft Hotel in New Haven during filming, where he would receive telegrams from studio boss Darryl Zanuck containing his notes. To my delight, when I opened Kazan's working script of *Boomerang!*, I found scrawled in pencil the names and phone numbers of two crucial and very familiar artistic allies: Arthur Miller and Harold Clurman. (Courtesy Wesleyan University's Reid Cinema Archives)

for ten minutes. He died two hours later at St. Vincent's Hospital. It was a complete mystery why someone would want to kill this much-loved priest. More than twelve thousand people showed up to his funeral, and swift action was demanded.

One week later, police picked up a twenty-year-old veteran named Harold Israel (played by Waldron in the film) in Norwalk who they said was "acting strangely." In his possession was a .32 caliber revolver—the same kind that had killed Father Dahme. Israel was arrested for carrying a concealed weapon. A savvy *Bridgeport Times* reporter (Dave Woods in the film) got wind of the arrest and fed information about the gun to Bridgeport police. On the basis of that tip, four detectives were dispatched to interview Israel in jail. (The brutality of the interrogation as depicted in the film is stomach-churning.)

The *Bridgeport Times* stoked public interest, writing, "If you have any information or are of the opinion that you saw a suspicious character that may be Harold Israel, you may help solve the most brutal murder in the history of Bridgeport." After the story appeared in the paper, witnesses came forward identifying Israel, including a waitress who said she saw Israel walk by her restaurant the night of the murder. That, along with Israel's own confession—after being subjected to twenty-eight hours of intense questioning—became the strongest part of the case against him.

Homer Cummings, state's attorney for Fairfield County, was brought in to prosecute. A jailhouse visit to gather evidence left him questioning Israel's guilt; he believed that Israel's confession had been coerced. He also thought that the witnesses' accounts placing Israel at the scene could not be accurate, since Israel had a ticket stub proving he was at a movie house nowhere near the Lyric Theatre at the time of the murder.

At the same time, there was enormous pressure on Cummings to convict Israel, as he himself was soon to be up for reelection. He began his oral arguments to the court by saying, "Upon its face, at least, it seemed like a well-nigh perfect case." As he continued, however, he surprised everyone. In what has become Cummings's most remembered line, he said, "Despite the facts, it goes without saying that it is just as important for a state's attorney to use the great powers of his office to protect the innocent as it is to convict the guilty." He then proceeded to rebut all the evidence the police had gathered against Israel, dropping the state's case against him. It was not a popular decision in Bridgeport, and Cummings wisely chose not to run again for county prosecutor, yet the integrity he showed in the case brought him a great deal of publicity, and in 1933 he was tapped by the newly elected president, Franklin D. Roosevelt, to become attorney general of the United States.

Harold Israel was once again a free man, but it would not be the last time he and Cummings would see each other. In 1941, Harold Israel was married and living in the coal-mining town of Gilberton, Pennsylvania. Out of work and "on the relief," he reached out to Cummings for help. "Dear

Friend," he wrote. "Just a few lines to let you know that I am well and that this will leave you the same. I guess you think that I have the nerve to write to you for what you have did [*sic*] for me. But you see I have to write to some one [*sic*]."

Cummings wrote back, acknowledging his plight, but writing, "I do not know at present what I can do."

Just five years later, though, fate intervened. Cummings received a call from Louis de Rochemont, who was considering producing a movie about Israel's case and wanted to know if Cummings knew how to get in touch with him. Cummings was concerned the studio might take advantage of Israel, so, without telling Israel, he negotiated on his behalf, getting him $20,000 ($200,000 in today's currency) for the rights to his story, setting aside $6,500 for an anticipated tax hit, and investing $8,995 in US savings bonds in Israel's name.

Cummings then asked Israel to take the train to Washington to see him. It was the first time the two men had seen each other since the trial. Cummings filled him in on Louis de Rochemont's plans and the amount he was able to obtain for the film rights. Israel had only one condition. He was upset that the newspapers had described him as a "vagrant" and a "moron," and wanted to make sure the film depicted him as an honorably discharged veteran—which he was. A mention in the script that Waldron suffered from "war nerves" was also later removed. Two men from very different worlds, brought together by circumstances, would now have their story immortalized in *Boomerang!*

There was one problem in adapting the story for the screen. They had the rights to Harold Israel's and Homer Cummings's stories, but the murder itself was still unsolved. Zanuck wrote in a telegram to Kazan, "We have a very engrossing story and an excellent movie, but in the last third, we run into trouble. There is nothing at stake; the suspense is over." His notes suggest a reframing of the facts to enhance the suspense. Zanuck later wrote: "You take the factual things and play them up, but you do not make the mistake of sticking with factual things. Instead, you bring in your movie technique, and if you have properly planted all your elements and developed them with dramatic and suspenseful scenes, the audience will accept your movie ending as factual."

Coming right after Kazan's credit, the first line in *Boomerang!* is seen as an on-screen book page, which reads: "The story you are about to witness is based on fact"—but, as is often the case in movies dealing with actual events, it's not entirely accurate. "Based on" is the operative phrase. One of the witnesses, Nellie Trafton, the waitress who claimed she saw Israel on the night in question, threatened to sue over the portrayal by Cara Williams of "Irene Nelson," a kind of loose woman who implicates Waldron out of revenge because he stood her up for a date. Trafton was paid $1,200 by the studio and backed down.

Bridgeport officials refused to allow filming in the city, so it was shot in Stamford. Since

Cummings had script approval, he may have provided his own insights, as the script implied that Bridgeport politicians put pressure on newspapers, the police, and Cummings to make Israel a scapegoat, because the unsolved murder of a priest would not bode well for their reelections. The rush to judgment had almost cost Harold Israel his life.

Homer Cummings's personal life may have inspired a key scene, in which Paul Harris (Ed Begley) threatens to blackmail Henry Harvey (Dana Andrews) about his wife's involvement in a shady real estate deal if he doesn't prosecute Waldron. This might be a reference to something that happened to Cummings. In what was meant to be a smear campaign to destroy his credibility, Cummings was blackmailed about an affair he was having, and love letters between Cummings and a married woman (who later became his second wife) were published in the local newspapers around the same time as the trial.

In the end, Kazan was able to weave the social causes he was so passionate about into what would be his first "neorealist" film. The semi-documentary approach to filming on real locations and using real people as background extras, mixing factual events with movie technique, all foreshadowed modern filmmaking. *Boomerang!* is a superbly acted, well-directed drama about a man who stood up for truth and saved another man's life. Although their later relationship is not depicted on-screen, Cummings remained a presence in Israel's life, dispensing financial advice and exchanging letters with his wife Olivia. In one touching exchange, Olivia wrote, "To him, Mr. Cummings, you are next to God. He worships you. He said he would trust you more than anybody in this world."

Homer S. Cummings on the right with attorney Harry J. Crawford in February 1929.

International Pictures
PRESENTS
Edward G.
ROBINSON
Loretta
YOUNG
Orson
WELLES
IN
The Stranger
WITH
PHILIP MERIVALE
RICHARD LONG · BILLY HOUSE
Directed by
Orson Welles
PRODUCED BY S. P. EAGLE
STORY BY VICTOR TRIVAS
AND DECLA DUNNING
SCREEN PLAY BY ANTHONY VEILLER

TWO FILM NOIRS SET IN CONNECTICUT

Connecticut provided the ideal backdrop for two film noirs, *The Stranger* (1946) and *The Man in the Net* (1959). What could be more disturbing than discovering there might be a Nazi, or a wife murderer, living in your quiet little corner of the state?

THE STRANGER (1946)

Although it was filmed entirely in Hollywood, *The Stranger* (1946), directed by and starring Orson Welles, is set in fictional Harper, Connecticut. Welles is Franz Kindler, an escaped Nazi war criminal who relocates to the small town of Harper and assumes the new identity of Professor Charles Rankin. His unsuspecting wife, Mary (Loretta Young), has a hard time believing she is in danger even as Kindler is making plans to kill her before she discovers his past crimes. His fascination with the clock tower in the town square will prove to be his undoing.

In 1939, two years before *Citizen Kane*, Welles utilized the Stony Creek Theatre in Branford, Connecticut, to stage his Mercury Theatre production of a play by none other than William Gillette, *Too Much Johnson*, hoping to move the production to Broadway. A silent film Welles wrote and directed, with the Mercury Players, meant to accompany the play, was unable to be screened because the theater was not equipped to show movies. The show ran for two weeks, but it never went to Broadway.

The Stranger (1946) is a film noir both starring and directed by Orson Welles. Orson Welles mounted an ill-fated production of *Too Much Johnson*—a comedy from 1894 written by William Gillette—in Branford. A filmed sequence of the play could not be shown because the Stony Creek Theatre lacked a means of projection. (Photofest)

The Man in the Net (1959), directed by Michael Curtiz, is a film noir set in Thompson and Woodstock, sometimes called part of the "Quiet Corner" of Connecticut. The unique architecture of the two early-nineteenth-century mansions complements the Gone Girl–style mystery.

THE MAN IN THE NET (1959)

John Hamilton (Alan Ladd) can't seem to do anything right. Now his wife has disappeared, and John—a mild-mannered artist whom everybody in town was already suspicious of—is accused of killing her. John and Linda (Carolyn Jones) had agreed to leave New York to get out of the rat race. That's the cover story they have told their neighbors in the rural community of Stoneville (sounding to me much like Stonington), Connecticut.

Part of the backstory is true. John left a lucrative job in New York at an advertising agency to try his hand at painting, but the move to Connecticut was to help Linda, who has severe mental health issues, kick the bottle. It didn't work. She's secretly back on the booze, and ready to cause some trouble. Adding to the pressure, John's paintings aren't selling, and his career is going nowhere.

Linda still lives for the excitement of New York. Her afternoon trips to the mysterious mansion, the Chimney House (Roseland Cottage), to meet her secret lover alleviate her boredom but will ultimately lead to her demise. John and Linda's relationship is stormy on a good day. She enjoys tormenting John, making fun of his failures as an artist, or taunting him that she's going to leave him for another man—and there are many in Stoneville.

Jones's arresting look in *The Man in the Net* is deliciously over the top—think beatnik nympho meets Goth girl—and the black-rinse Buster Brown hairdo and skin-tight silk capri pants and cha-cha sandals (not heels, as Ladd was very short) probably don't go over very well at the yacht club. In my research I came across a crazy publicity campaign, suggesting that women who saw *The Man in The Net* and favored Linda's "short straight bob" could enter a raffle, where the prize was getting the same hairdo for free at their local beauty parlor.

Jones, coming off Michael Curtiz's *King Creole* (1958), with Elvis Presley, was at the height of her career. *The Man in the Net* was one of four films she made that were released in 1959 (the others being *A Hole in the Head*, *Career*, and *Last Train from Gun Hill*).

The Man in the Net, with Barbara Beaird and Alan Ladd.

CONNECTICUT IN THE MOVIES

Postcard of the Vernon Styles Inn, from 1959—the same year *The Man in the Net* was released. The house, in Thompson, is now called the Cottage House. It was built in 1814 as a public house, then purchased by Captain Vernon Stiles and known as Stiles Tavern. Location was the key to its success, as it was situated between the routes from Boston to Hartford, and Providence to Springfield. Stiles Tavern boasted many famous visitors, including, reportedly, French nobleman and officer, the Marquis de Lafayette. Stiles was a gregarious host and also a justice of the peace. Stiles Tavern gained the nickname "the marriage factory," as Stiles married couples from out of state who had fled to Connecticut to marry. The hasty unions also earned Stiles Tavern the title "Gretna Green of New England." Of course, a colorful captain like Stiles would not leave this earth quietly. His ghost is said to "walk the house," and there have been many sightings of Stiles in his full uniform regalia. The Cottage House is currently a bed-and-breakfast.

A monument designating the Henry C. Bowen House as a landmark. Roseland Cottage in Woodstock is also known as the Pink House. Roseland Cottage was built in 1846 by Woodstock native Henry Bowen as a summer retreat for his large family. Bowen owned a newspaper called the *Independent*, in which he promoted religious values, temperance, and the abolitionist movement, though apparently he did approve of bowling (the house boasts one of the earliest versions of a bowling alley). The gingerbread vergeboards, quatrefoil trim, stained glass, oriel windows, steep gables, and soaring asymmetrical style were all hallmarks of Gothic Revival architecture. Bowen chose the bright pink color himself, to suit his own dynamic personality. Roseland Cottage is now a museum, and the interior remains largely untouched since *The Man in the Net* was filmed. (Since the movie is in black and white, you won't be able to appreciate its exterior's vibrant pink color.) The day I visited, I was lucky enough to be invited to the wedding that was taking place outside in the garden.

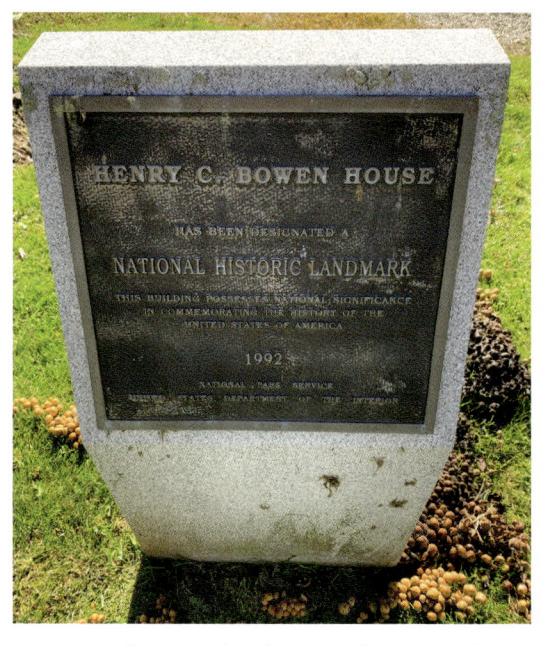

The gardens of Roseland Cottage. This staircase with gothic overtones, found inside beautiful Roseland Cottage, is featured in *The Man in the Net*.

John is doing his best to cope with what has become an unhappy marriage. They have no children of their own, but he forms a bond with a group of local kids whom he engages with while he paints. Linda finds country life—and her husband—dull, and she begins having affairs with other men, including the local sheriff, Steve Ritter (Charles McGraw). John is aware of her cheating and is humiliated by it, but he feels helpless to stop her. News of a job offer at his old advertising agency means a possible move back to New York, and Linda neurotically begs John not to leave her, promising she will see her psychiatrist.

That night they are supposed to attend a cocktail party at a neighbor's house, but Linda tells John she has a migraine and retires to her bedroom with a bottle of vodka, leaving him to go without her. Later, Linda crashes the party, drunk and sporting a black eye; and tearfully informs the partygoers that John hit her during an argument. Though it's not true, John doesn't deny it. His neighbors in this small community are alarmed, beginning to wonder what is going on in the marriage and what kind of man John is.

When John returns home from his trip to New York and finds his paintings slashed and Linda missing, suspicion naturally falls on him. It is the children he has befriended (played by Barbara Beaird, Susan Gordon, Michael McGreevey, Charles Herbert, and Steve Perry), who rally around him, hiding him from the police in a cave while he tries to prove his innocence. The children's faith in John never wavers, even when Linda is found dead and he is accused of her murder.

An off-screen dynamic may have affected *The Man in the Net*. Ladd was at times so ill he could not run, and had to be extensively doubled. Alan Ladd was never an energetic actor, but his portrayal of the quiet, reserved artist John Hamilton is noticeably moody and downbeat. Ladd was only in his forties, but he was drinking heavily, despondent about his failing career and recent breakup with actress June Allyson. Producer Walter Mirisch admitted he had never before witnessed such self-destructive behavior from the actor.

Although Ladd's deportment works within the framework of the movie, which is about a man suspected of murdering his wife, a certain doomed quality permeates his performance. It's as if Hamilton's failure to make any headway as an artist, his wife's lack of sexual interest in him, even being unjustly accused of a crime, all mirror Ladd's own sense of unworthiness. If not for the children fighting for him, John might have turned himself in for a crime he hadn't committed. Even when the real murderer is discovered, John exhibits no great sense of relief, or even outrage at his neighbors for falsely accusing him. John just goes back to his quiet life, painting in the meadow with his only friends—the children—beside him.

Although director Michael Curtiz was an industry icon who had directed many classic films, including *Casablanca* (1942), he was known to be notoriously difficult. Seventy-one when he made

The Man in the Net, and at the end of his storied career, he was grouchy and short-tempered with the cast. In Alan K. Rode's biography of actor Charles McGraw, who played Sheriff Ritter, child actor Michael McGreevey, who played the young Buck Ritter, recalled a situation between McGraw and Curtiz:

> *We were filming out in a dump . . . Charlie and I had to find something there that linked Ladd to his wife's murder in the story. Curtiz had this involved master shot with a lot of camera movements. It was not uncommon for Curtiz to go 25 takes when things were going well. Charlie had a lot of dialogue. He was missing words, blowing lines and getting more and more frustrated. Instead of calling a break, Curtiz just kept going. After about 45, 46 takes, Curtiz dressed down Charlie publicly, just humiliated him in front of everybody.*

Frank Stovall was the artist who provided the paintings to serve as the work for Ladd's character, John Hamilton. Art director Hilyard Brown arranged his paintings throughout the barn set that served as Hamilton's art studio. In the story, an intruder comes in the night and slashes Hamilton's paintings, but when the time came, Brown could not bring himself to damage Stovall's work. Curtiz stepped in and personally slashed the paintings. The only solace for Stovall was that they paid him three times what the paintings were worth.

MAN ON A SWING (1974)

Man on a Swing (1974) was based on the book *The Girl on the Volkswagen Floor* (1971) by William Arthur Clarke, about the unsolved murder of a schoolteacher, Barbara Ann Butler, in Kettering, Ohio. It's a moody little film, typical of the era in which it was made—the 1970s—that sneaks up on you with a slow-moving intensity that pulls you in, then has a quick, blunt ending, much like the murder it was based on.

Man on a Swing is a hard movie to classify—part neo-noir, part psychological thriller, part mystery. Now we'd call it very "Lynchian," meaning in the style of auteur David Lynch, who is best known for *Blue Velvet* (1986) and *Twin Peaks* (1990–1991, 2017). There's a woodsy setting, an eerie score by Lalo Schifrin (*Mission Impossible*), a beautiful young dead girl, an obsessed policeman, and weird characters who make psychic pronouncements. In fact, Frank Perry was doing mind-bending cinema (*The Swimmer*, 1968; *Diary of a Mad Housewife*, 1970; *Play It as It Lays*, 1972) long before David Lynch came on the scene. Aside from the stylish opening credits sequence—with its awesome lens flares from director of photography Adam Holender (*Midnight Cowboy*, 1968), to remind you it's the 1970s—Perry relies on the performances of the two lead actors: the very self-contained Cliff

Man on a Swing offers another murder in a small town. I had no expectations about Frank Perry's *Man on a Swing* (1974), mainly because I had never even heard of it. This film marked Perry's return to filming in Westport, where he had made *The Swimmer* (1968). (Photofest)

Robertson as Police Chief Tucker, and the very hyperactive Joel Grey as psychic Franklin Wills, who enter an unlikely partnership to solve a murder.

It was supposed to be a day like any other in the mundane little town of Laurel, Connecticut. (The film was shot in Westport and New Milford.) Chief Lee Tucker would push a few pencils at work, drink a few beers, shoot the shit with his buddies, then return home to his pregnant wife. Tucker seems to be ambivalent about his life, his work, and even his marriage. That changes when a beautiful local schoolteacher, Maggie Dawson (Dianne Hull), is found strangled to death in the front seat of her Volkswagen, which had been left in a supermarket parking lot. Tucker is at first unnerved, having never seen anything akin to what looks like a sex crime. Tucker interviews Maggie's parents, but they are mystified, believing theirs is a "nice neighborhood." When they break down in tears, Tucker is unable to offer any comfort to the grieving parents, having learned to compartmentalize his feelings.

Tucker seems to have feelings for Maggie that go beyond trying to solve her murder. He may even be in love with her, as his wife Janet (Dorothy Tristan) seems to imply. Or perhaps it's easier to feel something for someone after they are gone than while they are living. Tucker skips going home at night and begins poring over clues, looking at slides of the crime scene, trying to glean a motive as to who would kill this girl, and why.

When a fellow cop, Willie (Peter Masterson from *The Stepford Wives*), looks in on Tucker, he catches him staring at a photograph of the murdered, half-stripped Maggie Dawson, a spot of blood over her breast. Tucker says quietly, "Kinda pretty," but Willie just shrugs, seeing nothing beyond Maggie's blank expression. Tucker brings in a local delinquent, Richie Tom Keating (Christopher Allport), previously arrested for attempted rape, but he has nothing to hold him on, and he's released. Tucker can do nothing but open another can of beer and ponder his next move.

That's when the mysterious clairvoyant, Franklin Wills, enters the picture. Wills claims to be psychic and wants to share with the police information he saw in a trance. This was Grey's first screen role since his Oscar win for *Cabaret* (1972); his entrance has so much theatricality and razzle-dazzle, it's as though he's playing to off-screen applause. Grey as Wills—from the white shoes and *Music Man* seersucker suit to the musicality of his delivery—is a nice contrast to Robertson's masterful slow burn in their game of cat and mouse. Robertson was also an Academy Award winner for the film *Charly* (1968). In between sips of beer, he percolates, a barely perceptible shift in his jaw conveying his rage at Wills. It's a great game of chess between two great actors.

Of course, Wills enjoys toying with Tucker, as any good villain does. He's able to give Tucker such accurate details of the murder that he immediately becomes a suspect, purring, "Oh, I hope I haven't been so good you think I'm the killer." Wills's overt femininity (although he's happily married with a child) and pseudo-seduction make macho Tucker uncomfortable, but Tucker is also intrigued by Wills and the world of psychic phenomena. If he can prove Wills has special powers, it would be a gateway to a more magical way of looking at the world. If Wills is not psychic, he is a killer. Wills becomes Tucker's de facto partner, although Tucker sometimes wonders if Wills is helping him solve a crime that he himself committed.

Emboldened with a sense of power that his relationship with Tucker has given him, Wills goes to Tucker's home, meeting Tucker's pregnant wife, Janet. He appears to be helpful, telling her she will not have twins; "You were worried about that," he says cattily. Wills's familiarity disturbs her, and she later tells her husband that Wills is not welcome there again, ever. Soon the Tuckers are receiving mysterious and harassing phone calls and letters. Tucker can't prove Wills is behind these annoyances, and what's more frustrating is that he can't solve the case without him.

Tucker tricks Wills into meeting with two psychiatrists by telling him they are doctors who want to test his psychic abilities. Dr. Willson (Elizabeth Wilson) thinks that Wills's lack of empathy is indicative of a sociopath. Wills knows he has been set up, and to prove he is not the killer, he goes into a trance, writhing around the room, then predicting that soon a young girl would die. The next day a twelve-year-old girl, Virginia Segretta, is found strangled. A witness comes forward identifying the license plate of a car leaving the scene, a car that belongs to Richie Tom Keating, the delinquent that Tucker had originally questioned for the murder of Maggie Dawson.

Tucker forms a very dark theory: Richie and Franklin Wills may *both* be involved. Did Wills come forward using facts about the murder that he got from Richie so he could gain fame as a psychic? Or, an even more sinister thought: Did Wills hypnotize Richie in order to have him carry out the murders, so Wills could later claim he'd predicted them?

Tucker confronts Wills, and Wills just smiles, knowing in some way that he has made a fool of Tucker. Wills tells him they should probably stay in touch after his baby is born, predicting it will be "a little girl." Tucker had just told him that the victim, Virginia Segretta, was a twelve-year-old girl, and the suggestion is not only that Wills *knew* another girl would be killed (as in, he's the murderer), but also that he knows Tucker's baby will be a little girl (as in, he is psychic).

EVERYBODY WINS (1990)

In 1973, Peter Reilly, who was eighteen at the time, was charged with the brutal murder of his mother in Canaan, Connecticut. After eight hours of intense interrogation, Reilly confessed to the crime, but later recanted. He was convicted of first-degree manslaughter and sent to prison, but many locals believed the confession was coerced, and raised money for an appeal.

Among his chief supporters was a group of high-powered celebrities living in Connecticut that included writer William Styron, playwright Arthur Miller, actor Richard Widmark, and director Mike Nichols. They helped assemble a team to prove Reilly's innocence, hiring a new attorney for Reilly, a private investigator to study the case, and a forensic pathologist. They raised money for him to be freed on bond so he could complete his senior year in high school.

In 1976, Reilly won a new trial. The new presiding judge not only cleared Reilly of the charges, but sharply rebuked the police department, which never pursued any other suspects. The case remains unsolved to this day.

Two films have been made about the case. The first was an excellent television drama called *A Death in Canaan* (1978), shot entirely in Los Angeles and based on the book of the same title by Joan Barthel. It was directed by Tony Richardson and starred Stefanie Powers and Brian Dennehy. *A Death in Canaan* followed closely the real events of the murder and trial, and focused on the town's coming together to help prove Reilly's innocence.

Arthur Miller, who helped to free Reilly and get his conviction overturned, wrote a one-act play loosely based on the events, called *Some Kind of Love Story* (1984), which he adapted

Everybody Wins (1990) was the first pairing of Nick Nolte and Debra Winger since the infamous *Cannery Row* (1982), when their reported off-screen relationship was stormy. Apparently, they were up for a second go-round here. Previously filmed as *A Death in New Canaan* (1978), *Everybody Wins* (1990) had the potential of being a prestigious project. Director Karel Reisz was one of the gutsy British New Wave film directors, known for *Saturday Night and Sunday Morning* (1960) and *Morgan!* (1966). He also directed *The French Lieutenant's Woman* (1981). The script of *Everybody Wins* was Arthur Miller's first original screenplay since *The Misfits* (1961), and was based on one of the most controversial murder cases in Connecticut history. Miller and his neighbor Richard Widmark had been directly involved in the case, helping suspect Peter Reilly obtain legal counsel. Reilly was eventually acquitted, and the murder has remained unsolved to this day. (Photofest)

into *Everybody Wins* (1990). It strays from the facts, as the boy is accused of murdering his uncle. A private investigator is brought in, and, while trying to prove the boy's innocence, he stumbles into a hornet's nest of political corruption, but the film speculates on how small-town politics played a part in a rush to judgment.

The real-life events had occurred in Canaan, but what cinched Norwich as the location for filming *Everybody Wins* was the Norwich City Hall in the main square. The Victorian building, majestic but slightly crumbling, had what production designer Peter Larkin called "the smell of small-town politics." He added: "Norwich was a dream come true. The town was built on a series of hills, so the background is always interesting." The other notable location was the former Thermos factory in the Laurel Hill section of Norwich, which housed a major industry—the manufacture of vacuum flask bottles, or what the rest of the world calls thermos bottles. (The company failed to patent the name.) They also made metal lunch pails. The original plant was built in 1912 and was in operation until 1984. In the film, the abandoned building becomes a garage and hideout for a group of bikers and druggies.

The mystery-thriller *Everybody Wins* (1990) is a little like Connecticut weather. Wait a minute, and it will change. It begins as a true-crime story, switches to hard-boiled detective yarn, then it's a romance, and then it weaves in political corruption in the small town of Highbury, Connecticut, which sounds a little like Waterbury.

Set in Connecticut, but with all exteriors shot in California, *A Death in Canaan* (1978), directed by Tony Richardson, stars Stefanie Powers, Brian Dennehy, Paul Clemens, Doreen Lang, and Conchata Ferrell. The film, which is also about the Reilly case, was written by Spencer Eastman and Thomas Thompson, along with Joan Barthel, and based on her nonfiction book of the same name.

Tom O'Toole (Nick Nolte) is a former Boston cop turned private investigator who plays a little outside the law in the small town of Highbury. Emotionally remote since his wife died, he lives with his sister, Connie (Judith Ivey), and puts all his energy into helping clients. He has a strong sense of morality and often finds himself up against State's Attorney Charley Haggerty (Frank Converse). Something about Haggerty's enormous ego nags at Tom's sensibility, and he confides to his friend, Judge Harry Murdoch (Jack Warden), that he'd like to see him go down.

Tom's reputation for freeing clients falsely convicted of crimes precedes him. Angela Crispini (Debra Winger), a beautiful but seemingly flighty woman, seeks Tom's help for a teenage boy, Felix (Frank Military), she says has been wrongly arrested for the murder of his uncle, the respected Dr. Daniels. Angela has information about the murder but is afraid to come forward because the police may be involved in framing the boy. Tom is reluctant to take the case, but Angela is alluring and preys on his loneliness. No sooner is Tom turning up the radio to listen to Leon Redbone singing "I Want to Be Seduced" than he begins a torrid affair with her. Tom is smitten, telling Angela, "You're the most unex-

Will Patton and Nick Nolte at the Thermos factory in Norwich. (Photofest)

pected thing that ever happened to me."

Even more unexpected is his finding out from Connie, and just about everyone else in town, that Angela is the local hooker. Tom knows she's a kook—he tells his sister the clues Angela has given him are like "chasing feathers in a tornado"—but Tom has fallen hard for Angela, and won't give up on her. In addition to being a prostitute, Angela suffers from multiple personality disorder, so each time Tom sees her, she manifests a new personality that tells him a different version of the events of the murder.

Miller had written *The Misfits* (1961) for his then wife, Marilyn Monroe. They had once been madly in love, happily married and living in Connecticut, but something went wrong. Monroe's troubled psyche drove them apart, and Miller found himself unable to help her. They divorced not long after filming of *The Misfits* was complete, and Monroe died in 1962 of a possible drug overdose.

When Miller wrote *After the Fall* (1964), he was criticized for mining his relationship with his former wife, especially because she was no longer there to defend herself. (I would imagine as a writer it would be hard *not* to mine one's relationship with someone as fascinating as Marilyn Monroe.)

Whether it's Miller's writing or Winger's desire to channel the famous actress in her performance is up for debate, but the character of Angela in *Everybody Wins* is certainly reminiscent of Marilyn Monroe.

Postcard of the former American Thermos Bottle Company in the Laurel Hill section of Norwich, at 11 Thermos Avenue.

As the story unfolds, Angela first uses her sexuality to seduce Tom. Then, when he starts to express his love for her, she emasculates him for helping her, even boasting that his nemesis, Haggerty, is the love of her life (similar to the plot of *After the Fall*). At one point, Angela even adopts Marilyn Monroe's breathy voice and mannerisms. Later, when Tom seeks advice from Harry, Harry chides him: "A romantic fella like you always has to idealize the woman he's screwing."

Okay, get ready for some plot twists. Angela's lack of truthfulness is wearing on Tom. She implicates Jerry, a local thug and drug dealer, as the person who killed Dr. Daniels. Jerry (Will Patton) works out of a garage on the outskirts of town with a group of outcasts and druggies. Over coffee at the South Windham Diner, Jerry tells Tom that Dr. Daniels was involved in selling drugs and admits to killing him in a drug

A metal lunch pail made in Norwich at the Thermos factory.

192   CRIMES AND MISDEMEANORS

The Ripley-Woodhull House in Norwich and Norwich City Hall, where scenes from *Everybody Wins* were filmed.

While filming, Nolte frequented Wilson's Saloon on Broadway, close to Norwich City Hall.

deal gone wrong. When Jerry flies off the handle and smacks his girlfriend and fellow druggie, Amy (Kathleen Wilhoite), in the head, Tom realizes Jerry is unhinged and Felix is innocent. But now he's left wondering about Angela's involvement. Tom is about to get the police involved, but Jerry commits suicide by running his motorcycle into a truck. (Didn't see that coming!) Tom confronts Angela with what he has uncovered, but she warns Tom that "this case goes to the top of the mountain." Everyone in Highbury, including State's Attorney Charley Haggerty, is involved.

Tom wants to see Haggerty go to prison and to live happily ever after with Angela, but a backroom deal is struck with Judge Murdoch to free Felix. Tom reluctantly pimps Angela out to Murdoch, leaving them alone together long enough that Felix is sprung from jail. Tom has purchased Felix's freedom, but at a personal cost to his own ethics. Angela is content—"This way everybody wins," she says—but Tom is disillusioned, and decides to leave Highbury behind.

BRISTOL BOYS (2006)

It's sometimes challenging to admit that not every community in Connecticut is a picture-perfect Currier and Ives postcard, a land of wealth and privilege. One Connecticut native, Brandon David Cole, who wrote, directed, and edited his very independent feature, *Bristol Boys* (2006), sought to depict his very different life experience growing up in Bristol, Connecticut, where he saw firsthand the growing epidemic of young people getting involved with the usage and trafficking of drugs.

Cole had insights few others had. He was friends with the real-life protagonist Kevin Toolen—on whose life the story is based—the subject of one of the largest drug busts in Connecticut's history. On August 1, 2001, after a months-long investigation, extensive wiretapping, and help from an informant, the Statewide Narcotics Task Force raided twenty-two homes in Bristol. Toolen and twenty-one other people involved in selling drugs from Bristol, Plymouth, Southington, and Thomaston were arrested. Toolen's journey from local used-car salesman with a future to his downfall selling drugs is the focus of the film. Cole also wanted to examine the culture of Bristol that had drawn Toolen into selling drugs in the first place. (Toolen himself has a small role in the film, playing Detective Capobianco.)

Cole said he was not making the movie as an attack on Bristol, but Bristol officials, police, and residents had a negative response to the film, much as the city of Bridgeport had when Elia Kazan filmed his crime story *Boomerang!* back in 1947. There are at least two sides to every crime story, and different points of view about guilt and innocence, victims and perpetrators. The criticism of *Bristol Boys* was that Cole sought to make a martyr of Kevin Toolen and glorify the drug trade, bash the police, and give the town of Bristol a black eye. One of the characters in the film refers to Bristol as "an industrial wasteland," which would not be considered a travelogue moment for any town.

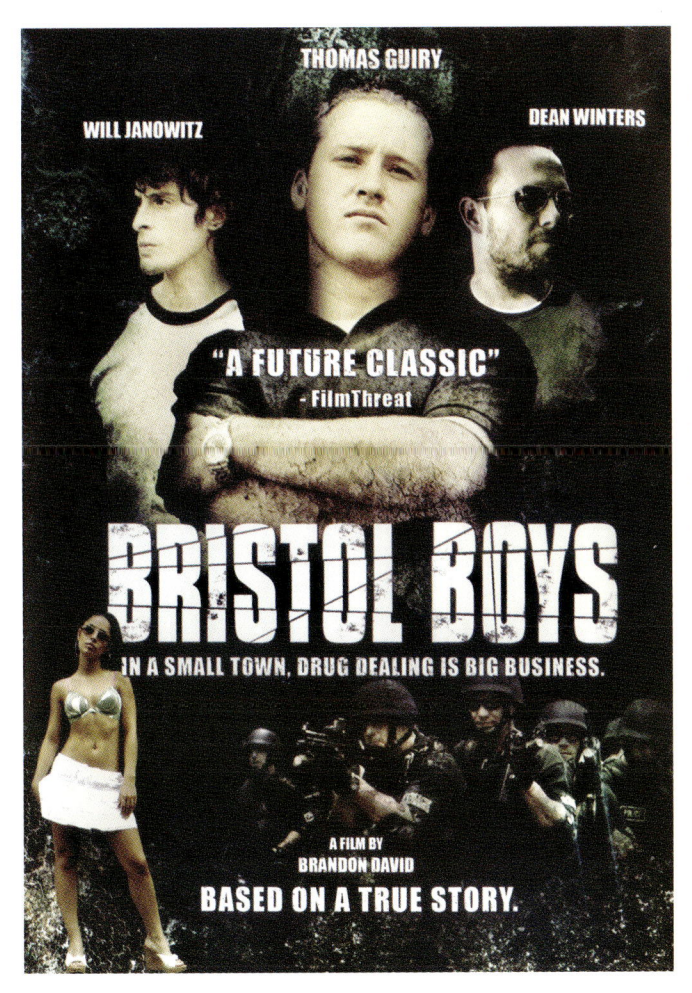

In an interview in 2007 for the film's release, Cole justified the narrative of *Bristol Boys*—which was made for a lean $500,000—saying, "The biggest message I want to get out is I didn't make a movie about Bristol. I made a movie about something that happened to people I know." That being said, *Bristol Boys* does seek to settle scores, albeit cinematically. For instance, after Toolen was arrested, he discovered that a longtime friend was the DEA informant whose testimony had led to his arrest. In the film, this informant, Donny (Max Casella), is later killed by a rival drug dealer. Cole felt this might have been fair justice for the friend, saying, "There was no murder, but if I were a guy that ratted everybody out, I'd be concerned."

The film carries this same streetwise point of view. You learn a lot about the psychology of the drug trade, the hierarchy among dealers, and the symbiosis between dealer and junkie. Less is devoted to the psychology of why Toolen became a drug dealer, and the story goes awry when Cole seems to get caught up in trying to make life in Bristol into a small-time version of *The Sopranos*. The film works best when we get to see the culture of blue-collar life in Bristol, the socioeconomic conditions, the aimlessness of the boys involved. It is then that it becomes a fascinating character study, not only of Toolen, but of the town that created Toolen.

The real person the film is based on—Kevin Toolen—gives an extended audio commentary on the DVD of what his life of crime was like. It's an intriguing interview, but vital questions are left unanswered. For instance, what was it that drove Toolen into the drug trade? The film ends with his arrest, but we don't learn whether he went to prison. The closing credits tell us that Toolen fulfilled his dream of becoming a real estate agent—but was it difficult for him to go straight?

Energetic Michael "Little Man" McCarthy (Thomas Guiry) is working as a used-car salesman and living with his drug-addicted mother (Gillian Foss), who turns tricks with her drug dealer to support her habit. Little Man wants to send his mother to rehab but doesn't have enough money. Then he loses his job. After a discussion with a friend, Randy (Dean Winters), a mechanic who supplements his income by selling marijuana on the side, Little Man decides to start selling weed, too. His master plan is to sell enough to go legit and become a real estate salesman.

Soon Little Man realizes he has an affinity for selling drugs and wants to invest in selling better marijuana to his clients. This leads him further into the drug trade, and he gets caught up in the lifestyle—fancy cars, strip clubs—and draws the attention of the police. Little Man makes enough money selling drugs to send his mother to rehab, but later she goes back to using, and eventually ODs on OxyContin. (Toolen's mother, in fact, died of cancer; she was not a drug addict.) Little Man is busted for selling marijuana, but makes a deal with police and his lawyer (Jerry Mond) to avoid prison.

He goes right back to selling marijuana, and soon moves up to the more lucrative business of selling cocaine, with a larger and more dangerous syndicate of drug dealers. This time, the police are determined to bring him down. His fellow dealer Donny has his own troubles with the law and makes a deal with a local cop, Detective Benson (David Zayas), to turn on Little Man, becoming an informant. Little Man is arrested, along with all his friends. Donny's fate is sealed: A rival drug dealer kills him for ratting on Little Man.

Bristol Boys is not an easy film to watch, but it is fascinating, and it took me to a world I knew nothing about, as films can do. The problems of drug addiction have only increased since this film was released in 2006, and hundreds of Connecticut residents die each year from drug overdoses. Bristol, like many cities across the country, established its own Opioid Task Force to deal with addiction and recovery. *Bristol Boys* is a reminder that by looking straight at the issue, we may better understand the problem.

ALL GOOD THINGS (2010)

Ryan Gosling plays David Marks, the wealthy but troubled son of New York real estate tycoon, Sanford Marks (Frank Langella). Initially his marriage to Katie McCarthy (Kirsten Dunst) and their move to Vermont bring them happiness, but cracks begin to appear after they return to New York and he goes to work for his father in his sleazy real estate empire. He begins to abuse Katie, and when she attempts to leave the marriage, she mysteriously disappears. David moves to Texas, where he is tried for the murder and dismemberment of his neighbor, Malvern Bump (Philip Baker Hall), but is found not guilty. At the same time, his friend Deborah Lehrman (Lily Rabe), who may have assisted him in Katie's murder, is found dead in California. The film ends with Marks escaping justice.

Ryan Gosling and Kirsten Dunst are seen here in *All Good Things* (2010), a crime drama inspired by real-life accused murderer Robert Durst, whose wife Kathleen McCormack disappeared in 1982. *All Good Things* also stars Connecticut-born actress Diana Venora as DA Diane Rizzo. The Vermont health-food store location was in Gaylordsville, Connecticut, across the street from the fire department. Additional scenes were filmed in Fairfield, and at the Hospital of St. Raphael in Waterbury. Standing in for Gracie Mansion was the Ridgefield Community Center in Ridgefield, Connecticut. The scene of the "crime" takes place in Brookfield. (Photofest)

Upon the release of *All Good Things* in 2010, Robert Durst contacted director Andrew Jarecki to praise the film. Durst agreed to be interviewed by Jarecki (*Capturing the Friedmans*, 2003), which resulted in the six-part documentary series *The Jinx: The Life and Deaths of Robert Durst*. The series' most memorable moment was when Durst was caught on a hot mic softly asking himself, "What the hell did I do? Killed them all, of course," in reference to his three victims. Durst was eventually convicted of the murder of his friend from California in 2021, and died in prison in January 2022. His wife's murder remains officially unsolved.

Many scenes in *All Good Things* were shot in towns in Connecticut, including Newtown, which had its own connections to high-profile murder cases. The Regina Brown cold case and the disappearance of the long-missing Elizabeth Heath, whose remains were discovered in 2010, both remain unsolved. Also notorious was the "woodchipper case," which inspired the 1996 Coen brothers' film, *Fargo*.

CONNECTICUT IN THE MOVIES

The lake house scenes from *All Good Things* were filmed in Brookfield, Connecticut. This is a private residence. David Marks (Ryan Gosling) got rid of his wife's body off the Shelton Bridge on the Housatonic River. I can relate, as I nearly went over the edge just snapping this shot!

On November 18, 1986, not long after meeting with a divorce attorney, a Danish flight attendant, Helle Crafts, mysteriously disappeared. Helle's friends immediately suspected her husband, Richard Crafts, who had a volatile temper. Helle had once said, "If anything happens to me, don't assume it was an accident." Though there was no body, Richard Crafts was eventually convicted of the murder of his wife after police determined he had fed her body through a woodchipper, disposing of her in Lake Zoar. The case marked Connecticut's first conviction without a victim's body. Crafts was convicted in 1989 and sentenced to fifty years, but was released from prison in January 2020. Until recently he was living in a halfway house in New Haven, but has since been released.

it's
all
about
women...
and
their
men!
"all about eve"
Darryl F. Zanuck
BETTE DAVIS
ANNE BAXTER
GEORGE SANDERS
CELESTE HOLM
ALL ABOUT EVE
Gary Merrill · Hugh Marlowe
Thelma Ritter · Marilyn Monroe
Gregory Ratoff · Barbara Bates
Walter Hampden
Produced by DARRYL F. ZANUCK
Written for the screen and
Directed by JOSEPH L. MANKIEWICZ

CHAPTER 9
CONNECTICUT CAMEOS

DRAGONWYCK (1946)

Miranda Welles (Gene Tierney) is a farm girl living in rural Greenwich, Connecticut, in the 1800s. Her parents are very strict, and life on the farm is stifling. A visit from a distant cousin, Nicholas Van Ryan (Vincent Price), brings romance, but after he takes her to his New York estate, called Dragonwyck, she learns that Nicholas may not only be mad, he may be a murderer.

Tierney was raised in Westport, and attended school in Waterbury and Fairfield. A chance

Vincent Price and Gene Tierney in *Dragonwyck*. (Photofest)

trip to Hollywood when she was just eighteen changed her life. She met director Anatole Litvak at Warner Bros., who suggested to her mother that with her looks, she should be an actress.

While Greenwich is mentioned throughout the Twentieth Century Fox film, *Dragonwyck*, directed by Joseph Mankiewicz, the historical melodrama was actually filmed in Hollywood. Anya Seton, the author of *Dragonwyck* (1944), was born in New York, but she grew up in Cos Cob, and died in Old Greenwich, in 1990. She's buried in Putnam Cemetery. Actress Gene Tierney was raised in Green Farms and went to school in Fairfield. She continued her education at Miss Porter's School in Farmington. In 1938, before she left for Hollywood, she made her debut at the Fairfield Country Club.

Fairfield Country Club, where screen icon Gene Tierney made her debut in 1938.

IT'S A WONDERFUL LIFE (1946)

George Bailey (Jimmy Stewart) is at the end of his rope, wishing he had never been born. On the eve of Christmas he contemplates suicide, until a guardian angel named Clarence (Henry Travers) steps in to help him. If Clarence can help George, he will receive his wings and head to heaven, and George will be able to celebrate Christmas in Bedford Falls with his family.

From watching *It's a Wonderful Life* (1946), we know that "every time a bell rings an angel gets his wings." But did you know that the bell was provided by the Bevin Brothers bell company in East Hampton, Connecticut? Bevin Brothers have been making bells since 1832. East Hampton is even nicknamed "Belltown," as it was once the heart of bell manufacturing in the country. Today it is only Bevin Brothers that still exists.

Some of the more iconic Bevin bells you've probably heard are those of the Salvation Army bell ringers around Christmas; the bell from a Good Humor truck, driving through your neighborhood; the opening and closing bell on the NYSE; the cowbell from the *SNL* skit with Will Ferrell and Christopher Walken, made famous by the line, "We need more cowbell."

It was indeed a Bevin Brothers bell that got Clarence the angel his wings in one of the most beloved Christmas films of all time. George's realization that it's not money but love from family and friends that make him "the richest man in town" is a heartwarming message.

It's a wonderful thought that the bell that got Clarence into heaven was made right here in Connecticut. Bevin Bells is located at 17 Watrous Street, East Hampton, Connecticut. (Photofest)

A CONNECTICUT YANKEE IN KING ARTHUR'S COURT (1949)

Bing Crosby and Rhonda Fleming star in the musical comedy from Paramount, *A Connecticut Yankee in King Arthur's Court* (1949), directed by Tay Garnett, based on the novel by Mark Twain, and produced by Robert Fellows. (Photofest)

Mark Twain was a resident of Hartford when he wrote and published his novel *A Connecticut Yankee in King Arthur's Court* in 1889, about a "Connecticut Yankee" named Hank who gets hit on the head and travels back in time to the reign of King Arthur. A silent film adaptation was released in 1921, and there was a 1931 sound version called *A Connecticut Yankee* starring Will Rogers. This musical adaptation was released in 1949.

Postcard of the Mark Twain House in Hartford, in the 1930s.

An earlier filmed version was *A Connecticut Yankee* (1931) starring Will Rogers, and also based on Twain's novel.

CONNECTICUT IN THE MOVIES

ALL ABOUT EVE (1950)—WE OPEN IN NEW HAVEN!

All About Eve won numerous Academy Awards, including Best Picture, and, for Joe Mankiewicz, Best Director. It is one of the greatest films about showbiz treachery, with a key scene occurring in New Haven.

The story follows aging Broadway star Margo Channing (Bette Davis), who hires a seemingly naive young hopeful named Eve Harrington (Anne Baxter), only to discover that Eve has cleverly gained entry to sabotage Margo's career, and start her own. With the help of the powerful columnist Addison DeWitt (George Sanders), ambitious Eve quickly manages to become Margo's understudy, eventually replacing her in the new play, *Footsteps on the Ceiling*, which is opening in New Haven.

It's in New Haven, during the play's out-of-town tryout at the Shubert, that DeWitt teaches Eve a lesson for crossing him, deliciously cutting her down to size in one of the most exhilarating scenes ever written for the screen.

All About Eve (1950). (Photofest)

After leaving the Shubert, they walk arm and arm down College Street, Addison escorts Eve back to the Taft Hotel, confronting her about her shady past, and her intentions to not only walk off with Margo's part, but, after failing to steal Margo's man, Bill (Gary Merrill), to entice Karen's (Celeste Holm) husband, the playwright Lloyd Richards (Hugh Marlowe), into marriage. As Addison tells Eve with quiet ferocity, "I have not come to New Haven to see the play, discuss your dreams, or to pull the ivy from the walls of Yale! I have come here to tell you that you will not marry Lloyd—or anyone else—because I will not permit it."

Here, in *All About Eve* (1950), the play *Footsteps on the Ceiling*, starring that temperamental actress, Margo Channing (Bette Davis), is opening. (Photofest) The Shubert Theatre today.

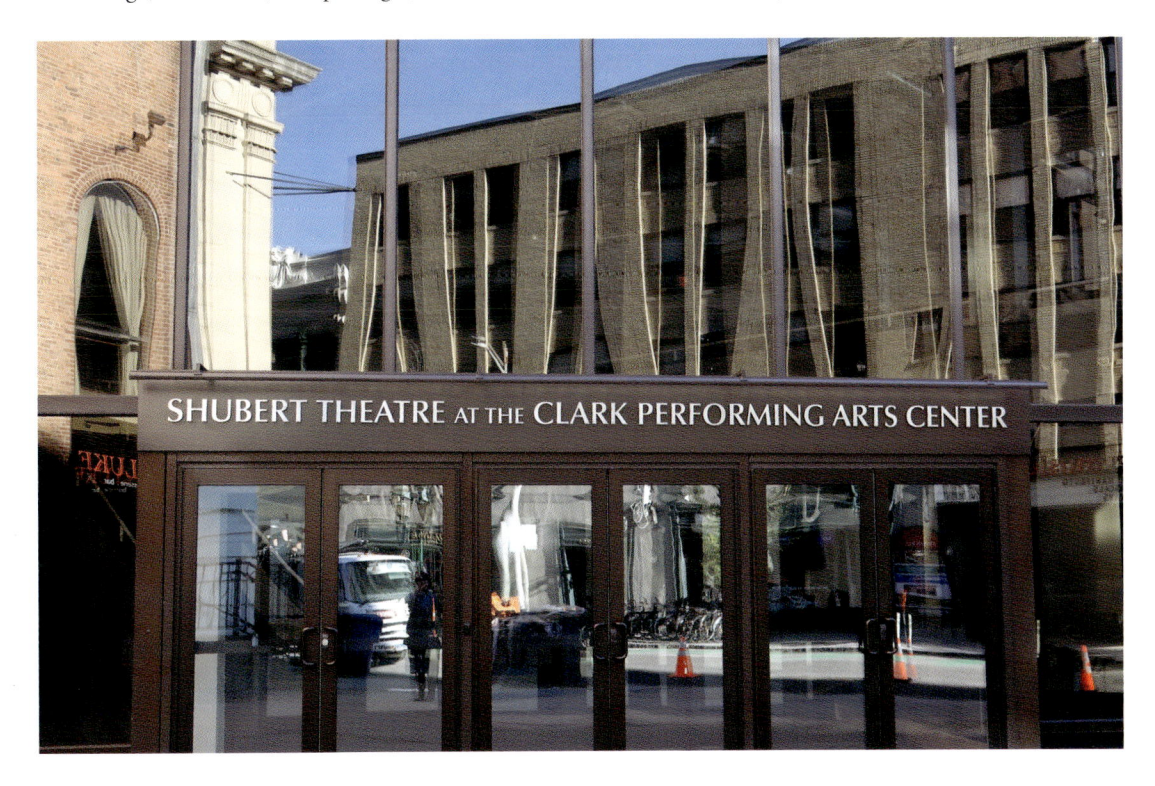

CONNECTICUT IN THE MOVIES

207

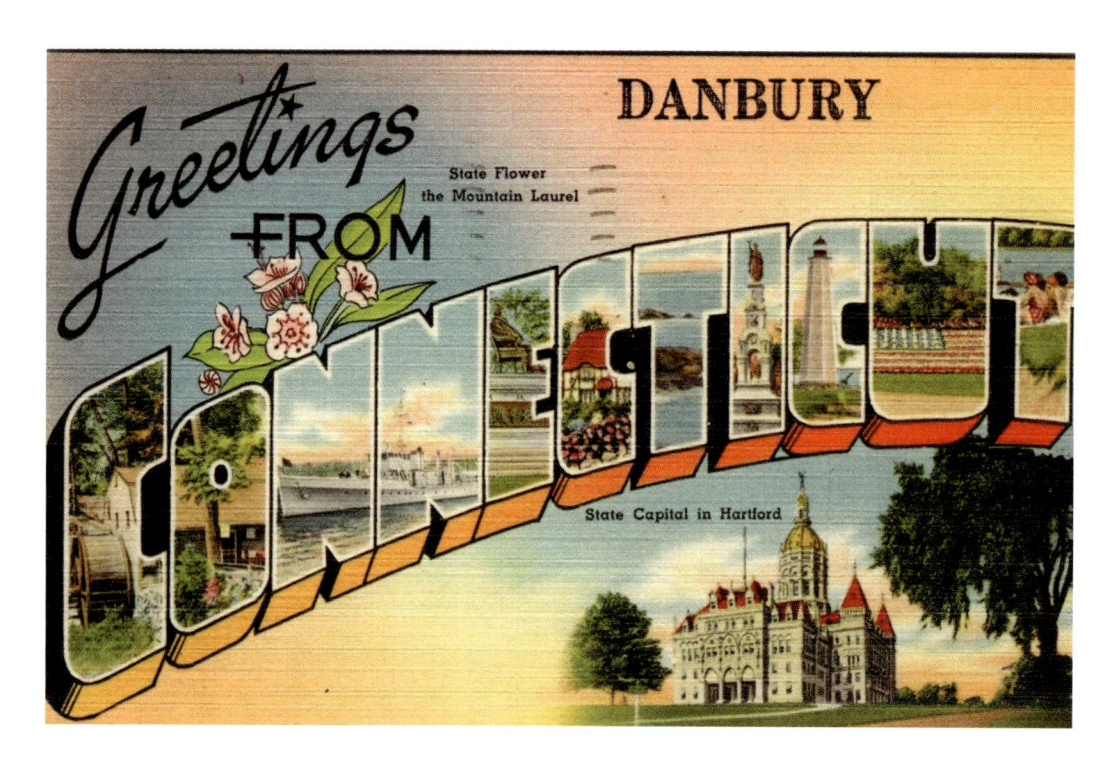

STRANGERS ON A TRAIN (1951)

A charming but lethal sociopath named Bruno Antony (Robert Walker) is looking to "switch murders" with tennis pro Guy Haines (Farley Granger), a stranger he meets on a train. Though scenes were filmed in Darien, Danbury, and at the Danbury railway station, in the film it's called Metcalf, and the Metcalf station. Warner Bros.' production notes indicate that they shot in Darien (that may be Bruno's house). Miller's Music Store, where Guy's wife works, was shot on Main Street in downtown Danbury.

Bruno follows Guy to Metcalf to try to set him up for the murder that he alone will be committing. Here's the only clue that they filmed in Connecticut, so look closely. In what appears to be a goof, as Bruno arrives at the Metcalf station, there's a sign in the background that reads "Danbury Diner." In subsequent shots the sign reads "Ray's Metcalf Diner." Director Hitchcock, known for his own cameo appearances in his films, can be seen getting on the train, carrying a large case for a double bass. The Danbury location is now the Danbury Railway Museum.

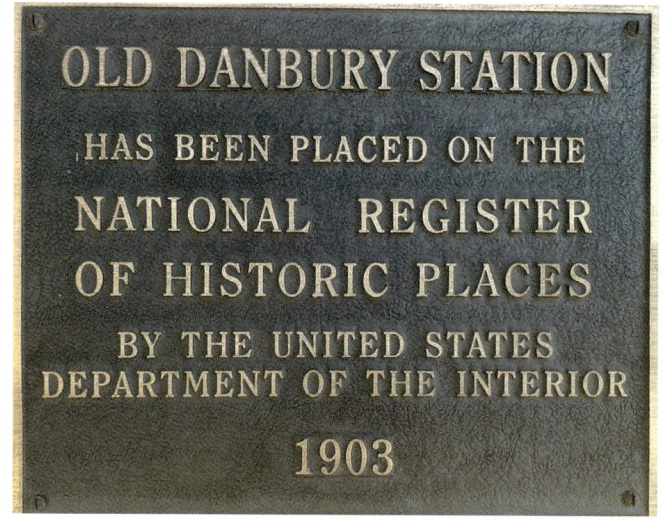

The Danbury Railway Museum is also home to the largest Uncle Sam—once on display at the Danbury State Fair—in the country.

Ray's Metcalf Diner (aka, the Danbury Diner), seen in the background, is still there. It's now called the Holiday Diner.

Alfred Hitchcock filmed his own cameo at the Danbury railway station in *Strangers on a Train* (1951). (Photofest)

AUNTIE MAME (1958)

A scene in *Auntie Mame* (1958) depicting the opening of Vera's (Coral Browne) play, *Midsummer Madness*, at the Shubert Theatre was re-created on a soundstage at Warner Bros. A dance number called the "Darien Dip" appeared in the later musical adaptation, *Mame* (1974). (Photofest)

Auntie Mame (1958) is based on the novel by Patrick Dennis and the later play by Jerome Lawrence and Robert Edwin Lee. It features the adventures of the free-spirited and independent Mame Dennis (Rosalind Russell), her relationship with her nephew, whom she has raised, and how her Bohemian lifestyle comes between them.

Rosalind Russell was born in Waterbury, Connecticut, in 1907, and raised in the Roman Catholic faith. In her book *Life Is a Banquet* (1977), she recalled a happy childhood in Waterbury, going to her first dance in Canterbury, and seeing the many theater companies that performed on the circuit there. She saw artists who played Temple Hall, even going with a girlfriend to see silent film star Valentino, dancing somewhere outdoors. Russell was a brilliant comedienne who had a legendary career in films like *The Women* (1939), *His Girl Friday* (1940), and *Gypsy* (1962). The title of her book, *Life Is a Banquet,* is based on a famous quote from *Auntie Mame*: "Life is a banquet, and most poor suckers are starving to death."

Mame has raised Patrick (Roger Smith) to be accepting of all races and religions. Now grown, he becomes engaged to a snooty young woman named Gloria Upson (Joanna Barnes), who lives in fictional Mountebank, "just above Darien," she says, "in Connecticut." Gloria—whose tight-jawed speech sounds like a cross between Katharine Hepburn and a honking goose—brags that Mountebank is "completely restricted." When Gloria's parents—who named their house "Upson Downs"—invite Mame to dinner, she decides to teach them a lesson in tolerance by planning an "invasion of Connecticut," filling their restricted community with "undesirables." Mame's worst fear is that Patrick will become "an Aryan from Darien," and she forces him to choose between life with Gloria or life with her.

WANDA (1970)

Barbara Loden had a small but memorable role in Elia Kazan's *Splendor in the Grass* (1961). She married director Kazan, but theirs was a stormy union. A well-respected actress, Loden won a Tony Award for Arthur Miller's *After the Fall* (1964), directed by Kazan. Despondent after being fired from *The Swimmer*, Loden set out to write, direct, and star in her own feature, *Wanda* (1970), which was shot in and around Kazan's home in Newton. It would be her only feature. (Photofest)

Barbara Loden developed *Wanda* while married to Elia Kazan, whom she had met while filming *Splendor in the Grass* (1961). She got the idea for the film after reading a story in the newspaper about an ordinary woman who took up with a bank robber, although there were also some auto-

Barbara Loden with Arthur Miller, Jason Robards, and husband Elia Kazan in Kazan's production of *After the Fall*. (Photofest)

biographical elements. She originally set her story—about an aimless woman who takes up with a drifter and petty thief (Michael Higgins)—in the South, but budget restrictions made her choose Pennsylvania and parts of Connecticut for filming. In addition to scenes in Waterbury, the last scene was shot in a saloon in Sandy Hook, where husband Kazan had a house. It also features the bizarre Connecticut roadside attraction, Holy Land USA, located in Waterbury, at 60 Slocum Street. Their website states: "Since opening in 1958, Holy Land continues to be a cornerstone of Waterbury, with visitors from all over coming together to behold the beauty of the land and unite through peaceful reflection and worship."

Shot in a cinema verité style, *Wanda* only gained recognition years later. After being widely dismissed at the time, it is now considered a feminist cult classic. Sadly, Loden died of breast cancer in 1980, at the age of forty-eight, and didn't live to see her film's resurgence.

THE OTHER (1972)

I am including *The Other* because I love this film, even though it's so obscure I could not locate a photo. The Connecticut cameo here has to do with the screenwriter.

This tale of the supernatural takes place on a Connecticut farm in 1935, but was filmed entirely in California. The author of *The Other*—former actor Tom Tryon (who was born in Hartford and attended Yale)—adapted his own novel about twin boys, one good and one very bad, for the screen. He had hoped to shoot the film in Connecticut, but the time of year made that impossible.

THE CANNONBALL RUN (1981)

The Cannonball Run (1981) and its equally all-star sequel (1984) did very well for Burt Reynolds, but he later lamented that following up the *Smokey and the Bandit* (1977, 1980) films with yet another car-chase movie series made the industry stop taking him seriously as an actor. The movie is loosely based on a real-life illegal cross-country race that begins in Connecticut and ends in California.

The Cannonball Run was based on an actual cross-country race called the Cannonball Baker Sea-to-Shining-Sea Memorial Trophy Dash, which began at the Lock, Stock, and Barrel restaurant in Darien, Connecticut, and ended in Redondo Beach, California. (Photofest)

A MIGHTY WIND (2003)

(Photofest)

A memorial concert for a famed folk producer who has died—Irving Steinbloom—reunites his best acts, including Mitch and Mickey, the New Main Street Singers, and, of course, The Folksmen. Director Christopher Guest does not disappoint, continuing his legacy for making the funniest mockumentaries around. The Mohegan Sun casino in Uncasville has cameoed quite a few times in movies, most recently in *Uncut Gems* (2018). Above, in *A Mighty Wind* (2003), the Folksmen (Harry Shearer as Mark Shubb, Michael McKean as Jerry Palter, and Chris Guest as Alan Barrows) is a fictional folk group whose members reunite after not performing together since the 1960s. Michael McKean is no stranger to Connecticut; in the 1970s, he performed at the Eugene O'Neill Theater Center in Waterford.

INDIANA JONES AND THE KINGDOM OF THE CRYSTAL SKULL (2008)

It took $10,000,000 to turn downtown New Haven into the fictional town of Bedford circa 1957 for this fourth installment of the Indiana Jones franchise, starring the most famous movie star to cameo in Connecticut, Harrison Ford. Here, Yale's New Haven campus becomes Marshall College

The scene of fictional Bedford was filmed in downtown New Haven. If you watch closely, you'll catch Indiana Jones (Harrison Ford) and Mutt (Shia LaBeouf) pass a New Britain, Connecticut, bus during a motorcycle chase. (Photofest)

(this may be a nod to the film's producer, Frank Marshall). Ford re-creates his iconic role as Indiana Jones, the archaeology teacher whose heart is bent on adventure. When Sean Connery declined to come back for this installment to play Indy's father, Ford joked that at sixty-four, he was old enough to play his own father.

In addition to an interior classroom scene at Yale, there's a motorcycle chase sequence that gives you a nice tour of the city. It begins at the Copper Kitchen diner on Chapel Street (called Bedford Coffee Shop in the film) and travels down Elm, College, Church, and High streets, and then onto the Old Campus. Production housed the actors at the Omni Hotel, and the New Haven Green was used for hair and makeup for extras and background actors.

Crystal Skull (2008) was the second film Spielberg directed in the state, after *Amistad* (1997). Executive producer Kathleen Kennedy said Yale was Spielberg's first choice for filming. She recalled that he thought Yale (which his son Theo happened to be attending) was "the most iconic-looking Ivy League school in the United States." High praise indeed from one of the greatest directors in history. You're welcome back anytime, Steven!

CONNECTICUT IN THE MOVIES

THE HAUNTING IN CONNECTICUT (2009)

The Haunting in Connecticut (2009) originated in the Snedeker family's paranormal experiences that occurred in Southington, Connecticut, in the 1980s. A team of investigators was called in, and out of this came the book *In a Dark Place: The Story of a True Haunting* (1992), on which the film was based. Later, one of the coauthors, Ray Garton, admitted he had sensationalized or made up many of the details for effect; however, the Snedeker family maintains that their house *was* haunted. (The family name was changed to Campbell in the film.) *The Haunting in Connecticut* was filmed in Canada. A sequel called *The Haunting in Connecticut 2: Ghosts of Georgia* (2013) kept Connecticut in the title to capitalize on the success of the first film, but they filmed in Louisiana.

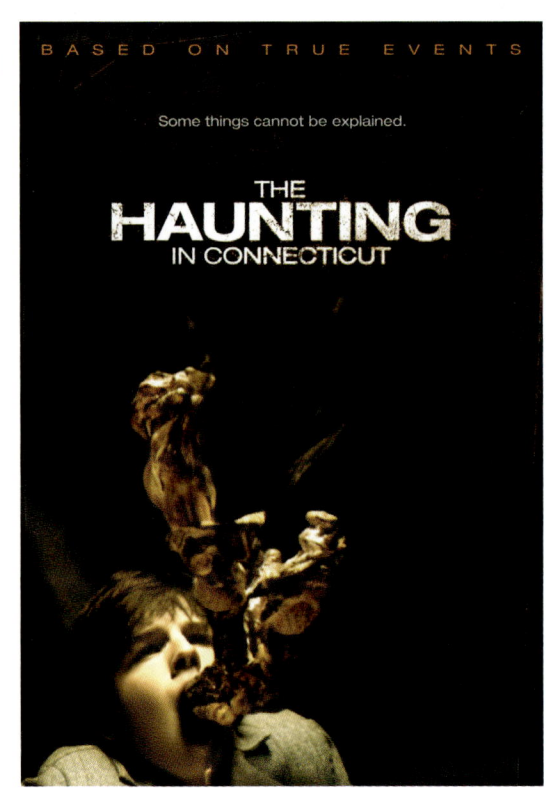

AWAY WE GO (2009)

After discovering they are expecting their first child, Verona (Maya Rudolph) and Burt (John Krasinski) decide to go on a road trip across America, hoping to discover the secret of good parenting. (In real life, Krasinski attended the National Theater Institute, housed at the Eugene O'Neill Theater Center in Waterford, Connecticut.) The film lists location shooting in Watertown, Wilton, Thomaston, Woodbury, New Haven, and Stamford, but even though they had all these Connecticut locations, they never took advantage of them. Night scenes filmed in New Haven are identified as Canada. Hope they at least tried New Haven–style pizza while they were here! Director Sam Mendes—and Connecticut—fared much better with his previous film, *Revolutionary Road* (2008) (see chapter 12).

Director Sam Mendes shoots his second film in Connecticut, a dramedy that shot all over the state but never mentions Connecticut. (Photofest)

Dean Stockwell and Katharine Hepburn in *Long Day's Journey into Night*. (Photofest)

CHAPTER 10

HOMEGROWN DRAMA: THE FILMS OF EUGENE O'NEILL

Though not born in Connecticut, the Pulitzer Prize–winning playwright Eugene O'Neill will always be associated with New London, Connecticut, where he drew from his experiences growing up in this vibrant seaside city. O'Neill set two of his most well-known plays, *Ah, Wilderness!* (1933) and *Long Day's Journey into Night* (1956), in his family's summer home, Monte Cristo Cottage. Both were later made into films, *Ah Wilderness!* in 1935, and *Long Day's Journey into Night*, in 1962.

Monte Cristo Cottage was built in an area known as the Pequot Colony Historic District of New London. From the 1850s through the 1920s, this district was one of the most socially prominent summer resort communities on the Connecticut shore. In 1852—

A smiling Eugene O'Neill and friends at the beach in New London, Connecticut, circa 1917. (Courtesy Eugene O'Neill Theater Center)

PEQUOT HOUSE, NEW LONDON, CONN.

New London would be the backdrop for both the optimistic *Ah, Wilderness!*, taking place over a joyous Fourth of July weekend in 1903, and *Long Day's Journey into Night*, which takes place in August 1912, during what would have been the decline of New London as a summer resort town.

Pequot Hotel Fire, May 7, 1908. Fire Veteran Powers second from left.

A postcard depicts the Pequot Hotel Fire of 1908. New London began to decline as a resort town soon after.

220   HOMEGROWN DRAMA: THE FILMS OF EUGENE O'NEILL

the same year the shoreline railroad connected New London to New York—the Pequot House Hotel and adjoining Pequot Casino were built. They attracted distinguished visitors, including diplomats, two nineteenth-century presidents, and a chief justice of the Supreme Court. Wealthy families began building their own summer cottages in a variety of architectural styles popular at the turn of the century.

James O'Neill, Eugene's father, came to New London and purchased the house on Pequot Avenue in 1884; he then expanded the original home, which had been built in 1840, and named it Monte Cristo, after his most celebrated role, that of Edmond Dantès in *The Count of Monte Cristo*. James O'Neill had purchased an adapted stage play of the Alexandre Dumas novel *The Count of Monte Cristo* in 1883. He achieved great fame, playing it over six thousand times, but it precluded him from being seen in any other role. James lived to see his son win his first Pulitzer Prize in 1920, but died shortly after, at Monte Cristo Cottage.

Another important section of New London that O'Neill mined for characters was the Montauk Historic District, a more affordable but no less stylish part of New London. The Montauk Hotel offered a less exclusive alternative for working-class families who wanted to vacation there. O'Neill also lived with a family named Rippen in New London in 1913–1914. They would become the inspiration for the loving and supportive Miller family in his play *Ah, Wilderness!*

O'Neill fueled his memories into two very different plays. In 1931, O'Neill paid a visit to Monte Cristo Cottage. Two months later he wrote *Ah, Wilderness!*, describing it as "the way I would have liked my boyhood to have been. It is more the capture of a mood, an evocation of the spirit of a time that is dead now with all its ideals and manners and codes—the period in which my middle teens were spent. Perhaps, if I give you a subtitle you will sense the spirit of what I've tried to recapture in it." *Ah, Wilderness! A Nostalgic Comedy of the Ancient Days when Youth was Young, and Right was Right, and Life was a Wicked Opportunity* premiered on Broadway in 1933. A few years earlier, in 1925, he had stopped at the family house on Pequot Avenue and written in his diary, "Decay and ruin—sad." In 1940, when a worsening tremor in his hand made O'Neill feel his writing career would soon be over, O'Neill penned *Long Day's Journey into Night*, "written in tears and blood." It's considered the greatest autobiographical drama of all time.

AH, WILDERNESS! (1935)

Ah, Wilderness!, the ensemble family comedy about the life of the Miller family in a quintessential New England town, inspired by O'Neill's childhood in New London, became an instant classic. Its themes of family values and small-town living inspired the successful MGM franchise known as the Andy Hardy movies. *A Family Affair* (1937), made two years after *Ah, Wilderness!*, was the first in that series, and starred Lionel Barrymore, Spring Byington, Mickey Rooney, Cecilia Parker, and Eric Linden, transitioning from Millers to Hardys. Andy Hardy movies were knocked for being corny and overly sentimental, but they were enormously popular. There were sixteen Andy Hardy films, and the series lasted until 1946 (with a one-shot revival with Mickey in 1958).

There was also a musical based on *Ah, Wilderness!* Thirteen years after the original film, *Summer Holiday* (1948) revisited the Miller family, with Mickey Rooney now taking a turn in the role of the idealistic Richard Miller.

It's summer in a small coastal town in Connecticut. Young Richard Miller (Eric Linden), having just graduated from high school, is about to experience the joys and sorrows of first love with his high school sweetheart, Muriel McComber (Cecilia Parker). Although they live across the street from each other, Richard and Muriel come from two different worlds. Richard comes from a large, boisterous middle-class family. Muriel's father, Dave McComber (Charles Grapewin), is a wealthy businessman who doesn't approve of Richard or the Miller family, who are too bohemian for his taste. Richard's benevolent father, Nat Miller (Lionel Barrymore), is the editor of a local newspaper who relies on advertising from McComber.

Ah, Wilderness! was purchased by MGM and adapted for the screen by the married team of Frances Goodrich and Albert Hackett, who wrote the screenplays for *The Thin Man* (1934), *It's a Wonderful Life* (1946), and *The Diary of Anne Frank* (1959). Clarence Brown (*National Velvet*, 1944; *The Yearling*, 1946) helmed the popular comedy. (Photofest)

In 1948, MGM made *Summer Holiday*, a musical adaptation of *Ah, Wilderness!*, directed by Rouben Mamoulian. It starred Mickey Rooney, now cast as Dick Miller. (Photofest)

On a balmy summer's eve before the Fourth of July, Richard and Muriel walk down a country lane in the moonlight. Richard is a dreamer, a romantic, and ready to experience life. He longs to kiss Muriel, but she keeps saying she is not ready. "You always do the conventional thing," he says, admonishing her for her lack of spirit.

Richard's uncle Sid (Wallace Beery) can't hold down a job as a reporter because he drinks too much. After being fired from a Waterbury paper, he moves back in with the Millers. Uncle Sid has been courting Essie Miller's (Spring Byington) sister, Aunt Lily (Aline MacMahon), but she refuses to marry him until he's sober. Unfortunately, she's been waiting years for that to happen.

Summer Holiday (1948), with Mickey Rooney and Gloria DeHaven. (Photofest)

The role of Uncle Sid had been tailored to the comic strengths of W. C. Fields, but Wallace Beery ended up getting the part. His brutish quality in many comic scenes—such as eating an entire lobster in its shell—isn't quite as funny as I imagine Fields would have played it. Albert Hackett was disappointed that Fields did not end up in the film, and said of Beery, "He wouldn't say any of the lines as written. He wouldn't say any of O'Neill's lines! Anything that came into his head he would say, but not O'Neill."

Richard's mother, Essie, sees only the best in Richard and her large and eclectic brood. This includes Richard's older brother Arthur (Frank Albertson), who is home from Yale for the Fourth of July weekend; Tommy (Mickey Rooney), who shoots off fireworks that scare the neighbors; and bratty Mildred (Bonita Granville), who sticks her tongue out at a girl who's prettier than her. Richard's father, Nat, has high hopes for Richard to fulfill his aspirations of becoming a writer, but he cautions his son that he needs to concentrate more on his work and less on spreading the politics of socialism or sharing racy poetry with Muriel. Nat chuckles at his son's impudence, but it's the last straw for Mr. McComber, who forces Muriel to break up with Richard over the purple prose he has shared with her.

Heartbroken, Richard sneaks out with an older college friend of Arthur's to drown his sorrows. He ends up at a speakeasy with a woman of ill repute named Belle (Helen Flint), who spikes his drink.

Having never had alcohol before, he passes out, and Belle steals his money. When Richard returns in the morning, his father is wise enough not to punish him, realizing it's been a learning experience for his son.

As the Fourth of July comes to an end, Muriel comes to her senses, realizing she does love Richard after all, and defies her father to be with him. Nat Miller, inspired by the young lovers, looks up at the moon, sighs, and tells Essie, "I can only remember a few nights as beautiful as this," thereby signaling a happy ending for all.

DESIRE UNDER THE ELMS (1958)

Looking for what he called "a safe harbor," O'Neill purchased Brook Farm in 1922 on North Salem Road in Ridgefield, Connecticut, and lived there with his second wife, Agnes, until 1927. Brook Farm would be the setting for his play, *Desire Under the Elms*. The title refers to the earthy nature of human passion. *Desire Under the Elms* infused elements of Greek tragedy into a New England farm setting. A film was made of the play in 1958, directed by Delbert Mann. The story follows a greedy farmer (Burl Ives) who would rather go to his grave than leave his farm to his son Eben (Anthony Perkins). O'Neill mined his feelings for his family for this work.

Desire Under the Elms (1958) starred Anthony Perkins and Sophia Loren. It was a filmed version of the O'Neill play performed in 1924. O'Neill penned his play in Ridgefield, Connecticut. (Photofest)

LONG DAY'S JOURNEY INTO NIGHT (1962)

Long Day's Journey into Night (1962) is based on many of the demons that O'Neill and his family had faced. James Tyrone (Ralph Richardson) is an actor at the end of a once-thriving career. (James O'Neill's last performance in *The Count of Monte Cristo* was a silent-film version produced by Adolph Zukor in 1912—the same year that *Long Day's Journey into Night* is set.) James's ambitions of becoming a great artist were abandoned over his fears of the poorhouse. His wife, Mary Tyrone (Katharine Hepburn), has just returned from a sanitarium, where she went to cure her morphine addiction. (O'Neill's mother, Mary Ellen, or Ella, was born in New Haven. After Eugene, her third son, was born, she was administered morphine for pain and became addicted.) Jamie Tyrone (Jason Robards) is the older of two sons. He tried to follow in his father's footsteps, but his cynical nature and tendency to abuse alcohol

Eugene, Jamie, and James O'Neill on the porch at Monte Cristo Cottage in New London, 1900. (Courtesy Eugene O'Neill Theater Center)

The Tyrone family has gathered for what should have been a joyous reunion. It will instead become a night of recriminations and anger. Pictured here are Jason Robards and Katharine Hepburn in Sidney Lumet's filmed adaptation of *Long Day's Journey into Night* (1962). (Photofest)

ruined any chance of success as an actor. (Eugene O'Neill's eldest brother, James, suffered all his life from alcohol addiction, and drank himself to death in 1922. O'Neill's play, *A Moon for the Misbegotten*—in which Robards starred—was based on him.)

Edmund (Dean Stockwell), the younger son, has just returned home from working as a merchant seaman. It's soon confirmed that Edmund has tuberculosis and must be sent to a sanitarium to be cured. (Eugene O'Neill contracted TB after a stint at sea.) Playing O'Neill was a burden for the actor. Lumet recalled a nervous Dean Stockwell showing up with a bottle of vodka at the beginning of rehearsals. Hepburn, who did not approve of drinking, put an end to that. Stockwell recalled, "It was as intense and rewarding an experience as I've had." In the end, he, Richardson, and Robards would share the Best Actor Award at the Cannes Film Festival. Stockwell began his career as a child actor, and also costarred in two other films made in Connecticut, *Gentleman's Agreement* (1947) and *Deep in the Darkness* (2014).

In the film, Mary's release from the sanitarium has brought the family together to celebrate, but the fear regarding Edmund's diagnosis causes Mary to start using morphine again. Fueled by alcohol, long-held grudges surface between the estranged father and sons. While they argue, Mary slips into a drug-induced stupor. What follows is a painful examination of a family coming apart and their long day's journey into night.

Director Sidney Lumet rehearsed the cast for three weeks and shot the scenes in sequence

Ralph Richardson and Jason Robards. (Photofest)

Ralph Richardson and Sidney Lumet. (Photofest)

Sidney Lumet and cast on the set of *Long Day's Journey into Night*. (Photofest)

from beginning to end on a soundstage, making no attempt to "open it up." It's closer to a photographed stage play than a film, but Lumet and cinematographer Boris Kaufman (*On the Waterfront*, 1954) keep it visually interesting with staging, and by using different lenses or soft-focus close-ups of Hepburn to capture her losing touch with reality. Hepburn wanted her longtime love, Spencer Tracy, to be cast as James Tyrone, even insisting the producers meet with him, but he was in poor health, and they moved on.

Lumet wrote in his memoir, *Making Movies*, "There are many reasons for accepting a movie . . . *Long Day's Journey into Night* is everything one can hope for. Four characters come together and leave no area of life unexplored." The film rests on O'Neill's brilliant words and the perfectly balanced performances of the four actors, speaking and living truthfully through those words.

Hepburn said of the film, "Lumet brought out something different in me. I guess it's called simplicity. I said to myself, don't act. Don't do anything. Let the audience hear the lines. The part is so brilliantly written it just carried me along. The overwhelming loneliness of that lost, drug-addicted woman." Hepburn worked with her own physical vulnerabilities, incorporating her own body and head shakes from her progressive essential tremor issues into Mary Tyrone's drug addiction. She was nominated for an Academy Award—the only member of the cast to receive that distinction.

English actor Ralph Richardson (*The Heiress*, 1949) was a natural to play James Tyrone. Aside from his melodious speaking voice, he brought a pathos and dignity to a man filled with regret. Classically trained, he responded to Lumet's method of working. Lumet comically recalled that, after

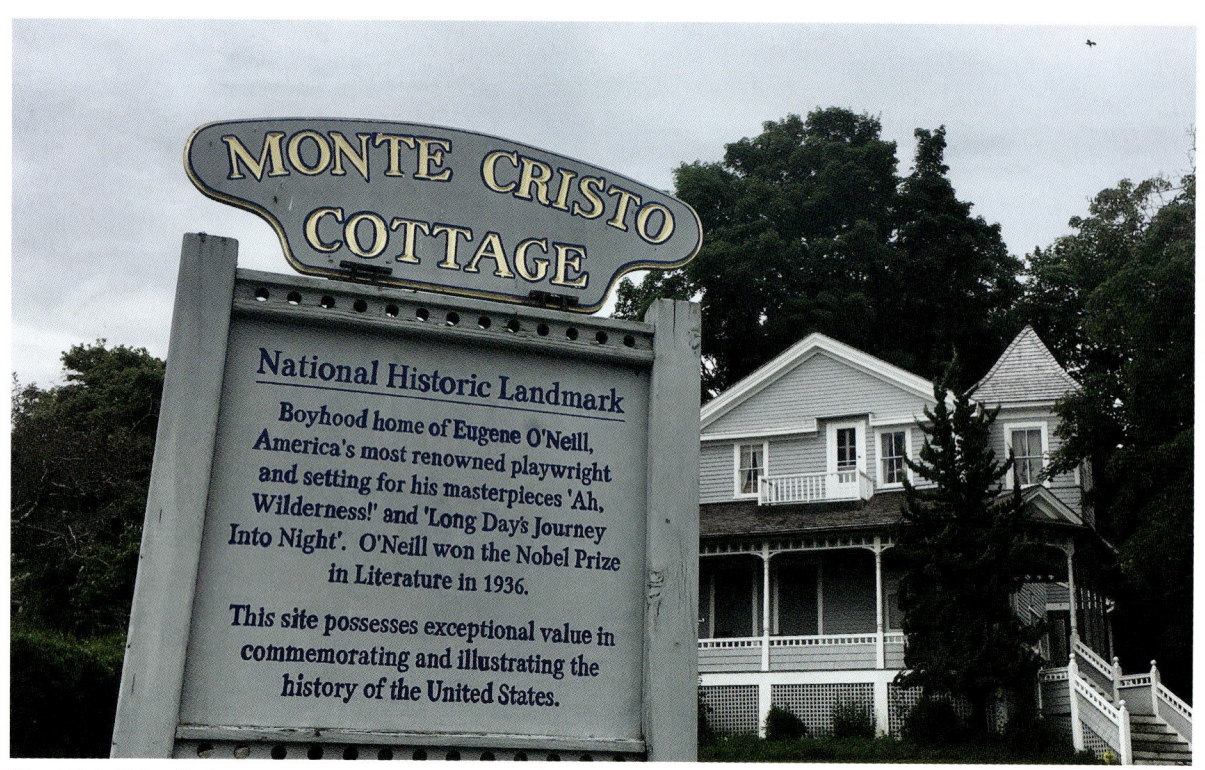

The O'Neill family home is now a museum. In 1964, George C. White founded the Eugene O'Neill Theater Center in Waterford, Connecticut, dedicated to new voices in the theater and named in honor of O'Neill, a four-time Pulitzer Prize winner, and America's only playwright to win the Nobel Prize in Literature.

giving him a lengthy bit of direction about the playing of a scene, Richardson said, "Ah, I think I know what you want—a little more flute and a little less cello."

Jason Robards was regarded as one of the foremost interpreters of O'Neill. He created the role of Jamie Tyrone in the original production of *Long Day's Journey into Night* on Broadway. He starred in O'Neill's plays *Hughie* (1964), *A Moon for the Misbegotten* (1973), and *A Touch of the Poet* (1977). He starred in the Broadway revival of *The Iceman Cometh* (1985). He starred in both the Broadway revival of *Long Day's Journey into Night* (1988) as James Tyrone and a revival of *Ah, Wilderness!* (1988) as Nat Miller, alternating nights in what I recall as perhaps the greatest stage performance of all time. Jason Robards moved to the Southport section of Fairfield, Connecticut, living what he called "a quiet life on the water."

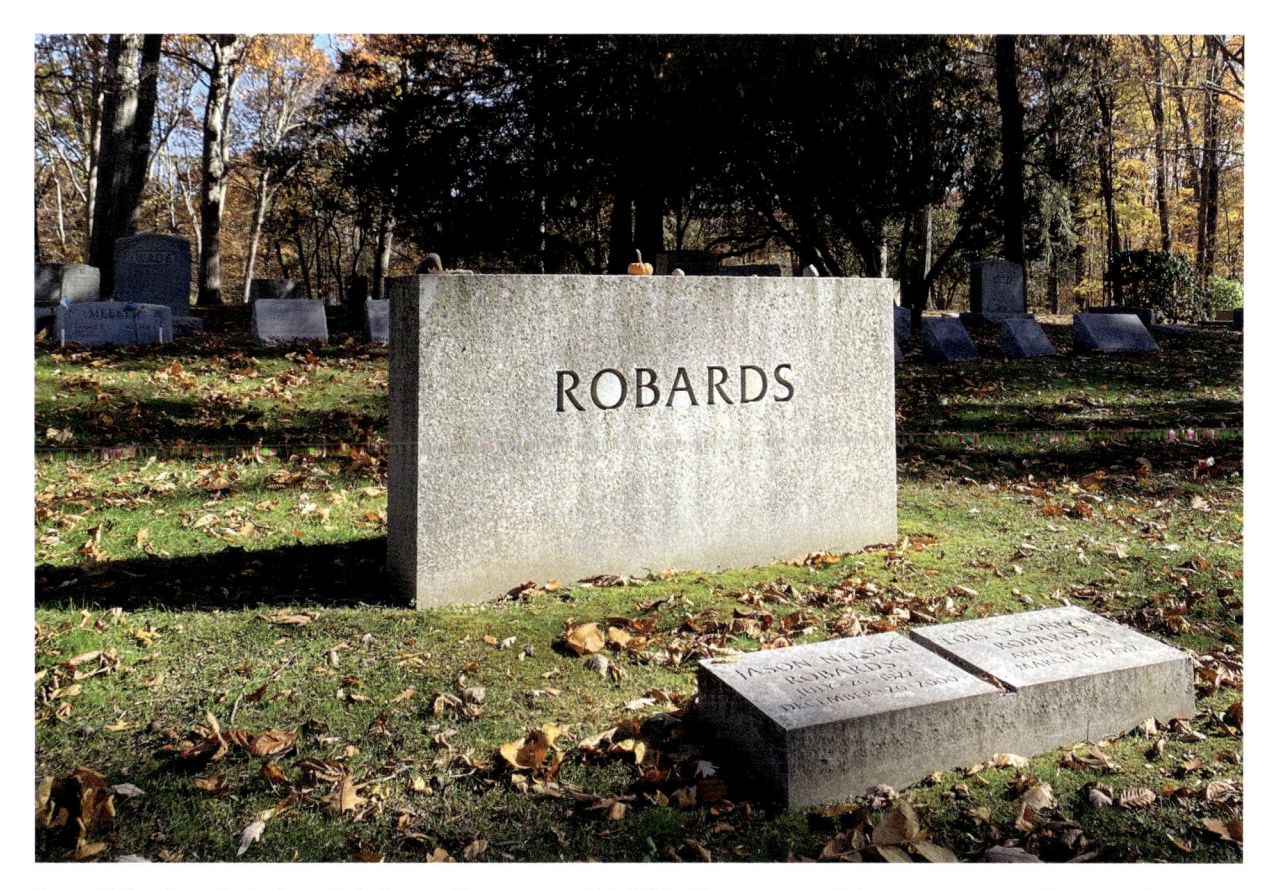

Jason Robards is buried in Oak Lawn Cemetery in Fairfield, Connecticut. I have my own recollections of meeting Connecticut resident Jason Robards . . . sort of. It was sometime in the mid-1970s. I was dining with a friend's family at a restaurant called Back Porch at 142 Ferry Road, right on the water in Old Saybrook. I was munching on my fried clams when I spotted Jason Robards—scruffy and looking like he'd just gotten off a boat—walking through the restaurant and taking a seat at the bar. This would have been around the time he'd won his second Oscar, for his supporting role in the film *Julia* (1977). I ripped off a piece of the paper menu and ran to get his autograph. I approached him with my little piece of paper, and he looked at me and slowly put his finger up to his lips, making a shushing gesture, signaling in a nice way to buzz off, and that maybe he wished to be incognito. I smiled, a little disappointed, but he rewarded me with a nod and crooked smile of appreciation for keeping his visit a secret.

Your heart will fall in Love with
LORETTA YOUNG
CELESTE HOLM
in
Come TO THE STABLE
20th CENTURY-FOX
HUGH MARLOWE · ELSA LANCHESTER · THOMAS GOMEZ
SCREEN PLAY BY OSCAR MILLARD & SALLY BENSON — FROM A STORY BY CLARE BOOTHE LUCE
Directed by HENRY KOSTER · Produced by SAMUEL G. ENGEL

CHAPTER 11
CONNECTICUT HISTORY

COME TO THE STABLE (1949)

If you build it, they will come. *Come to the Stable* (1949) is not a religious movie, but it is one where characters are guided by religious principles. Since it's a miracle I even discovered *Come to the Stable*— it was a late entry, my very, last in fact—I'm prepared to admit that someone from above may have intervened, to have me include it. I'm glad they did. It's an enchanting little comedy, beautifully acted. Today you might call it a "faith-based film," and its origins and history began right here in Connecticut.

The story follows two very dedicated nuns—one American, Sister Margaret (Loretta Young), and one French, Sister Scholastica (Celeste Holm), who have come to Bethlehem, "New England," determined to build a hospital for children. The nuns' arrival in Bethlehem seems out of the ordinary; after all, what are two French nuns doing in Connecticut? We soon learn that while everything they do appears to be random, they seem to be guided by divine intervention, leading them where they need to go, and getting them what they want. Take, for instance, the first person they meet. The nuns come upon a barn where a painter is painting a nativity scene. The eccentric woman's name is Amelia Potts (Elsa Lanchester), and it turns out Amelia has had a hand in their destiny.

Come to the Stable (1949). After making a pact with God, two French religious sisters, Sister Margaret (Loretta Young) and Sister Scholastica (Celeste Holm), come to the small New England town of Bethlehem to fulfill a mission: to build a children's hospital and abbey, finding help from local artist, Amelia Potts (Elsa Lancaster). The film is based on the true story of the Abbey of Regina Laudis in Bethlehem, Connecticut. (Photofest)

During the war, the two nuns were assisting at a children's hospital in Normandy that was under German control. American soldiers arrive and they want to shell the hospital, but since the children can't be evacuated, Sister Margaret prays for a miracle. The children are spared, although it results in American casualties. Nonetheless, Sister Margaret's prayers were answered, and now she must repay a vow she made—that if the children lived, she would go to America and build a children's hospital.

The nuns remembered a beautiful painted religious postcard of a biblical scene, and the artist was Amelia Potts. On the card was the phrase "Come to the Stable." They had noted that the card and artist were from a town in America called Bethlehem. The religious connotations of the name "Bethlehem," its association with the birth of Christ, sent them on a pilgrimage there.

Now that they are here and have met Amelia, and they have seen the natural beauty of Bethlehem, they're convinced it's not just fate, but God, who has led them here to build their hospital.

Loretta Young, Celeste Holm, and Dooley Wilson in *Come to the Stable* (1949). (Photofest)

And it does seem as if the hand of God keeps intervening to get them what they need. Walking in a meadow, they see an old witch-hazel factory and remark that it would be perfect for a church. As they stand there admiring the old brick building, a real estate salesman puts up a "for sale" sign on the side. They get him to agree to a small down payment until they can afford to pay for the whole property, and with Amelia's help, they start selling homemade crafts to be able to raise enough for a down payment.

The land next to the old factory is another story. It's owned by a kind of mysterious underworld gangster named Luigi Rossi (Thomas Gomez). His associates laugh at the thought of the gruff Rossi even meeting with the nuns, and at first, he does turn them down. The idea that he would donate his land to them is laughable—a noble pursuit, perhaps, but laughable.

Rossi does meet with the nuns, and after revealing to them that his son died in action in France, near where the nuns were located, in Normandy, he softens. Feeling now the pull of faith, he says he will give them his land if they will honor his fallen son and his memory by installing a stained-glass window of him in their church.

The nuns have been able to transform every hardened heart they have come in contact with. The last holdout is Miss Potts's neighbor, a composer named Bob Mason (Hugh Marlowe). He rents the barn on his property to Amelia so she can paint. Bob's property is right next to where the sisters want to build the hospital.

At first Bob is amused by the nuns. They are a curiosity. He lends them his jeep because he thinks them harmless and rather charming, but he certainly does not have any religious beliefs. And after learning they not only want to build a church, but a hospital, right next door, he thinks the noise will interrupt his work, and the idea of a hospital is morbid. Mason goes behind their back to buy the abandoned building out from under them. It turns out that Bob's handyman, Anthony (Dooley Wilson), is religious, however, and while Bob is working against them, Anthony is doing everything he can to help the sisters.

Once again, God seemingly intervenes. Bob has written a love song, "Through a Long and Sleepless Night," that impresses his music critic friend. He feels the song can be sold to Hollywood. The music critic is played by *Come to the Stable*'s own film's music composer, Alfred Newman. The song, and the chant the song is based on, were actually written by Newman. "Through a Long and Sleepless Night" was nominated for an Academy Award.

As Bob excitedly plans his trip to Hollywood and dreams of future royalties, the nuns begin singing their daily Gregorian chant. That's when the music critic notices that Bob's song and their chant have the same exact melody. How could it be? Bob is mystified, insisting he did not plagiarize the chant—that the melody had come to him while he was stationed during the war. Where was he stationed? Why, France, of course. Once again, the sisters seem to have God on their side, doing their bidding.

Bob acknowledges their plight, puts their needs above his own, and agrees to let them have the building. As the sisters believed, and came to Bethlehem, others soon follow. Soon, many more nuns begin arriving to farm the land, selling crafts and baked goods to make money to build the hospital. Sister Margaret and Sister Scholastica have fulfilled their mission because they worked hard, but also because they had faith, and believed it was possible.

As the sun sets, they are joined by their new friends and allies including Amelia, Bob, and even Luigi Rossi who have

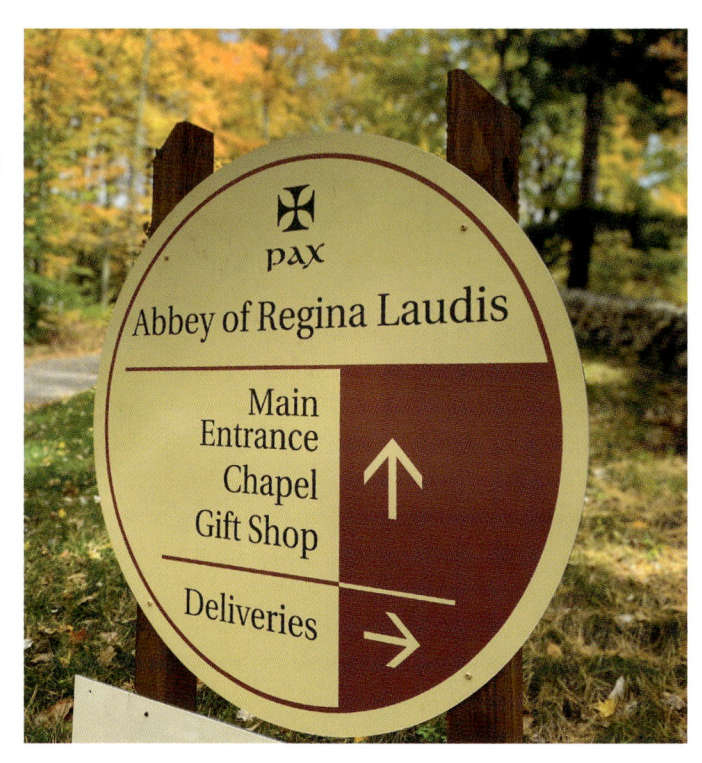

The Abbey of Regina Laudis in Bethlehem, Connecticut, which inspired the Hollywood film.

The entrance of the Abbey of Regina Laudis. Every year, people flock to Bethlehem, Connecticut, before Christmas so their Christmas cards will have the Bethlehem postmark. Thus, the post office of Connecticut's "Christmas Town" provides a large quantity of Christmas-themed postage stamps, and the town also holds an annual holiday market.

CONNECTICUT IN THE MOVIES

gathered together in their makeshift church to celebrate.

Come to the Stable was based on a story by writer and congresswoman Clare Booth Luce, famous for writing the play *The Women* (1936), on which the classic MGM film was based. Luce was a resident of Litchfield County, Connecticut. She was also a recent convert to Catholicism, and had been inspired to tell this fact-based story about the Abbey of Regina Laudis. This was fortuitous, because Darryl Zanuck, the head of Twentieth Century Fox, was looking for what he called "a religious picture," after seeing the success of religious-themed films like Paramount's *Going My Way* (1944) and *The Bells of Saint Mary's* (1945).

The Abbey of Regina Laudis was founded in 1947, in Bethlehem, Connecticut, by Mother Benedict Duss and Mother Mary Aline Trilles de Warren, both nuns of the Benedictine Abbey of Notre Dame in France, who had settled in Bethlehem at the invitation of the painter, Mrs. Lauren Ford. Ford lived in Bethlehem and painted biblical scenes, placing them in the rural setting of her farm. Ford's most famous painting is called *Nativity*. In *Come to the Stable*, the painter Miss Potter is shown re-creating a nativity scene in her barn, to paint.

It was an industrialist named Robert Leather who donated fifty acres of his land so the nuns could build their abbey. (There is a road named for Leather in Bethlehem.) Just as in the film, the Priory was housed in an old factory, though I'm not sure if it had been a "witch-hazel factory," although that is a nice Connecticut touch. Luce employed Greta Palmer, a member of the executive board of the Priory, to act as her researcher, and as a go-between for the Benedictines, the Catholic authorities, and Twentieth Century Fox. The reason that Connecticut is not mentioned in the film is that the nuns asked that their names and the locale not to be mentioned.

Additionally, they asked—I love it that even nuns had notes—that for the movie, instead of building the abbey as a place of spiritual fellowship, if it could be a maternity ward for GI wives. I imagine that a "children's hospital" conjured up war orphans and tugged more at the heartstrings, so that is what appears in the film. A $25,000 donation was made to the Priory for the rights to their story, and studio notes say that "Mother Benedict was highly pleased with what we were doing and gave me and us her blessings."

Darryl Zanuck could envision only one actress to play Sister Margaret, and that was Loretta Young. Young was a notable and outspoken Catholic. She had won an Academy Award the year before for *The Farmer's Daughter* (1947). Zanuck had the magic casting touch, as Young was nominated for an Academy Award for her role as Sister Margaret, as was Celeste Holm for her role as Sister Scholastica, along with Elsa Lanchester as Miss Potts. The following year, Holm would reunite with the actor who plays the composer, Bob Mason, when she played Hugh Marlowe's wife in *All About Eve* (1950).

People often think *Come to the Stable* is a Christmas film. That may be because Loretta Young also stars in *The Bishop's Wife* (1947), which is a Christmas film and has spiritual overtones. Elsa Lanchester is also in *The Bishop's Wife*. Both films also have the same director, the terribly unsung Henry Koster. Koster, in addition to having a long and successful career making family-friendly comedies like *Come to the Stable* and *The Bishop's Wife* (his only nomination for Best Director), and *Harvey* (1950), directed the first-ever CinemaScope film, *The Robe* (1953). He also directed musicals like *Flower Drum Song* (1961) and *The Singing Nun* (1966).

Today, the Abbey of Regina Laudis in Bethlehem owns 450 acres, including a working farm. Their website states that the Abbey is "A community of contemplative Benedictine women dedicated to the praise of God through prayer and work." If you go there you will see, very much as depicted in the film, nuns doing farm work, riding the tractors, caring for the cattle, harvesting the apples and hay, and gathering wood for sale. In the gift shop they sell hand-knit and -woven products made from the convent's sheep, and food from the farm, including their famous cheese, honey, and homemade granola. They also sell arts and crafts, greeting cards, pottery, soaps, candles, and religious paintings and objects, along with CDs of the nuns singing their Gregorian chants.

One more fascinating story about the Abbey of Regina Laudis: Many may be aware of the story of actress Dolores Hart, who, at the height of her career, having starred opposite Elvis Presley in back-to-back films, *Loving You* (1957) and *King Creole* (1958), decided to leave Hollywood and seek a higher calling to become a nun. Mother Dolores Hart, O.S.B. (as she is now called), came to the Abbey in the mid-1960s. She still resides there, and has continued to promote the arts. In collaboration with her friend and fellow actress, the late Patricia Neal, they helped found The Gary-The Olivia Theater on the grounds of the Abbey, which presents live productions. The HBO documentary, *God is the Bigger Elvis* (2012), was made about her extraordinary life.

OTHER PEOPLE'S MONEY (1991)

Other People's Money was based on Jerry Sterner's play that began its original run in 1988, right here in Connecticut, with the Hartford Stage Company. It transitioned to off-Broadway, where Hollywood came calling for the theatrical rights, but HSC still retains a credit in the end titles.

The film would have a lasting significance in Seymour, Connecticut. The employee-owned Seymour Specialty Wire Company—then one of the state's last remaining copper and brass plants—was selected as the central location for the fictional New England Wire and Cable that corporate raider Larry "the Liquidator" Garfield (Danny DeVito) wants to take over. Not only did much of the action of the film take place at the plant, but many of the factory workers were employed as background extras to give the film some grit and authenticity. Director Norman Jewison said, "There are faces out there,

Piper Laurie, Gregory Peck, and Penelope Ann Miller rehearse a scene in *Other People's Money* at the Seymour Specialty Wire Company. (Courtesy Penelope Ann Miller)

workers and townspeople. I wanted to show how all this affects the workers of America."

Other People's Money marks the third time Gregory Peck would return to Connecticut to make a film (*Gentleman's Agreement*, 1947; *The Man in The Gray Flannel Suit*, 1956). The beloved star even had his hair cut at a local barbershop, filming a scene (that didn't make the final cut) at Pete's Hollywood Barbershop on Bank Street, with owner Pietro Cristani.

In *Other People's Money*, Peck would add Andrew Jorgenson—the stoic owner of New England Wire and Cable, defending the rights of the workingman—to his canon of principled men. Though Jorgenson stands to make a profit, he doesn't want to sell the company his father began because he knows it will displace the workers. Even as Jorgenson delivers a powerful speech extolling their virtues, we also see how out of touch he is in the debate. "A business is worth more than the price of its stock," Jorgenson says. "It's the place where we earn our living, where we meet our friends, dream our dreams. It is, in every sense, the very fabric that binds our society together." He also says, "One day . . . when we finally begin to rebuild our roads, our bridges, the infrastructure of our country, demand will skyrocket. And when those things happen, we will still be here, stronger because of our ordeal, stronger because we have survived." (These were concerns back in 1991. Here we are in the present, still dreaming about how spending on infrastructure will rebuild the working class.)

Director Norman Jewison and Penelope Ann Miller on set at the Seymour Specialty Wire Company. The Connecticut-based company was once the largest employee-owned business in the United States. In a *New York Times* publicity story about the making of *Other People's Money*, which was then shooting in Seymour, and the Gilbert & Bennett Mfg. Co. wire mill in Georgetown, Connecticut, Canadian director Norman Jewison (*In the Heat of the Night*, 1967; *A Soldier's Story*, 1984; *Agnes of God*, 1985; *Moonstruck*, 1987) described the love–hate relationship reflected in the many films he's made about American culture. "That is the one thing that a Canadian does have—objectivity about America," he said. His opinion about the post-Reagan era of greed, "ten years of corporate takeovers," and its effect on blue-collar workers, was concise: "Where have our values gone?" *Other People's Money* brings us back to a time in history when this debate was still a solvable issue. (Courtesy Penelope Ann Miller)

Jorgenson tries to appeal to Garfield's sense of decency in an effort to convince him to not swallow up his company. When that fails, he reluctantly gets tough, hiring his stepdaughter, Kate Sullivan (Penelope Ann Miller), a high-profile lawyer, to stop Garfield. Her sex appeal keeps Garfield at bay for a while, but Garfield desires money and winning more than love. Kate worries that Jorgenson underestimates the greed of his fellow shareholders, and in the end, his partner, Bill Coles (Dean Jones), goes behind his back and sides with Garfield, which gives him an edge to win. "Everybody looks out for themselves," he says. The proxy vote is won by Garfield, and Jorgenson loses control of his own company.

In an era when union membership is on the decline and just a few corporations seem to own everything, *Other People's Money* may come across as naive by today's standards, warning about the

CONNECTICUT IN THE MOVIES

The workers from the Seymour Specialty Wire Company were able to successfully purchase what was a failing business. In *Other People's Money*, Gregory Peck attempts to persuade his workers to do the same thing. He delivers a powerful speech, but in the end he loses his company to a hostile takeover. Both the Seymour Specialty Wire Company and the Gilbert & Bennett Mfg. Co. mill are now closed. (Photofest)

slippery slope of corporate takeovers by ruthless capitalists. For Connecticut, the meaning hit close to home. It foretold the end of the Seymour Specialty Wire Company. A few short years before the film was made, in 1984, the workers had purchased the failing business from its owners, and it was the biggest employee-owned industrial firm in the United States. But in 1992, one year after *Other People's Money* had immortalized the company on-screen, the plant on Franklin Street, which had been in business since 1878, closed. The Seymour Specialty Wire Company site is now a Super Stop and Shop grocery store. I'm not sure if that's progress.

AMISTAD (1997)

The 1997 film *Amistad*, filmed in part in Mystic and New Haven, brought national attention to one of Connecticut's greatest historical legacies. The *Amistad* trial that began in New Haven had an impact across the nation and became a symbol for abolitionists in the nineteenth century.

The story begins in 1839. The ship *La Amistad* was traveling from off the coast of Cuba. On board were Africans captured by rival tribes and sold into slavery to Portuguese slave traders. (Slave trading was illegal in the United States beginning in 1808, but still legal in many other parts of the world.) The African captives, led by a rice farmer named Sengbe Pieh, also called Joseph Cinqué, took over the *Amistad*, killing the captain, the cook, and others, but sparing the navigators, so they could steer them back home. Instead, they misdirected the ship toward the American East Coast, where it was seized off Long Island by the brig *Washington* of the US Navy and towed to New London, Connecticut. The fifty-two captives on board (including some women and children) were taken to New Haven and held in prison for murder and mutiny. (The prison was close to City Hall and the First Church of Christ, near New Haven Green, where there is now a memorial.)

This painting of Joseph "Cinqué," depicted in the film *Amistad* (1997), is by New Haven artist Nathaniel Jocelyn (1796–1881), and is located at the Connecticut Historical Society, 1 Elizabeth Street, in Hartford.

There was much financial support in New Haven from residents, fellow abolitionists, and the clergy, who raised funds for the Africans to return home after the trial. Two lawsuits were filed—one involving the mutiny and the legality of the Spanish enslaving the Africans, and one brought for salvage rights to the contents of the seized *Amistad*—the captive Africans. Cinqué became the spokesperson of the group; a translator was found to help him communicate. Lewis Tappan, a prominent abolitionist, arranged for Yale students to teach the Africans English. In Connecticut there was much sympathy for the group, but President Martin Van Buren was trying to maintain

CONNECTICUT IN THE MOVIES

This painting of the *Amistad* is in the New Haven Historical Society at 114 Whitney Avenue. The museum has a permanent exhibit related to the *Amistad*.

political relations with Spain, which wanted the return of what it considered their property.

In January of 1840, the Hartford court ruled that the Africans had been illegally taken to Cuba, but after trials in New Haven and Hartford, found in favor of the *Amistad* captives. The Van Buren administration appealed the case to a circuit court. John Quincy Adams at first did not want to be involved, as he was ambivalent about slavery, but eventually he felt compelled to speak on their behalf, and argued the case when it went before the Supreme Court. Adams's transformation is one of the highlights of the film.

The showdown between President Van Buren (portrayed by Nigel Hawthorne) and ex-president John Quincy Adams (Anthony Hopkins) became known as "the trial of the presidents." Adams successfully argued on the *Amistad* Africans' behalf. (Hopkins, as Adams, transports us to another era in an eleven-minute speech, giving us a history lesson in the law, circa 1841.) After two years of imprisonment, the African captives were finally free.

It was the noted actress, producer, and choreographer Debbie Allen (*Fame*, 1980) who brought the story of the *Amistad* to Steven Spielberg after seeing *Schindler's List* (1993), saying he was "the right person for the job." Spielberg said, "*Amistad* is a story that people had to know about," but acknowledged he would not have gone forward had he not found the right actor to play Cinqué. He found the

Amistad (1997) is based on historical events. Matthew McConaughey is seen here as Roger Sherman. Sherman (1793–1863) was born in New Haven. He was an attorney, served as a Connecticut senator, and was the thirty-second governor of Connecticut. (Photofest)

qualities he was looking for in Djimon Hounsou: "He was courageous, he was sympathetic, he was angry. He had dignity."

Djimon Hounsou had grown up in West Africa, but his parents had sent him to Paris, hoping to give him a better life. He ran out of money and was living on the streets. His destiny changed when a photographer discovered him. Hounsou began a career in modeling, and had recently started acting. Now, after appearing in only one film, he landed the lead in a Steven Spielberg movie portraying one of the greatest heroes of the civil rights movement: Cinqué, a man who refused to be taken as a slave.

It was not an easy shoot. The Black actors cast in *Amistad* portraying the captives went through much personal and emotional trauma in re-creating the past and the horrors of slavery. Hounsou described feeling humiliated and angry, and the cast and crew were often reduced to tears during filming.

No one is more adept than Spielberg at taking historical events and infusing action and adventure into the narrative to create a dramatic and compelling story; however, he was criticized for his so-called "Disneyfying" of historic events. There was a certain amount of hypocrisy with everyone who

Steven Spielberg directs Anthony Hopkins as John Quincy Adams and Morgan Freeman as Theodore Joadson. The Joadson character was fictional, but based on several key historical figures involved with the *Amistad*. Austin F. Williams was a noted abolitionist in Farmington who housed some of the *Amistad* captives during their trial. (Photofest)

was involved with helping the *Amistad* Africans. While they were imprisoned, New England abolitionists used them to promote their cause by charging curious onlookers money to come take a look at them, as if they were animals in a zoo. The well-meaning New England missionaries teaching them religion also sought to change their names or get them to drop their language in favor of English. In the film, Morgan Freeman plays a Black abolitionist named Theodore Joadson who assists Adams with the case. Joadson is meant to be a composite of several different historical figures.

The film takes place in 1840, a time when a Black man would not have been allowed to sit in a court, let alone work side by side with white associates, or visit the home of John Quincy Adams, but Spielberg wanted to depict people from different backgrounds coming together to pursue freedom.

Adding popcorn to a serious subject is never easy, and while some facts have been omitted or simplified for entertainment value, the film is a starting point to learn not only about the trial, but about some of the prominent Connecticut citizens involved. For instance, Matthew McConaughey's

The *Amistad Memorial* is a bronze sculpture by artist Ed Hamilton, honoring Joseph Cinqué and the African captives on the spot where they were held for two years. It is located outside at 165 Church Street. A replica of the *Amistad* is located at Mystic Seaport. *Amistad*'s Djimon Hounsou (below) as "Cinqué." (Photofest)

character, real estate attorney Roger Baldwin—an ordinary man caught up in an extraordinary situation—was loosely based on Roger Sherman Baldwin, a member of city government in New Haven who became governor of Connecticut from 1844 to 1846, and was elected to the US Senate in 1846. At the time of the *Amistad* trial (1840–1841), he represented the town of New Haven in the General Assembly; he held public office until 1851. His notebooks referring to the *Amistad* case are located in the Yale University Archives in New Haven. New Haven residents formed the *Amistad* Committee and volunteered aid to the captive Africans, taking them food and clothing and offering housing before their return to Africa.

One of the *Amistad* captives, named Tamie, lived with the family of Dr. Chauncey Brown in Farmington. In the *Farmington Magazine* in February 1901, Brown's wife, Julia Strong Brown, reminisced about the experience:

> *It was a most singular episode in the quiet life of Farmington which brought to us the . . . three Mendian girls. One of these, by name Tamie, . . . remained with me until their departure for their native land . . . About fourteen years of age, she was tall, straight as an arrow, and lithe as a willow, with a soft low voice and a sweet smile . . . She was fond of flowers and particularly enjoyed a little garden which she tended carefully. I remember her joy when I had been preparing pineapples; she asked for the green crowns to plant and was so delighted when they began to grow.*

Williams and his wife, Jennet Cowles Williams, were abolitionists. During the Africans' imprisonment, Williams corresponded with the *Amistad* Committee and helped arrange, with Samuel Deming and John Treadwell Norton, housing for the Africans after their release. His house later became a station on the Underground Railroad.

Though *Amistad* has been criticized for taking liberties with the facts, adding extraneous fictional characters or fictional motives to strengthen the narrative, one cannot deny that Spielberg cares deeply about the subject. In the film, it is John Quincy Adams who opines that "Whoever tells the best story wins." This compelling (though scripted) argument brings sympathy to the cause and ultimately wins the case for the *Amistad* Africans. The same may be said for Spielberg, who feels that the audience must first know and care about the participants in order to care about the story.

The breathtaking scope and sheer talent that went into making *Amistad*—from the all-star cast to the cinematography, art direction, costumes, production design, and score—are at the highest levels of filmmaking, and helmed by the greatest epic director of our era, Steven Spielberg.

MARSHALL (2017)

Marshall is a terrifically acted courtroom drama and biopic directed with verve and style by Reginald Hudlin. Once again, the opening credits inform us that *Marshall* is "based on true events," and we remember what that means. In this case, these events impacted not only Connecticut's history, but America's. The movie purports to retell the events surrounding a famous Connecticut crime case, *State of Connecticut v. Joseph Spell*, which played a memorable role in the early career of civil rights attorney, and later, the first Black Supreme Court justice, Thurgood Marshall. *Marshall* also highlights the remarkable career of the Connecticut attorney Samuel Friedman, who helped gain Spell his freedom.

Marshall (2017) has Chadwick Boseman as Thurgood Marshall, Josh Gad as Sam Friedman, and Sterling K. Brown as Joseph Spell. Director Reginald Hudlin said, "Thurgood Marshall has always been a hero of mine. To get a script this good about, to me, one of the greatest Americans who ever lived, is a dream come true." The writer of *Marshall*, Michael Koskoff (a cousin of *Come to the Stable* composer/actor Alfred Newman), was a renowned civil rights and personal injury attorney who lived and worked in Westport, Connecticut. His father, Theodore Koskoff, had defended members of the Black Panthers in the 1969-1971 trials in New Haven. Michael took up screenwriting as a hobby, working on the script of *Marshall* for seven years, and ended up co-writing it with his son, Jacob. (Photofest)

CONNECTICUT IN THE MOVIES

It was a Connecticut lawyer-turned-screenwriter, the late Michael Koskoff, who had long been intrigued with the case. He penned the script over the course of seven years (with some help from his son Jacob), and got it to producer Paula Wagner. Wagner had wanted to film where the story is set, but the state had suspended its tax credit program in 2013, which made it financially unfeasible. *Marshall* was filmed entirely in Buffalo, New York.

In December 1940, a socialite named Mrs. Eleanor Strubing was found soaking wet and wandering along Route 22 near Westchester County, New York. Strubing claimed she was "a victim of a beastly attack" by her Black servant, a man named Joseph Spell, who was working at her estate on Round Hill Road in Greenwich. Strubing claimed Spell had come into her bedroom, dragged her from her shower, raped her four times, then gagged her and drove her to nearby Kensico Reservoir, where he threw her into the water.

"Mrs. J. K. Strubing is Kidnapped and Hurled Off Bridge by Butler" read the *New York Times* headline. The accompanying article described her alleged night of horror in great depth. Spell was later picked up by the Greenwich police at Strubing's house and held for kidnapping and rape.

The papers had a field day with the story, sensationalizing the events with a distinct racial bias. Spell maintained his innocence. He never denied having sex with Strubing, but he asserted that "she had agreed to it." Fearing they would be seen by her neighbors, she had asked Spell to drive them to a discreet location; she later panicked, jumped out of the car, and told Spell to drive home without her. This was an era when a mere accusation by a white woman against her Black servant for such a crime could send a man to prison for life.

Though this was not a civil rights case, the NAACP feared Spell would be a victim of racial bias. The organization selected a thirty-two-year-old Black attorney named Thurgood Marshall to defend him. They needed a lawyer familiar with Connecticut laws, so the Bridgeport branch of the NAACP found an unlikely ally in attorney Samuel Friedman. Friedman, who was white, later recalled that he was initially reluctant to try the case with Marshall, saying, "I don't think you could find a man on the street that in any way had any sympathy for Spell or believed that this was consensual, including me." Friedman was merely supposed to assist Marshall as co-counsel, but his colorful and theatrical defense ended up gaining sympathy for Spell. Friedman's strategy: He pitted the Greenwich upper-class socialite Strubing against the working-class man, Spell. Both took the witness stand, and Friedman pointed out inconsistencies in Strubing's story. In the end, the jury believed Spell, and his unlikely acquittal was a big win for the NAACP and for Thurgood Marshall.

At first the film stays pretty close to the facts. Connecticut socialite Eleanor Strubing (Kate Hudson) is found wandering on a country road near her Greenwich mansion. When police pick her up, she accuses her Black chauffeur and servant, Joseph Spell (Sterling K. Brown), of raping her. Ster-

Kate Hudson as Eleanor Strubing takes the stand in *Marshall*. (Photofest)

ling K. Brown's performance delicately balances the fear a Black man accused of a crime by his white employer might face in 1940s America, but also adds plenty of charm, to show that Spell might just be a ne'er-do-well playboy not to be believed.

Spell is then picked up at Strubing's house and held in a Greenwich jail, where Thurgood Marshall (Chadwick Boseman) arrives to defend him. As Marshall, the late Boseman shows another side of our future Supreme Court justice—a charismatic, gentle man who loved music. Marshall felt the burden of responsibility in winning the case for the NAACP. At the time of the trial, he had been crisscrossing the country, fighting racial injustice, looking for cases that would educate the public on segregation.

Sam Friedman, the NAACP-recruited local personal injury attorney who takes on the case

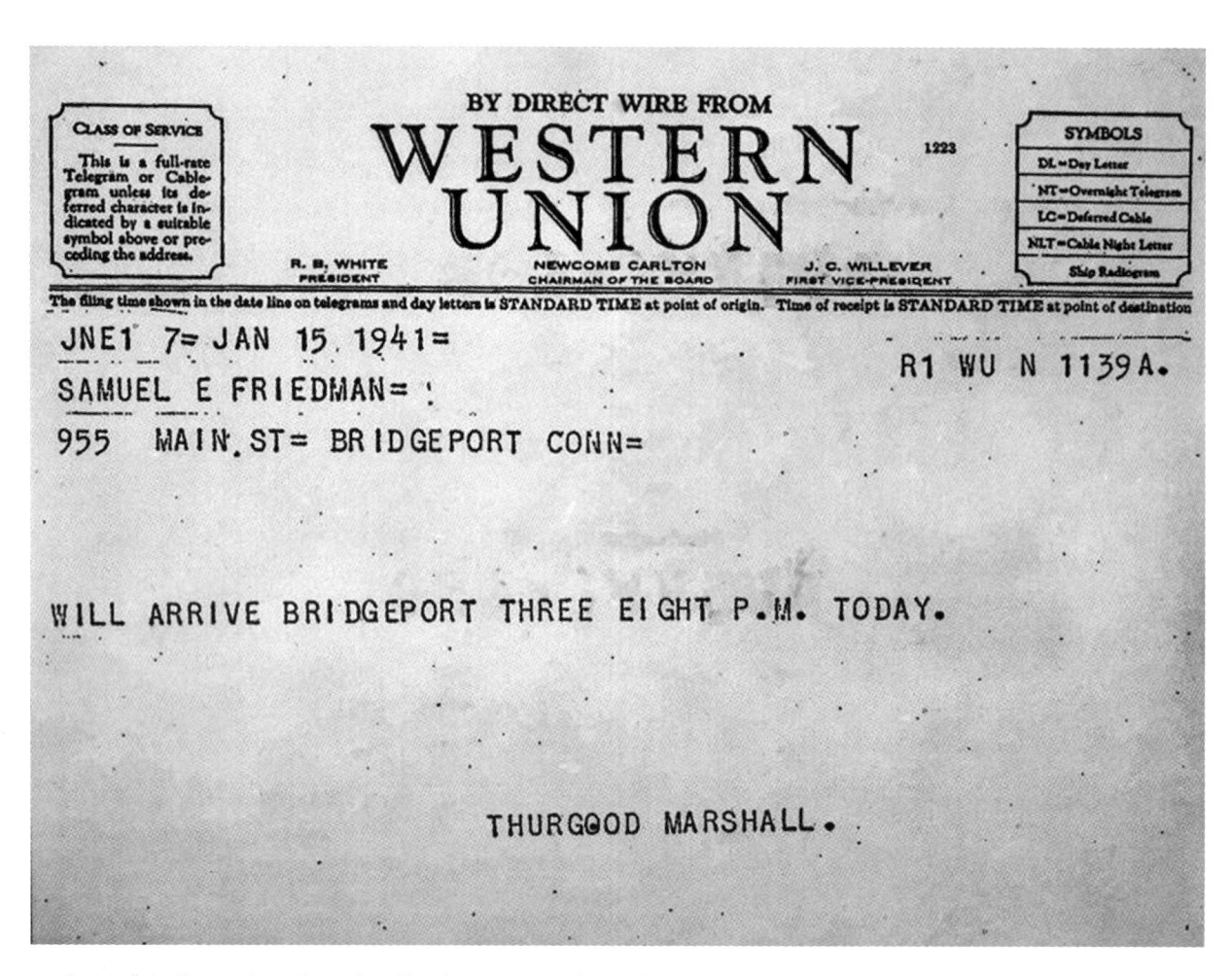

> **WESTERN UNION**
>
> BY DIRECT WIRE FROM
>
> JNE1 7= JAN 15 1941=
> SAMUEL E FRIEDMAN=
> 955 MAIN ST= BRIDGEPORT CONN=
>
> WILL ARRIVE BRIDGEPORT THREE EIGHT P.M. TODAY.
>
> THURGOOD MARSHALL.

with Marshall, is played in the film by actor Josh Gad. Known more for his musical comedy work onstage in plays such as *The Book of Mormon* (2011), and also his voice work in *Frozen* (2013) and its subsequent sequels, Gad shines in *Marshall*, in one of his few dramatic roles.

There are a few facts-vs.-fiction moments that have riled critics, as well as inaccuracies with which the family of Samuel Friedman has taken issue, but overall, the film makes the point that at the time, Marshall and the NAACP had the big picture in mind, and securing these small victories would bring much-needed attention and money to fight racial injustice across the country.

One example in the film is that the judge assigned to the case, Judge Carl Foster (James Cromwell), decides that Marshall can attend court but not speak on Spell's behalf. The filmmakers wanted to depict the challenges of Northern racism that existed by showing the humiliation of Marshall—an experienced trial lawyer—when he was not allowed to speak in the courtroom simply because he was Black. He therefore has to teach Friedman how to try the case. In truth, Marshall was sent as a consultant. In an effort to create dramatic conflict in their relationship, the film depicts Friedman as having never tried a criminal case. Fearing his reputation would be ruined by defending a Black man, Friedman tells Marshall, "I have to live in this city after you're gone."

Friedman was in fact not a novice. He was a respected Bridgeport attorney who had been practicing law for fourteen years. In the film, Friedman begins experiencing anti-Semitic attacks for defending Spell, and is beaten up. This becomes a motivation for Spell to fight even harder. In reality, this never happened. Though both Friedman and Marshall did receive death threats, it was Friedman's skill at out-lawyering his opponent and picking apart Mrs. Strubing's story that were instrumental in gaining Spell his freedom.

In the end, an unlikely partnership was forged between Thurgood Marshall and Samuel Friedman. How did Marshall and Friedman get Spell—who was less than a model citizen—cleared of rape charges? With an all-white jury, no less? As *Marshall* depicts him, Spell was a gambler, with a wife and children, and another common-law wife on the side. He freely admitted he had had sex with Mrs. Strubing, but insisted it was consensual. Mrs. Strubing, on the other hand, was a model citizen, married to a very wealthy and established man. Why would she make up this outlandish story? Clearly, Strubing's relationship with Spell may have been a more complicated affair. Kate Hudson as Eleanor does her best to convey that there is more to this story than we know, like when she is led from the courtroom and tearfully smiles at Spell, mouthing the words "I'm sorry."

After the trial, Eleanor and John Strubing moved to Old Lyme, Connecticut. The publicity did not harm her reputation. Her husband John became president of the country club. After Spell was acquitted, he received fan mail sent to the *Amsterdam News* office. He moved with his wife to East Orange, New Jersey.

In 1954, Thurgood Marshall won the landmark case of *Brown v. Board of Education*, which outlawed segregation in public schools. He later argued thirty-two civil rights cases before the US Supreme Court, and won all but three. In 1967, he became the first Black Supreme Court justice, appointed by then-president Lyndon B. Johnson.

The Ice Storm (1997), filmed in New Canaan, Connecticut, is one of the best examples of the Dark Suburbia Redux genre. Kevin Kline, Joan Allen, and Christina Ricci shooting a scene in *The Ice Storm* at the New Canaan train station. The anonymity of the commuter is expressed in Kline's everyman trench coat, reminiscent of Gregory Peck's attire in *The Man in the Gray Flannel Suit*. (Photofest)

CHAPTER 12
DARK SUBURBIA REDUX

Dark Suburbia Redux is a category of modern films that redefine Connecticut culture and the suburban malaise of the past. Director Ang Lee cited the 1950s horror movie *Invasion of the Body Snatchers* (1956), about aliens growing human bodies, as an inspiration for his modern take on Dark Suburbia: *The Ice Storm* (1997), which takes place in the 1970s. Director Sam Mendes said the ending of *Revolutionary Road* (2008), which takes place in a storybook 1950s Connecticut neighborhood, looks at the "emptiness of suburbia," and was about "enduring." Todd Haynes's *Far from Heaven* (2002) shattered the myth of a perfect marriage and examined bigotry, circa 1958, in Hartford, Connecticut.

All three films share stylized interpretations and specific points of view about Connecticut culture, a postmodern analysis that would give voice to the perceived angst that men and women surely must have felt but were never allowed to talk about. While no one is happy in the past, they do suffer artfully. In Dark Suburbia Redux films, the past was reimagined to feel more intense but look less real. Ang Lee, describing the look of *The Ice Storm*, set in the 1970s, said, "It was not realistic. It was realist, almost painted."

Sometimes the dark storylines about adultery, insanity, abortion, alcoholism, racism, homosexuality, and wife-swapping are filmed so elegantly, or set against such sumptuous production values—with lush scores or groovy soundtracks behind them—that the savagery is muted by the beauty of the sets and the photography. Women who live in modern glass houses or well-appointed mansions are imprisoned by circumstances they cannot escape, but their hair is amazing! Men are emotionally detached, or struggle to free themselves from feelings of pain through drugs, alcohol, or sex, but their trench coats look so cool that it's distracting. Characters dressed in period costumes sleepwalk through their own personal nightmares. Welcome to Dark Suburbia Redux.

THE ICE STORM (1997)

The Ice Storm (1997), filmed in New Canaan, is one of the best examples of the Dark Suburbia Redux genre. Based on the 1994 novel by Rick Moody, *The Ice Storm* takes place during what was considered to be the worst ice storm in Connecticut's history, on December 17, 1973. (In the film, this date is moved to Thanksgiving weekend.) It began as a snowstorm, but the snow soon turned into freezing rain, covering the ground with solid ice. Falling trees and branches brought down power lines. One-third of the state lost power, which would take a week to restore.

Director Ang Lee was determined to shoot the film in New Canaan, where the novel took place. Some events in the novel, particularly a scene involving wife-swapping, made the town wary of filming. New Canaan residents were not thrilled about being depicted as "key partying" swingers, and were quick to point out that the author, Moody, had also lived in Darien. The town relented, but there is still debate to this day about where the notorious key party scene was filmed. (Some have it on Dairy Road in Greenwich, while others insist it's on Laurel Road.) An older New Canaan resident was blasé, claiming she had attended "quite a few" key parties in New Canaan in the 1970s. Who says Connecticut is boring?

The tranquil setting of New Canaan juxtaposes nicely against the inner turmoil of the adults, who are all coping with one drama or another, but are unable to talk about it. For instance, in one scene, Ben is furious after discovering his teenage daughter, the precocious Wendy, and the Carvers' son Sandy, "playing doctor" in the basement. Ben yanks Wendy by the arm and marches her out of there, but doesn't yell at her. Instead, he and Wendy walk back home through the woods in silence, Ben, lost in his own thoughts, Wendy trailing glumly behind him.

As the wind picks up, signaling the beginning of the storm, Wendy's red poncho starts to flap, standing out against the gray trees. Wendy is Little Red Riding Hood, all alone and frightened in the woods. Ben looks down at his daughter, this creature that he created, and suddenly, our hearts break for both of them. She looks so small and scared; he looks so confused and helpless. Ben realizes that even though Wendy is sexually active, she is merely a child, and may need some guidance. He leans down to pick her up, and holding her tightly in his arms, he carries her through the storm.

The Ice Storm. (Photofest)

This is a beautiful foreshadowing of how parents need to hold on to their children, because you never know what dangers may be coming. Parents are often unreliable, and children are left to parent themselves. Ben is attempting to be a good and loving father, but at the same time, he is so immersed in his own life, his own unhappiness, that he is not equipped to watch after his children. The ice storm will be a reckoning. While a storm rages outside, the parents are attending a wife-swapping key party, testing the boundaries of their marriages, attempting to feel . . . something.

Another major element of Dark Suburbia Redux seems to be that although everyone is engaging in frivolous sexual activity, unlike the '60s sex comedies, there is no joy in it. There is a reexamination of the behavior of the past, a moral questioning. Elena (Joan Allen) is trying to be a happy 1950s-style housewife, but she is furious at her husband's indiscretions and lack of attention. He has stopped sleeping with her. When she attempts to let it all hang out by doing the same thing, and having a sexual encounter with Janey's husband, Jim, in the front seat of the family station wagon, she regrets it, and just feels degraded (a similar scene occurs in *Revolutionary Road*).

Although the children's behavior largely mimics what they have learned from their parents, in one instance, we see Ben's son, Paul (Tobey Maguire), choose right over wrong. In a New York City

The Ice Storm stars Christina Ricci and Elijah Wood. Its haunting score incorporates Native American flutes. Composer Mychael Danna said, "Ang and I wanted to remind people of the power of nature; that nature was there before anyone else, and that nature will be there when we've gone. As the characters walked through the woods to their mod houses, the ground beneath their feet used to belong to civilizations that are long gone." (Photofest)

apartment, Paul has been drinking with a classmate he is wildly attracted to, Libbets (Katie Holmes). When she passes out, drunk, he contemplates taking advantage of her, but ultimately, he can't go through with it. The parents have no such qualms about questions of morality.

During the key party, one of the children, Janey's son Mikey (Elijah Wood), goes outside, curious to explore the beauty of the ice storm. He is accidentally electrocuted. Darkness descends on each family as it can and often does in a small town. The Carvers and the Hoods are now forever linked by tragedy.

Coming off his period drama *Sense and Sensibility* (1995), Ang Lee took a contemporary approach to a film about family dysfunction in the 1970s. He was strongly influenced by twentieth-century art, specifically the Cubism movement, and wanted to introduce that look and feel to the film. He also chose two architecturally significant New Canaan houses to tell the stories of two very different families. Each created a unique emotional effect.

The Hood family—Ben, Elena, Wendy, and Paul (Kevin Kline, Joan Allen, Christina Ricci, and Tobey Maguire)—live in a classic split-level home with a brick exterior that embraced a 1960s feel. (Lee liked the house so much he considered purchasing it after filming was finished.)

The Carver family—Janey, Jim, Mikey, and Sandy (Sigourney Weaver, Jamey Sheridan, Elijah Wood, and Adam Hann-Byrd)—live in a modern glass house. This was a nod to Philip Johnson's famous glass house in New Canaan. The glass house was used to literally expose the interior lives of the characters. In one scene, after Ben Hood has been stood up by his neighbor Janey Carver, with whom he's having an affair, he stares out from her modern glass house, completely alone, in his underwear. The trees and sky reflected across his body emphasize his loneliness and isolation.

The New Canaan train station where scenes from *The Ice Storm* were filmed.

The Ice Storm's director, Ang Lee, with Sigourney Weaver in New Canaan. (Photofest)

Janey Carver's (Sigourney Weaver) ultra-mod house in *The Ice Storm* is located in New Canaan. It is a private residence.

DARK SUBURBIA REDUX

Production designer Mark Friedberg, who later worked on *Far from Heaven* (2002), used the interiors of the houses to create a mood for each family. It's a pastiche of the best and worst of 1970s design, from sleek Swedish furniture to cringeworthy but very popular waterbeds and avocado kitchens. After seeing the first cut of the film, Lee told Friedberg, intending it to be a compliment, "It looks really good. It's not the 1970s, but it's interesting."

FAR FROM HEAVEN (2002)

Far From Heaven (2002) was filmed as an homage to the 1950s Hollywood melodramas of German filmmaker Douglas Sirk, but included updated themes such as bigotry and homosexuality in 1950s Hartford. The film was clearly a labor of love for its writer and director, Todd Haynes. Haynes cited Sirk's films *All That Heaven Allows* (1955) and *Imitation of Life* (1959) as inspiration. He borrowed liberally from the plot of *All That Heaven Allows*, in which Rock Hudson plays a poor but caring gardener who falls in love with his wealthy client, an older woman played by Jane Wyman. In Haynes's *Far from Heaven*, the gardener (Dennis Haysbert) is Black, which ups the stakes considerably. Haynes's original concept for *Far from Heaven* was about a perfect married couple, Frank and Cathy Whitaker (Dennis Quaid and Julianne Moore), living the perfect 1950s life in Hartford. Frank is an executive at Magnatech (Haynes was not able to secure the rights to the Magnavox brand and had to rename the company), who happens to be hiding a very big secret.

After they are profiled by a local magazine as "Mr. and Mrs. Magnatech," Cathy makes the discovery that her husband is homosexual. He is arrested in a sting operation. He initially denies the accusation, saying it was a misunderstanding, but Cathy realizes that she is in a sham marriage. Her identity as the perfect wife, hostess, and mother has been taken from her, and she begins to withdraw into herself. She can't confide in her best friend, Eleanor (Patricia Clarkson), for fear she will lose her social status.

Cathy finds comfort from an unlikely source—her gardener, Raymond, played sensitively by Dennis Haysbert, who finds beauty in nature, and possibly, in Cathy. Finally, Cathy has someone she can communicate her feelings with, but there might be something more to it for her, too. Cathy's friends are women, and Raymond is a welcome male companion who treats her like a woman, not a trophy wife. They have an easy compatibility; he's handsome, and he has an empathy Frank lacks. She's drawn into a deeper friendship with him after she sees him at a local art show. Sensing her loneliness, Raymond encourages Cathy to step outside the confines of her strictly white neighborhood. He kids her, "There's a world, even here in Hartford, where people look just like me."

There's a bit of irony in this line. I worked with Dennis Haysbert, and I was able to ask him about *Far From Heaven*, and what that line meant to him in terms of the story. His answer made me

A postcard from the 1950s, when the film takes place.

Dennis Quaid, Julianne Moore, Ryan Ward, and Lindsay Andretta in *Far from Heaven*. (Photofest)

Far From Heaven (2002) with Patricia Clarkson and Julianne Moore. (Photofest)

laugh. "I've never been to Hartford; I've never even been to Connecticut." On a more serious note, he told me that when the film came out, "I had a lot of women come up to me and say that was my story. It was a generational divide. A line you didn't cross."

To re-create the look of a 1950s studio melodrama, cinematographer Ed Lachman employed colored gels or bright 50 K studio-style lighting for interiors, giving them a glossy look. To give it a Technicolor feel, the outdoor scenes were filled with falling red autumn leaves and pink spring blossoms to bring home the romance. Production designer Mark Friedberg (*The Ice Storm*, 1997) made the Whitaker home a study in artifice, with grand staircases for characters to enter and exit as actors once had in studio films.

Raymond invites Cathy to lunch, and she accepts. As they eat at an all-Black diner, the town gossip, Mona Lauder (Celia Weston), sees them together and begins spreading the news all over town. Her friend Eleanor warns Cathy that a "mixed-race" friendship won't be tolerated by the neighbors. Her husband, Frank, is enraged, worrying about their reputation in the community, which Cathy sees as hypocrisy, considering his situation. Cathy, who has developed feelings for Raymond, regretfully tells him she cannot see him again. She attempts to rebuild her marriage to Frank, but he confesses he's fallen in love with a young man and wants a divorce.

CONNECTICUT IN THE MOVIES

Far from Heaven's Dennis Haysbert and Julianne Moore (above); director Todd Haynes with Julianne Moore (below). (Photofest)

While the 1950s film *All That Heaven Allows* had a happy ending, with the gardener and the older woman getting beyond the stigma of "what other people think," *Far from Heaven*, a film that re-creates the 1950s, ends in sadness. Cathy, who has rejected Raymond because of what the neighbors will think, ends up alone after her husband leaves her. Raymond, too, decides to leave Hartford and move to Baltimore after an incident where his daughter is bullied by local boys because she is Black. Cathy goes to the train station to see Raymond off. As much as I wanted to see Cathy bravely face society and get on the train with Raymond, she waves good-bye to him, and any future happiness in Connecticut.

REVOLUTIONARY ROAD (2008)

"We all have dreams, and *Revolutionary Road* deals with unfulfilled dreams," said director Sam Mendes. *Revolutionary Road* (2008) is the darkest of the Dark Suburbia Redux genre. Based on a 1961 novel by Richard Yates about postwar disillusionment, the story took many years to be brought to the screen. It was adapted by screenwriter Justin Haythe for Kate Winslet. Winslet had but one costar in mind, and convinced her friend Leonardo DiCaprio to sign on to play her husband. Reunited after their blockbuster romantic hit, *Titanic* (1997), they would once again head into dark waters, this time as a 1950s couple who compromise their dreams after moving to Connecticut.

Frank and April Wheeler (Kate Winslet and Leonardo DiCaprio) fight against being just like everyone else in *Revolutionary Road* (2008). The contemporary film takes place in the 1950s. For the look of the film, director Sam Mendes took inspiration from the photographs of Saul Leiter, a prominent photographer of the 1950s New York School. (Photofest)

Leonardo DiCaprio and Kate Winslet shooting at Pinewood Lake on 33 East Lake Road in Trumbull. (Photofest)

Winslet wanted her husband at the time, Sam Mendes, to direct. British director Mendes was no stranger to sadness in suburbia. His debut film about family dysfunction, *American Beauty* (1999), garnered five Academy Awards, including Best Picture and Best Director.

"We begin the movie in crisis," said director Sam Mendes on the Blu-ray commentary for *Revolutionary Road*. The same might be said of his relationship with his wife, lead actress Kate Winslet. Mendes continued, "You somehow find yourself living a life you hadn't quite expected and certainly one that you didn't really want to live." His words may be reflective of the filming. The consequences of a married couple working on a film about a rocky marriage led to off-screen tensions. The couple divorced not long after the film opened.

Revolutionary Road begins in 1950s New York City. Aspiring actress April (Kate Winslet) meets handsome war hero Frank Wheeler (Leonardo DiCaprio) at a bohemian party in Greenwich Village. They have an instant attraction and are soon making love in Frank's studio apartment and planning their future, which includes a trip to Paris. They marry, but April soon discovers she is pregnant, and gives up her dream of becoming an actress. Frank is still searching for his "passion in life," but he takes the easy path by following in his father's footsteps and working at Knox, a business machine company.

Production designer Kristi Zea was tasked with finding just the right Connecticut house. Director Sam Mendes said, "The house so full of promise becomes a prison." Other filming locations include Bethel, Darien, Greenwich, Stamford, Southport, Beacon Falls, Fairfield, Norwalk, New Canaan, Shelton, and the Thomaston train station. Neighbors David Harbour and Kathryn Hahn as the Campbells in *Revolutionary Road* (2008). (Photofest)

With a baby on the way, they begin looking for a home in Connecticut. The American Dream, right? Their realtor, Helen Givings (Kathy Bates), suggests Revolutionary Road Estates, an exclusive community. As Mrs. Givings describes their future in suburbia, however, we see April apprehensively looking out the car window in a scene reminiscent of the fearful Katharine Ross looking out her car window while her husband drives her to her doom in Stepford. April quietly notes how the houses, though beautiful, all look the same. Frank reassures April that they will be happy.

Leonardo DiCaprio shooting a scene at the Thomaston train station. As in *The Ice Storm*, echoes of *The Man in the Gray Flannel Suit* show commuters and a loss of identity, but it is heightened in Dark Suburbia Redux. (Photofest)

It's a promise he does not keep. They fall into a pattern of drinking and smoking too much and blaming each other for their unhappiness. April spends hours looking out the window, watching life pass her by. Frank commutes back and forth to New York for a job that in his own words is dull and inconsequential. On his thirtieth birthday he begins a casual affair with his secretary, Maureen Grube (Zoe Kazan, granddaughter of Elia Kazan), out of boredom. Though on friendly terms with another newly married couple, Shep and Milly Campbell (David Harbour and Kathryn Hahn), April is determined not to end up like them. She despises the idea that Milly Campbell loves her domesticity, loves her place in suburbia.

In Dark Suburbia Redux there is often contempt for things that used to be touted, such as The American Dream—as if to say that no one who is intelligent ever found joy in marriage or parenting or owning a home. April feels she and Frank are compromising on ideals they once shared, and hopes that moving to Paris will put them back on track. Initially he agrees that they are in a slump, but the trip is postponed after Frank receives a promotion at work and April becomes pregnant again.

After that, April is resigned to the knowledge that happiness will always be out of reach for them. She has an epiphany, and tells him, "Our whole existence is based on this great pretense that we're special, that we're superior to the whole thing, but we're not. We're just like everyone else! We bought into the same, ridiculous delusion, that we have to resign from life and settle down the moment we have children. And we've been punishing each other for it!" She continues, "It's what you are that's being stifled. It's what you are that's being denied and denied in this kind of life."

Further proof of this comes when she invites the Givings family for dinner, including their troubled son, John (Michael Shannon), recently released from a mental institution. He blurts out uncomfortable truths about Frank and April's marriage. Frank is outraged and ready to punch John in the face. Mrs. Givings jumps up from the table, screaming, "He's not well. He's not well!" But John's words have a deep effect on April; they foreshadow her own break from reality.

During a night of heavy drinking with the Campbells, April is determined to hurt Milly and destroy her supposed happiness. At a bar, she first entices Shep in a seductive dance. Later, he takes her home and they have sex in the front seat of his car. It's a crude and meaningless experience for them both, and Shep blames April for encouraging him. Mendes and screenwriter Justin Haythe were concerned about similarities they discovered between Yates's novel and Rick Moody's 1994 novel-to-screen adaptation of *The Ice Storm*. (A similar scene of an extramarital affair occurs in *The Ice Storm*, and the April–Shep scene was restaged to avoid drawing comparisons.) Haythe said that both films are about "couples striving to feel something, to feel anything."

Frank, who has been lost most of his life, has found peace in his work, his marriage, and his role as a father, but April descends into madness, as John Givings predicted. She escapes to the woods, but after spending the day running away, she returns, realizing she has nowhere else to go.

Mendes described the ending of *Revolutionary Road* as April finally "setting herself free." She rises early to make Frank breakfast before his commute. She wears a simple cotton dress and apron—a symbol of docile domesticity. Frank is relieved. Maybe April has finally accepted his pronouncement about the move to Connecticut: "They will be happy." When Frank leaves for work, April goes upstairs and self-induces an abortion that leads to her death.

FOUR CONTEMPORARY DARK SUBURBIA REDUX FILMS

RACHEL GETTING MARRIED (2008)

The screenwriter of *Rachel Getting Married*, Jenny Lumet, makes one thing perfectly clear on the DVD commentary: "Sorry if you're from Connecticut but, ech." It's an intriguing tidbit, since her debut screenplay, *Rachel Getting Married*, was shot in and around Stamford. Lumet is a child of the cinema. Her father is the famed director Sidney Lumet, whose dark family drama film *Long Day's Journey into Night* (1962) is discussed in chapter 10. Both films revolve around families gathering for what should be happy occasions before then turning on each other.

A joyous wedding will become one family's "long day's journey into night" in Sony Pictures Classics' *Rachel Getting Married* (2008). The film marked a turning point in Anne Hathaway's career, earning her an Oscar nomination for Best Actress. The script's author, Jenny Lumet, went on to become a top screenwriter in films and on television. (Photofest)

Rachel Getting Married is a fine example of contemporary Dark Suburbia Redux. Here, years of family dynamics and dysfunction will lead to a cathartic resolution at a family wedding. If it feels at awkward, tense, and painful to watch, that may be exactly what the filmmakers were hoping for.

Rachel Getting Married (2008) was made at a time when filmmakers were beginning to experiment with low-budget digital technology. Academy Award–winning director Jonathan Demme (*The Silence of the Lambs*, 1991) and cinematographer Declan Quinn employed a cinema verité semi-documentary style, using a wandering Steadicam that makes you feel as if you're one of the guests at the wedding. As a "guest," however, you soon discover that there is a lot of tension in this family.

Demme used the Altman technique (director Robert Altman is credited at the end of the film) of long, extended takes of overlapping dialogue mixed with live music that swings the party through emotional highs and lows. Kudos to editor Tim Squyres for keeping the footage straight. (There are quite a few accidental sightings of cameras and crew members.)

Jonathan Demme was a friend and mentor to many. This small and personal film reflects his loving hand. His directing career began in the 1970s, working for the low-budget master, Roger Corman. He later made quirky arthouse films like *Melvin and Howard* (1980) and *Something Wild* (1986), delved into music with *Stop Making Sense* (1984), and then made his most important film, *Philadelphia* (1993), which dealt with the subject of AIDS. After a career that spanned fifty years, Demme died in 2017.

Rachel Getting Married benefits greatly from having been shot on location. The Buchman family house, where most of the action takes place, is a classic turn-of-the-century Victorian on Westview Lane in Stamford, chosen for what Jenny Lumet said was its "haunted feeling." The green "painted lady" is very much a character in the film, and its cluttered interior reflects a family that has lived there for many years. The Ukrainian Museum and Library in Stamford was used also, for the wedding dinner.

Kym (Anne Hathaway) has been released on a weekend pass from rehab to attend the wedding of her sister, Rachel (Rosemarie DeWitt), to Sidney (Tunde Adebimpe). Her unexpected appearance dredges up the central family tragedy. We learn that Kym—driving under the influence—was responsible for the death of their youngest brother, Ethan. The family has been fractured since that accident, and Kym has not been able to maintain her sobriety.

Kym's feelings of being shut out by the family play out in a dangerous way. She enjoys making a spectacle of herself, and first attempts to steal the spotlight from her sister's wedding by endlessly talking about her addiction. Kym further complicates the day by having sex with Sidney's best man, a fellow recovering addict, Kieran (Mather Zickel), she just met that morning. Their father, Paul Buchman (Bill Irwin), tries to make everything right by being the perfect host and the perfect dad, but he is on the verge of a breakdown. He is busy feeding everyone, or talking too much, hoping no one will notice just how fragile he is. Fretting is his coping mechanism. Their mother Abby (Debra Winger) copes by being aloof to everyone and everything. Abby must distance herself from her daughters, as they are a painful reminder of their missing dead sibling. Each family member is isolated in their own pain. In the end, Kym recognizes that the only way she can help the family is by leaving them and saving herself. She will return to rehab and get help for herself—but once saved, will she ever return to suburbia?

THE PRIVATE LIVES OF PIPPA LEE (2009)

Cinematographer Declan Quinn (*Rachel Getting Married*, 2008) is once again behind the camera in *The Private Lives of Pippa Lee* (2009). This never-boring, well-acted, and well-directed film is about a modern-day Connecticut "Stepford wife," whose unresolved secret life, and rocky relationship with

The Private Lives of Pippa Lee sees Robin Wright as Pippa Lee, coping with contemporary life in suburbia. Writer/director Rebecca Miller lives with her husband Daniel Day-Lewis on her father Arthur Miller's farm in beautiful Roxbury, Connecticut. Locations include Grove Pond Lane off Krueger Circle in Southbury and Heritage Inn, where cast members Robin Wright and Keanu Reeves stayed while shooting. (Photofest)

her mother, is now causing trouble for her family and marriage. Filmed on location in New Milford, Southbury, Danbury, and Stamford, *The Private Lives of Pippa Lee* explores familiar territory: the dangers of losing one's identity, and the importance of discovering who one is before it's too late.

I chose this film because it examines Connecticut suburbia of both the past and the present, and also reflects on how the past affects the present. Like other Dark Suburbia Redux films, the scenes depicting the past—in this case, the 1960s—editorialize that the self-sacrifice of women being good wives and mothers is neither rewarded nor respected, and eventually leads to pill-taking and/or a crack-up.

The Private Lives of Pippa Lee was written by a Roxbury native, Rebecca Miller, based on her novel of the same title. Miller, a talented writer in her own right, is the daughter of the playwright Arthur Miller (whose film *Everybody Wins* appears in chapter 8). Miller has cited the photographs of William Eggleston, known for his everyday subject matter and refined compositions, as an inspiration for the look of the film, stressing a "realist" versus realistic approach. As in *The Ice Storm* and

Revolutionary Road, reflections once again dominate the frame, representing the loneliness of suburbia, and the duality of the two main characters, the beatific yet mysterious Pippa Lee (Robin Wright) and the soulful and caring Chris (Keanu Reeves).

Pippa Lee begins to look back on her life with regret after her husband, Herb (Alan Arkin), who is thirty years her senior, moves them to the retirement community in Connecticut called Marigold Village (Heritage Village in New Milford). When we first meet Pippa, she is presenting herself as the perfect Stepford wife-hostess. Her demeanor is calm and placid and accepting. She speaks softly and seems to be devoted to her one and only skill of making the perfect butterflied lamb. Having put aside her own needs for the needs of her family—her husband, Herb, a successful and wealthy book publisher, and her twin children, Ben (Ryan McDonald), a lawyer, and Grace (Zoe Kazan), a photojournalist (Miller's mother was photojournalist Inge Morath)—she's pleased that her children outshine her and content to be a wife and nursemaid to a much older man.

Their writer friend Sam Shapiro (Michael Binder) damns her with faint praise, dubbing Pippa "the one true artist's wife left in the modern world." But, trapped in suburbia and surrounded by retirees, Pippa's Stepfordesque facade begins to disintegrate, and she starts to hallucinate about her former life as a wild teen.

We then meet young Pippa (Blake Lively), who left home as a teenager because she couldn't bear watching her Dexedrine-addicted, overachieving mother, Suky (Maria Bello), slowly kill herself. Her aunt Trish (Robin Weigert) takes her in, but then kicks her out after she catches her posing for her girlfriend Kat's (Julianne Moore) pornography photos. On her own in New York City, Pippa falls into the party life existence and becomes more and more self-destructive. This changes when she meets Herb Lee. Herb is fascinated by Pippa, and he offers her a much-needed sense of security. Herb wants a divorce from his wife, Gigi (Monica Bellucci), who then kills herself at the dinner table—an act for which Pippa will always blame herself.

Pippa settles into her new role as a wife, determined to please Herb for "saving" her. Pippa never quite fit into the snobby elitist New York crowd, and though the marriage has lasted, the age difference—he's now eighty, and she's fifty—makes her realize she has settled for half a life, and is merely "willing" herself to be happy. As she explains to her friend and neighbor Sandra Dulles (Winona Ryder), it's not love that holds a marriage together; a woman must "will" it.

Not long after that declaration, Pippa's repressed past lives begin bubbling to the surface. She wakes up realizing she has gone back to smoking and has started sleepwalking. Miller said she wanted Pippa to be a sleepwalker because "her unconscious is moving her." In the Dark Suburbia Redux genre, we have seen characters metaphorically sleepwalking through their lives in *The Ice Storm*, *Far from Heaven*, and *Revolutionary Road*, and now a main character is literally sleepwalking through her life.

Pippa discovers Herb is having an affair with her friend Sandra (Ryder, in a wonderfully wacky performance). She's upset by the betrayal but also sees it as a way out. Pippa loses herself in a sexual relationship with Chris (Keanu Reeves), the troubled young son of her neighbor, Dot Nadeau (Shirley Knight). Chris is adrift and working at a convenience store. (Rebecca Miller fell in love with this convenience store in New Milford, and the owners gave her permission to film there.) Other local locations include Grove Pond Lane off Krueger Circle in Southbury and Heritage Inn, where Wright, Reeves, and Ryder signed autographs while filming.

Chris's ability to see Pippa for who she is—whoever that is—gives her a North Star to head toward. After Herb has a heart attack and dies, Pippa has an opportunity to turn a corner and begin a new life out west with Chris. Pippa's journey of self-discovery is never entirely resolved, but, hey, she does escape Dark Suburbia and gets to go off in a van with Keanu Reeves—so who's complaining?

THOROUGHBREDS (2017)

Something sinister is happening in Connecticut . . . again. *Thoroughbreds* examines the culture of the uber wealthy in Connecticut. It also warns that growing up wealthy, white, and privileged in suburbia might well breed a couple of sociopaths—Dark Suburbia Redux with a dash of Gothic horror. *Thoroughbreds* showcases the talents of a young Anya Taylor-Joy as Lily, a well-bred killer. With her black hair and delicate china doll looks, she was perfectly cast as a murdering suburban teen. Taylor-Joy would go on to star in *The Queen's Gambit* (2020) and *One Night in Soho* (2021).

The story revolves around Lily's overbearing stepfather, Mark (Paul Sparks), who wants to ship her off to an elite boarding school, so she and her childhood friend Amanda (Olivia Cooke) enter into a pact to kill him. At first, Lily and Amanda seem an unlikely pair to pull this off. Lily is an overachieving and spoiled rich girl who has a thick veneer of poise and good breeding. Amanda is the ambivalent outsider with mental health issues. Though she, too, comes from a wealthy family, she's not quite in the same social class as Lily.

As teenagers they had drifted apart, but they are brought back together when Lily is hired by Amanda's mother to tutor Amanda for her upcoming SATs. The tutoring is a pretense. Amanda had earned a reputation as a psycho for euthanizing a wounded racehorse with a knife, so her mother, Karen (Kaili Vernoff), reached out to Lily's mom, Cynthia (Francie Swift), hoping a renewed friendship might help Amanda regain entrée to her social world.

Amanda's millennial philosophy—"Not feeling anything doesn't mean I'm a bad person; it just means that I have to try harder than everyone else to be good"—appeals to Lily, who has her own feelings of ambivalence toward her family and suburbia. Amanda has recognized that she and

Thoroughbreds, writer/director Corey Finley's debut feature, centers on two disaffected teenage girls living in an affluent Connecticut community—Lily and Amanda (Anya Taylor-Joy and Olivia Cooke)—who have murder on their minds. (Photofest)

Lily are more alike than she first thought.

If Amanda seeks to indoctrinate Lily to do bad things, she doesn't have to try very hard, for under Lily's veneer of good breeding is a very bad girl, waiting to be awakened. Lily and Amanda seem to be aware that they are a product of their upbringing, and share the same coldhearted opinion that, if they are bad, it's because suburbia—and growing up wealthy and privileged—made them bad.

Amanda begins a subtle seduction, manipulating and encouraging Lily's suppressed rage toward her stepfather, and soon they are forging a plan to kill him, along with another disaffected teen, a local drug dealer named Tim (Anton Yelchin). The film is interested not so much in condemning their socially privileged lifestyle as it is in providing a road map to get inside of it.

Director Cory Finley hails from St. Louis, not Connecticut, but he graduated from Yale University in New Haven. After college, he found work around the state as a tutor, where he gleaned insights that inspired him to write *Thoroughbreds*. "I could feel the weight of the wealth around me, not just the love in it, but also the violence. At the same time, I also came to really like the kids I was working with, as any good teacher would. They would never knowingly hurt someone; on the other hand, they would never have to. And one day in the future—whenever life finally put something real in their path—some of them might find that apathy was their deadliest asset."

Thoroughbreds is artfully studied, cold-blooded, and stylish. Finley wanted the look to reflect a "pseudo-suburban world." The super-stagy blocking reminds me a little too much of Ingmar Bergman's *Persona* (1967), and cinematographer Lyle Vincent gives it a few too many tracking shots, à la *The Shining* (1980), but the film rests on its slow dance, watching the girls eventually turn on each other, in marvelously fiendish performances by Cooke and Joy.

Like other Dark Suburbia Redux films, it's highly atmospheric. The Georgian brick mansion where most of the action takes place is massive and foreboding. The avant-garde soundtrack by Erik Friedlander is juxtaposed with the actions of two very naughty girls. *Thoroughbreds* embraces the most nihilistic vision of suburbia—the key to happiness, wealth, and success is to feel nothing.

THE LAND OF STEADY HABITS (2018)

The Dark Suburbia Redux genre continues with the small but powerful *The Land of Steady Habits* (2018), a melancholy saga about two families unraveling in suburban Connecticut. It is based on the novel *The Land of Steady Habits* (2015) by Connecticut native, Ted Thompson, who grew up in Westport. Channeling the suburban angst of John Cheever (*The Swimmer*), Thompson also cited William Yates's novel *Revolutionary Road* (1961) as an inspiration. Thompson writes of his protagonist, Anders, that he is "living in an affluent hamlet of Connecticut along the commuter rail line and about to reap the rewards of a sensible life." Deciding he's had enough of "steady habits," he leaves his wife, buys a condo, and waits for his newfound freedom to transform him.

The title refers to a familiar Connecticut nickname made popular in the 1800s. The phrase "the land of steady habits" refers to New Englanders' always reelecting the same state officials and the resulting safe, predictable political stability. Like *The Stepford Wives*' association with Connecticut being Stepford-like, many of the reviews of *The Land of Steady Habits* interpreted the phrase to mean that Connecticut itself, along with anyone who lives in the state, is safe and predictable—that this environment, this imprisonment in suburbia, is what causes Anders to self-destruct. I don't think this interpretation serves this Dark Suburbia Redux film, which is a more personal look at an internal struggle one man is having, about why he can't find happiness in himself, or his environment.

Though the movie was made entirely in Tarrytown, New York, the "wealthy enclave of Westport" (where the central action of the film takes place) was identified in all the press production notes I found.

Anders Hill (Ben Mendelsohn) is in search of some deeper meaning. After walking away

Tragedy will once again destroy a family in the contemporary Dark Suburbia Redux film, *The Land of Steady Habits* (2018), starring Ben Mendelsohn as Anders Hill. A man bent on slow and steady self-destruction, Anders tells one of his lovers, "I couldn't do what I was doing and feel good about myself." Nicole Holofcener directing actor Ben Mendelsohn. (Photos by Alison Cohen Rosa / Courtesy Nicole Holofcener)

from a lucrative job as a "finance guy" in New York and leaving his wife, Helene (Edie Falco), and their large colonial house, he purchases an unassuming condo. He's in a "Now what?" phase. Not wanting to get deeply emotionally involved, he begins a series of sexual relationships with younger women. When he finds he's unable to consummate any of them, his anxiety about aging deepens. His cruelty toward one woman, Barbara (Connie Britton), whom he met at a strip club, makes him rethink his newfound freedom.

When Anders shows up at Helene's annual Christmas party, he realizes that his ex-wife and his former neighbors in suburbia are doing pretty well without him. Helene is dating another middle-aged "finance guy," the affable Donny (Bill Camp); his friends Sophie and Mitchell Ashford (Elizabeth Marvel and Michael Gaston) disapprove of how he is living, and keep their distance. Anders is also alienated from his son, Preston (Thomas Mann), who is aimlessly drifting after graduating from college and completing a stint in rehab for drinking.

Anders soon strikes up a friendship with the Ashfords' troubled teenage son, Charlie (Charlie Tahan). He begins secretly doing drugs with him, perhaps striving for some kind of connection to his own son. When Charlie's parents discover he is using again, they try to ship him off to rehab. Anders continues to get high with him, and doesn't think it's serious enough to let his parents know. Charlie runs away and is later found by Preston, dead of an overdose.

Australian actor Ben Mendelsohn said of his role, "People like watching bad behavior because they can live vicariously through the characters," but because the cause of Anders's angst is never identified, it's hard to root for him. He reveals that his marriage faltered because of a lengthy home renovation; when Helene wanted just one more thing, "a warming oven," he decided to walk out of the marriage. Is this a condemnation of the relationship, or of a wife who preferred an upwardly mobile Westport lifestyle? Or is it Anders himself, feeling like a fraud, playing the role of husband and father, and taking it out on his wife?

Throughout the story Helene comes across as a sympathetic woman who seems genuinely damaged by Anders, while he is unapologetic and attempts to thwart any future happiness for her. As in *The Ice Storm*, the death of a child is a wakeup call. Anders accepts responsibility that he was to blame, but I'm not sure he ever wakes up from sleepwalking through his life, now that he's also been damaged by his reckless actions.

The Land of Steady Habits is the least hopeful of the Dark Suburbia Redux genre. While no one lacks material things, the spiritual things—love, happiness—are unobtainable.

The Horror of Party Beach (1964) never met a gimmick it didn't like. It's a kitchen sink of genres: '60s beach movie, biker flick, and cautionary tale of illegal dumping of radioactive waste. It was directed and co-produced by Del Tenney, and filmed in Stamford. (Photofest)

CHAPTER 13
CREEPY CONNECTICUT

VIOLENT MIDNIGHT (1963)

Filmmaker Delbert "Del" Tenney carved out a niche for himself making a series of successful low-budget horror movies in Stamford, Connecticut, in the 1960s, some of which are now considered cult classics. Del Tenney was Connecticut's own Roger Corman. Corman, too, became famous churning out highly successful, low-budget exploitation and horror films. Like Corman, Tenney was writing, producing, and directing these B pictures—sometimes in less than two weeks—then selling them for a nifty profit. Tenney began his

Violent Midnight premiered in Hartford in 1963. It was later rereleased as *Psychomania* (1964). (Photofest)

career in California doing extra work in films like *Stalag 17* and *The Wild One* (both 1953) before relocating to New York to do theater. It was there he met his future wife and collaborator, Margot Hartman.

The Tenneys' association with Connecticut began when Del and Margot co-wrote (uncredited) and Del co-directed (uncredited) and produced the suspense thriller *Violent Midnight* (1963), shot entirely in Stamford. Margot has a small role in the film playing Lynn Freeman. *Violent Midnight* revolves around a series of slashing murders that take place at a women's college in a small New England town. Tenney got the idea from a notorious case that had occurred while Margot was attending Bennington College in Vermont.

In 1946, eighteen-year-old Paula Jean Welden went missing after going on a hike in the woods. Welden came from a prominent Stamford family, which engaged the Connecticut State Police to find her. Though there was a "person of interest," no one was ever arrested, and Welden's body was never found. Adding to the mystery is the fact that between 1945 and 1950, four additional people vanished from the same area in the woods where Welden disappeared.

Violent Midnight was an ambitious slasher film with a bona fide star, James Farentino, in one of his earliest gigs. The movie also marked the screen debut of Dick Van Patten. Combined with as much nudity as they could get away with in 1963, this made *Violent Midnight* successful.

THE CURSE OF THE LIVING CORPSE (1964)

The Tenneys were on their way, following up *Violent Midnight* with *The Curse of the Living Corpse* (1964). It's another murder mystery that takes place in New England, but this time in 1892. It concerns a man's corpse that comes alive and starts killing his family off one by one. Though again uncredited, it was Del Tenney's wife, Margot Hartman—who also stars in *The Curse of the Living Corpse*—who co-wrote the script with her husband. A producer friend of the Tenneys mentioned that he wanted some horror pictures, and Hartman, herself a writer and later a novelist, thought, "I could do that." Filmmakers often wore many hats on these low-budget B movies, and cinematographer Richard Hilliard, credited with directing and co-writing the earlier *Violent Midnight*, gets a dual credit in *Corpse* as director of photography and production director. Hilliard is credited as the writer, editor, and director of photography for *The Horror of Party Beach* (1964), and went on to have his own career directing exploitation films such as *I, Marquis de Sade* (1967).

The Curse of the Living Corpse is the most successful of Tenney's three horror films made in Connecticut. It marks the screen debut of Roy Scheider (billed as Roy R. Scheider). It was his costar, Candace Hilligoss (*Carnival of Souls*, 1962), who knew Scheider from the theater, who suggested him. Scheider, who became a big star after films like *The French Connection* (1971) and *Jaws* (1975), claimed *The Curse of the Living Corpse* "haunted" him. This may have had something to do with his more-than-haunting demise as the mad son Philip in the muddy "bogs" of Connecticut, drowning in what looks like piles of chocolate pudding.

THE HORROR OF PARTY BEACH (1964)

Twentieth Century Fox flipped for *The Curse of the Living Corpse,* and asked Tenney if he could make another movie as a double bill for the drive-in circuit. *Corpse* was a sophisticated and moody costume picture, but, faced with much less money and very little time, Tenney went for total camp. The result was *The Horror of Party Beach.* Like *Violent Midnight* and *The Curse of the Living Corpse, The Horror of Party Beach* used the grounds of the famed sculptor Gutzon Borglum's estate in Stamford. At the time it was owned by Tenney's father-in-law, Jesse Hartman. Borglum, who died in 1941, is the artist and sculptor best remembered for carving four presidents' faces on Mount Rushmore in South

The radioactive "monsters" wreaking havoc in Stamford in *The Horror of Party Beach* (1964). (Photofest)

The former home of sculptor Gutzon Borglum in Stamford. Borglum's studio was utilized to build the rubber monsters in *The Horror of Party Beach* when Del Tenney and Margot Hartman were living here in the 1960s.

Dakota. Hartman and his wife purchased the property in the early 1900s. The work that Borglum did on Mount Rushmore began in that sculpture studio in Stamford, Connecticut. Now art of a very different kind would be immortalized there. It was in Borglum's art studio that the rubber sea zombie outfits were created.

Originally, the costumes were made for stuntmen, but water made them shrink. The son of the production assistant Ruth Freedman, who was sixteen at the time, was enlisted to play one of the sea monsters when the rubber suit proved to be too small to fit the stuntman. The production also used local teens who jumped at the chance to dance to "Zombie Stomp" by the musical group the Del-Aires at Shippan Point, or become edible snacks to sea zombies in the slumber party scene. Tenney later said, "I think we paid for their lunch or something."

The Curse of the Living Corpse (1964), produced, written, and directed by Del Tenney and filmed in Stamford. It was actress Candace Hilligoss (above) who suggested Roy Scheider, who made his screen debut in the picture. (Photofest)

Del Tenney and wife Margot Hartman backstage at the Hartman Theatre in 1983. Margot was starring in their production of *Absurd Person Singular*. After twelve seasons, the Hartman Theatre closed in 1987.

Part of the charm of *The Horror of Party Beach* is that it fits the bill for the so-bad-it's-good kind of movie. (Fans of *Mystery Science Theater 3000*, the comedy film review TV series created by Joel Hodgson, may recall seeing it on the show.) The sea zombies look, at various times, depending on which rubber suit is being worn, like half-men / half-jellyfish, a rip-off of *The Creature from the Black Lagoon*, a Cobb salad, or a combination of all of the above.

For some biker appeal—another popular trend at the time—Tenney hired the Charter Oaks

Motorcycle Club of Greenwich to add some color. Hiring a motorcycle gang may have been Tenney's undoing. One of the gang members was showing off and caused a serious accident. After that, Tenney said, "They didn't want me to shoot in Stamford anymore." With his new partner, Alan V. Iselin, the Iselin-Tenney Productions horror double bill, which was made for a $120,000 investment, went on to earn $1,000,000 in its initial release on the drive-in circuit. When Tenney was criticized for making such terrible films, he replied, "Listen, I cry all the way to the bank."

Subsequent films of Del Tenney's, such as *Voodoo Bloodbath* (1971), retitled *I Eat Your Skin* when featured on a double bill with *I Drink Your Blood* (1970), did not fare as well, and Tenney and Hartman dropped out of the horror genre. The legacy of the Tenneys in Connecticut goes beyond their B-movie history. Living quietly in Greenwich in 1975, they decided to go back to their theater roots and founded the acclaimed Hartman Theatre, located in Stamford. Del Tenney produced and directed many plays there, while Margot acted and also produced.

Tenney and Hartman's philanthropic and artistic support of a multitude of theaters was widely known throughout the state. In recognition of Hartman's contributions to regional theater, the United Nations Association of Connecticut honored her with its Lifetime Achievement Award and Outstanding Connecticut Woman Award. The Tenneys continued to produce films, including *Clean and Narrow* (2000) and *Descendant* (2003). Del Tenney may not have been as prolific as Roger Corman, but his legacy in the horror genre, and his and Margot Hartman's association with Connecticut, are well worth remembering. And hey, these movies are fun!

LET'S SCARE JESSICA TO DEATH (1971)

Filmed in only twenty-five days, the low-budget independent feature *Let's Scare Jessica to Death* (1971) is truly a classic Connecticut horror film. The Middlesex County locations of Chester, East Haddam, Essex, and Old Saybrook, as well as the Chester Hadlyme Ferry, were a perfect backdrop for a genre known as "folk horror," in which people move from the city to the country, hoping to find peace and quiet, but instead find themselves in the middle of strange happenings—victims of ghouls, ghosts, or blood-sucking vampires. This film has all three.

Let's Scare Jessica to Death has gained in popularity over the years, with both Rod Serling (*The Twilight Zone*) and Stephen King (*The Shining*) singling it out. It's also been cited as a fine example of the "vampire cinema" popular in the 1970s. A 2019 DVD release with commentary by director John Hancock and the film's producer, William Badalato, reveals that fans of the film send Hancock selfies taken where Jessica once stood, or in front of the mysterious Bishop House on the Old Saybrook Turnpike.

As is true of many Connecticut movies I've written about, a house becomes central to the

Emily (Mariclare Costello) is undead, and Jessica (Zorah Lambert) is her next victim in *Let's Scare Jessica to Death* (1971). The scene above was filmed in the attic of the E. E. Dickinson Mansion. Lake scenes were filmed at Pattaconk Reservoir and Jennings Pond in Chester. The actors swam in freezing water, as the scenes at the Pattaconk were filmed in November. Additional scenes were shot on Petticoat Lane in East Haddam. The antique store and chicken coop scenes were filmed in Chester, and locals stepped in to play zombies. (Photofest)

The E. E. Dickinson Mansion in Essex is a private residence. No zombies live here . . . I think.

storyline, but this time the house needed to have a certain personality that would suggest it was haunted. (Boy, did they guess right!) It was Badalato, whose family had a country house in Chester, who suggested the location. He loved the area, and suggested the New England atmosphere would lend itself well to the story. They chose a beautiful white Victorian house atop a hillside, once part of a working farm called Fairview Farm. It would now stand in as Bishop Farm.

The day was overcast when the crew and the actors arrived to start filming, and the house was encased in a thick layer of fog. Rather than wait for the weather to clear, Hancock decided to utilize the fog-enshrouded house as an establishing shot, to be used throughout the film. The fog gave the scene an ominous, unwelcoming feeling. The interiors were shot at another famous house in the area, the E. E. Dickinson Mansion, on North Main Street in Essex, which also housed the cast and crew. Hancock and Badalato stayed at the Old Saybrook Hotel, where they used the swimming pool to shoot inserts of one of the ghostly apparitions rising out of the water.

Let's Scare Jessica to Death begins with the fragile Jessica (Zohra Lampert), who's just been released from a psychiatric hospital, arriving with her husband Duncan (Barton Heyman) and their buddy Woody (Kevin O'Conner) at what she discovers is her new home, a Victorian farmhouse in a small town called Brookfield. Once again, as happened in *The Stepford Wives*, Jessica's demise will be directly caused by her husband's moving her to Connecticut.

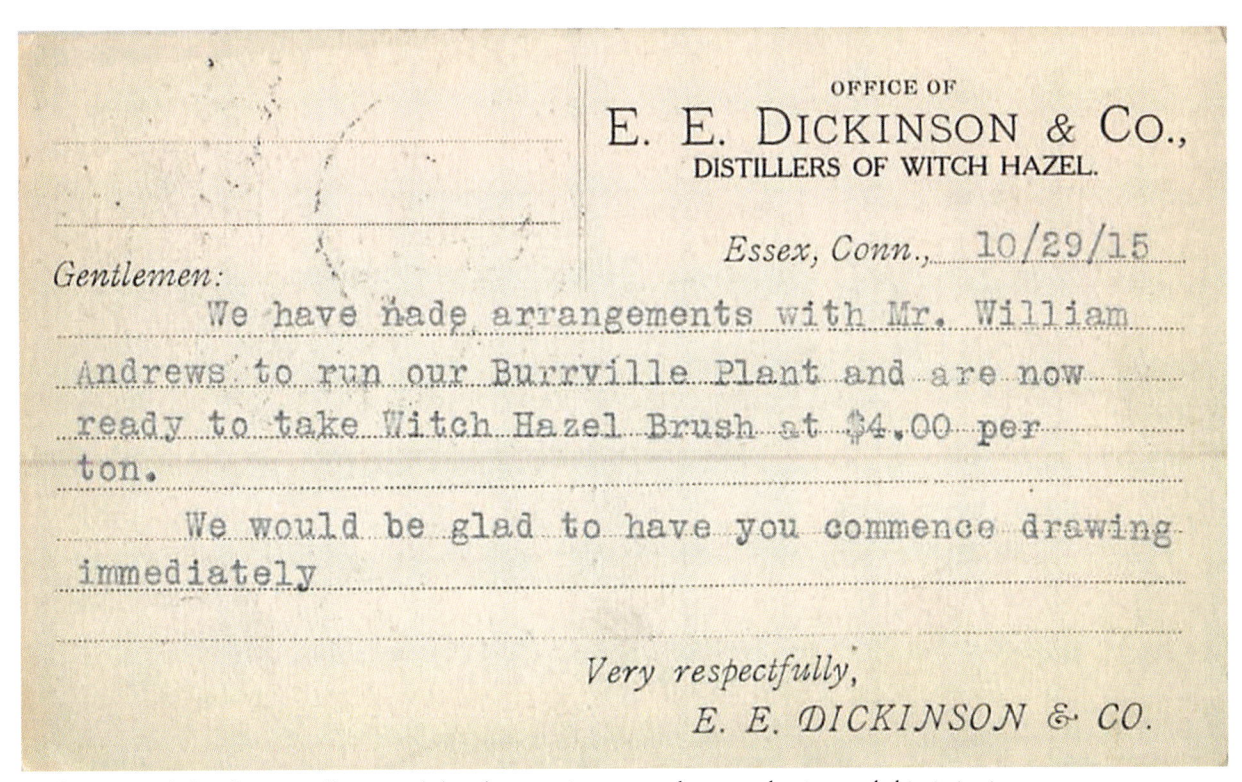

> OFFICE OF
> **E. E. DICKINSON & CO.,**
> DISTILLERS OF WITCH HAZEL.
>
> Essex, Conn., 10/29/15
>
> Gentlemen:
>
> We have made arrangements with Mr. William Andrews to run our Burrville Plant and are now ready to take Witch Hazel Brush at $4.00 per ton.
>
> We would be glad to have you commence drawing immediately
>
> Very respectfully,
> E. E. DICKINSON & CO.

Dickinson made his fortune selling witch hazel, an astringent used to treat bruises and skin irritations.

We learn that Duncan bought the farmhouse while Jessica was in the hospital. While he seems to be happy with his purchase, Jessica immediately senses that it's haunted, but she doesn't want to say anything to Duncan because that would be—well, crazy!

They discover a young, red-headed hippie named Emily (Mariclare Costello) mysteriously living in their house. Emily seems to cast a spell on Jessica, and Jessica invites her to stay. Big mistake. What was supposed to be a restful summer in the country recovering from a nervous breakdown now becomes a battle as Jessica fights off the undead. She can't tell if she's in great danger, surrounded by evil, or if she is sinking back into madness. Jessica hears voices and sees apparitions, such as a mysterious girl in white, beckoning her to run for her life.

When Jessica goes to town to get some eggs, strange men with scars on their necks menace her. Next, she finds a bloody dead body at the bottom of a dam near their house, but when she fetches Duncan to show him the body, it has disappeared. Emily's presence accompanies these strange events. She seems to enjoy tormenting Jessica. When Jessica tries to go for a swim, Emily first tries to push her under the water, and she later attempts to bite Jessica's neck, but Emily waves it off as if she's just kidding. Jessica spends a lot of time convincing people she's not crazy and trying to escape people who are, as is typical of many horror films. Eventually she realizes the only way to survive is to get out of this crazy town.

CONNECTICUT IN THE MOVIES

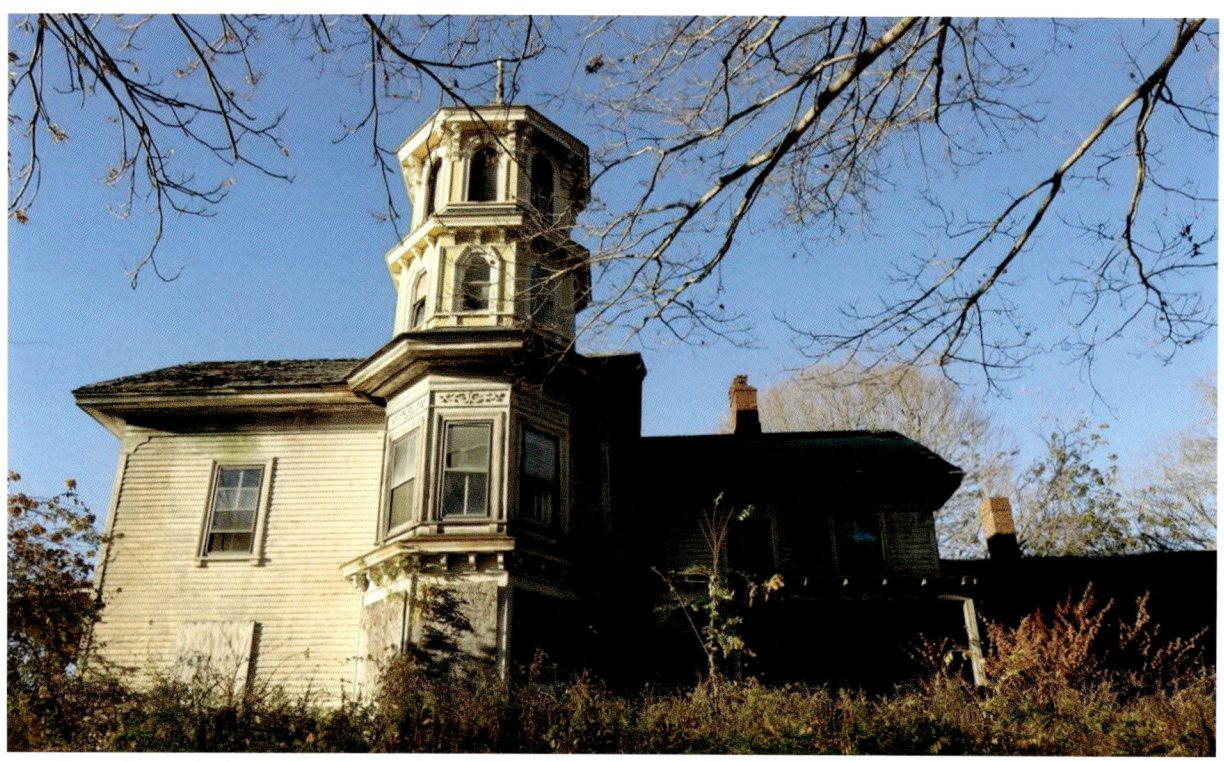

Would you live in the house from *Let's Scare Jessica to Death?* It's for sale. The Victorian house is so famous that a local realtor in Essex created this display for the town's annual Halloween contest.

Let's Scare Jessica to Death began as a horror satire titled *It Drinks Hippie Blood*. It was about a group of hippies who are killed while camping in the woods by a creature living in a lake. When Hancock came on board, he rewrote the script with the intention to "make a movie that was legitimately terrifying." Hancock would go on to direct *Bang the Drum Slowly* (1973) and *Weeds* (1987). In writing the script, Hancock turned to Henry James's gothic novella, *The Turn of the Screw* (1898), for inspiration, as well as Robert Wise's film *The Haunting* (1963) and Hitchcock's *Suspicion* (1941). As a first-time director, he credits the producer Charles Moss, who financed the project (Moss has a cameo as the strange chicken farmer), with knowing what would scare audiences and advising him on adding scenes such as the séance to increase suspense.

Hancock chose the actress Zohra Lampert for the leading role of Jessica, whom he knew from the theater. (She has a small role in *Stanley & Iris*, 1990.) She was not a typical scream-queen type of actress you'd see in a horror movie, which gives the film real credibility. Lampert, who had trained in the Method style of acting, remained "in character" when off-screen, to enhance her on-screen performance, and added little improvisations of her own to the dialogue.

Let's Scare Jessica to Death has been linked with other actresses in films of the era depicting women in distress, such as Carrie Snodgrass in *Diary of a Mad Housewife* (1970), Susannah York in *Images* (1972), and Gena Rowlands in *A Woman Under the Influence* (1974). In all of these films the women experience a break from reality. Jessica says, "Madness or sanity, I don't know which is which." Are ghosts and vampires trying to kill her, or is it all in her mind? As paranoia overtakes her, death becomes an option for ending her nightmare.

The history of the Victorian house known as Fairview Farm, located in a section of Old Saybrook called Obed Heights, has its own mystery. It was built in 1875, and the surrounding land used as a farm by J. B. Newton. There he raised dairy cows, sheep, and chickens and sold the produce at several Hartford markets. In the 1930s, during the Great Depression, he sold the farm to Fred Piontkowski for a mere $1,000.

It is not known what happened to Newton or why he sold the house, but from what I have read, from that point until today, the house has been handed down to various Piontkowski family relatives. They still own the property, which includes 124 acres of land and is currently listed for sale, but no one has lived in the house for many years. Questions about why the house was abandoned have led to many rumors that the property may be haunted. Over the years, interested horror movie fans and historians have visited the property to see if those rumors are true. (Not me!) In the meantime, you can always revisit *Let's Scare Jessica to Death* to get a glimpse of it in its prime.

THE LAST HOUSE ON THE LEFT (1972)

Filmed in part in Westport and Weston in 1971, *The Last House on the Left* (1972), written, edited, and directed by Wes Craven, would launch Craven's legendary career in the horror genre. It was the film's producer, Connecticut native Sean S. Cunningham, who had enlisted Craven and skillfully marketed the sexually graphic and gore-filled saga. Cunningham would go on to produce and direct several horror films himself, but is most famous as the co-creator and director of *Friday the 13th* (1980), written by Victor B. Miller, whom Cunningham met when the writer was living in Stratford. Before *Friday the 13th*, Cunningham and Miller collaborated on a couple of low-budget family films shot around Bridgeport: *Here Come the Tigers* and *Manny's Orphans* (both in 1978).

The Last House on the Left was an exploitation film meant to push the boundaries of the horror genre. It was originally titled *Night of Vengeance*, and Craven intended the violence to be hardcore, but once shooting began, the decision was made to make the film a little more commercial. The final result was still so sickening and depraved that it was banned by many theaters, which only made more people flock to see it.

The story revolves around two teenagers, Mari (Sandra Peabody), on the eve of her seventeenth birthday, and her friend Phyllis (Lucy Grantham), who are on their way to a concert. Unfortunately for them, they run into a gang of strung-out criminals led by Krug Stillo (David Hess, previously known as a songwriter who had written numerous hits for the likes of Andy Williams, Pat Boone, and Elvis Presley). A night of celebration turns to hell. The girls are taken to the woods near Mari's house, tortured, and eventually killed. Later Mari's parents seek re-

Wes Craven, a former professor turned filmmaker, cited Ingmar Bergman's *The Virgin Spring* (1960) as an inspiration for *Last House on the Left* (1972), but I don't recall anyone being sawed in half by a chain saw in *The Virgin Spring*. Actors in the film complained that the violence was at times too real. It was a big hit on the drive-in circuit. The low-budget film, which shot scenes in Westport and Weston, was made for $87,000, but it would go on to make $3.1 million. Craven remade *Last House on the Left* in 2009. (Photofest)

venge on the criminals, killing them in an equally revolting manner.

Shot in a gritty, grindhouse style, *The Last House on the Left* strips the beauty from Connecticut's countryside. The woods are a sinister place where monsters lurk. The trees join forces, becoming witnesses to torture, and the once-peaceful lake becomes filled with blood. These gruesome scenes were shot in the woods of Westport, and the lake sequence was filmed at the town reservoir in Weston.

While filming, the cast and crew stayed with Cunningham at his family's home. I'm picturing family dinners with the cast coming back from the set, drenched in blood, and Sean's mom asking, "And how was your day, dear?"

FRIDAY THE 13TH PART 2 (1981)

The original *Friday the 13th* was filmed entirely in New Jersey, but *Friday the 13th Part 2* (1981), directed by Steve Miner, was filmed in New Preston, Kent, and Waterbury, Connecticut. A documentary about the making of the *Friday the 13th* series, called *Crystal Lake Memories: The Complete History of Friday the*

Connecticut can lay claim to being part of one of the most famous slasher franchises of all time. Producer Sean Cunningham (*Last House on the Left*) founded Crystal Lake Entertainment, named after the lake in *Friday the 13th*. Here, sitting around the fire, Paul (John Furey) retells the story of Jason in *Friday the 13th Part 2* (1981). KenMont and KenWood Camp in Kent was the location for this scene at Camp Crystal Lake. There's a real Crystal Lake located on Crystal Lake Road in Middletown, Connecticut. (Photofest)

13th (2013), gives just that: a complete history of the series. The opening scenes in *Friday the 13th Part 2*, where Ted meets Sandra, are set on Church Street in New Preston. The exterior of Alice's house was shot in Waterbury, but has since been demolished. The counselor training center was filmed on Kenmont Road in Kent, and it too has been demolished.

In *Friday the 13th* (1980), you may remember, young Jason Voorhees drowned at Camp Crystal Lake, which made his mother, Pam Voorhees (Betsy Palmer), lose her head and go on a killing spree. (She loses her head literally at the end of the film!) *Friday the 13th Part 2* (1981) follows a similar storyline, with a crazed stalker once again killing a group of counselors at another summer camp, not very far from Camp Crystal Lake. There are theories that Jason may still be alive, living in the woods and avenging his mother's murder.

An uncut version of the film was recently discovered in 2020 by Scream Factory / Shout! Factory. Some of the highlights (no surprise: this is *not* a family film) include a bloodier version of Alice being killed with an ice pick, a longer, bloodier version of Ralph's death, a policeman being killed with a claw hammer, and, yes, a longer, bloodier version of Scott getting his throat cut. As the first sequel in what became an entire slasher series, *Friday the 13th Part 2* was our initial reminder that Jason is not going anywhere.

MY SOUL TO TAKE (2010)

After *The Last House on the Left* (1972), Wes Craven, along with his partner and producer, Sean S. Cunningham, tried to move away from horror, but he was unsuccessful in getting any film projects off the ground and returned to the genre that would lead to his greatest successes. Subsequent films, such as *The Hills Have Eyes* (1977), and, most notably, *A Nightmare on Elm Street* (1984) and the

Bull's Covered Bridge on Schaghticoke Road in Kent overlooks the Housatonic River. It's a great place to hike and fish. Other shooting locations include Danbury, New Milford, Fairfield, Norwalk, and Tolland High School.

Scream franchise—*Scream* (1996), *Scream 2* (1997), and *Scream 3* (2000)—cemented Craven's reputation as "the master of horror."

Craven returned to the woods of Connecticut to make *My Soul to Take* (2010). The slasher film depicting a "Riverton Ripper" killing teenagers one by one turned out to be one of his less successful horror films. After finishing *Scream 4* (2011), which would turn out to be his final film, Wes Craven confined himself to writing online—first, an active blog, then collaborating on a digital comic book mini-series called *Wes Craven's Coming of Rage* in 2014. In 2015, he died from a brain tumor.

CONNECTICUT IN THE MOVIES

I had the opportunity to meet and eventually work with Craven on 2005's *Cursed*. His quiet demeanor and professorial air reflected his former career as a teacher. *Cursed* was aptly titled, as nothing seemed to go smoothly on the production. Through various reshoots, my part was eventually cut, but I have fond memories of Wes on the Santa Monica Pier, sitting just off camera, his hands cupped next to his face as if imparting some great lesson and whispering at me in a low sinister voice before every take, "Remember . . . you're cuuuurrrrsssed." Wes Craven fans were excited in 2021 to learn that his original unfinished director's cut of *Cursed* was unearthed and may be released in the future.

Having watched the absolutely terrifying *The Last House on the Left*, I turned on every light in the house to prepare for watching *My Soul to Take*, but it turned out to be for naught. The scariest part of the movie was the first ten minutes, which showcases one of my favorite actors, Raúl Esparza, as the madman Abel Plenkov, "the Ripper," going on a killing spree. He dies at the hospital that night and his soul enters seven children, who are born at the same time. We pick up sixteen years later as the teens, who call themselves the Riverton Seven, gather in the woods to celebrate "Ripper Day," hoping to ward off the Ripper's return. Unfortunately for them, they are in a horror movie, so pretty soon the Ripper is killing them off, one by one.

Craven has a knack for combining humor with scares, but *My Soul to Take* is heavy on over-explaining the legend of the Ripper, and lacks both humor and jump-out-of-your-seat moments. In what appears to be a happy mistake for the Connecticut audience, look for the scene filmed at Tolland High School, where the character Alex (John Magaro, also in *The Life Before Her Eyes*) looks up at the sky, sees a condor, and quips to his buddy Bug (Max Thieriot), "Connecticut Condor?" Of course, who can blame him for forgetting the movie takes place in fictional Riverton, Massachusetts. Connecticut has a way of getting in your brain.

The Cayles (Sean Patrick Thomas and Athena Grant) are going to meet some zombies when they move to Connecticut in *Deep in the Darkness*. (Courtesy Colin Theys)

DEEP IN THE DARKNESS (2014)

Connecticut's Moodus Village and the quaint community of Johnsonville are the backdrop for a folk horror tale about a married couple who purchase a country house, only to learn, as the film's synopsis says, "the town's deepest secret: a terrifying and controlling race of creatures that live amongst the darkness in the woods behind [their] home."

Based on a novel by Michael Laimo, *Deep in the Darkness* (2014) shares many Connecticut connections in addition to being shot on location here. Director and producer Colin Theys grew up in Danbury and graduated from Wesleyan University. The film was produced through his independent production company, Synthetic Cinema International, located in Rocky Hill. Although Theys is known for his work in the horror and sci-fi genre, a love he has had since childhood, his other ties to Connecticut cinema include producing and directing a number of the beloved Hallmark Christmas

CONNECTICUT IN THE MOVIES

movies (see chapter 3), including *Rediscovering Christmas* (2019), *A Very Nutty Christmas* (2018), *Christmas at Pemberley Manor* (2018), and *Romance at Reindeer Lodge* (2017). He also produced a host of others, including, most recently, *Sugar Plum Twist* (2021), which was filmed in Norwich and Old Saybrook.

The screenplay for *Deep in the Darkness* is by another Connecticut native, John Doolan, who hails from Waterbury. He and Theys have collaborated on many other films together. This film also marks Dean Stockwell's third and final appearance in a movie connected with Connecticut, after *Gentleman's Agreement* (1947) and *Long Day's Journey into Night* (1962), although here, his gory demise means that he becomes dinner for a bunch of cave-dwelling cannibals.

Dean Stockwell in *Deep in the Darkness*. (Courtesy Colin Theys) Emory Johnson Homestead in Johnsonville (below).

Dr. Michael Cayle (Sean Patrick Thomas), his wife Cristine (Kristen Bush), and their young daughter Jessica (Athena Grant) have just moved to the small town of Ashborough, New Hampshire, where Michael has assumed a former doctor's practice. Things begin to get strange when, after meeting his oh-so-friendly and helpful neighbor Phil Deighton (Dean Stockwell), he comes upon Deighton's disfigured wife Rosy. Phil takes him on a walk in the woods and explains that cave dwellers known as Isolates have lived hidden among the townspeople for centuries, and that they butchered Rosy. They perform ritualistic killings unless the town does what they want . . . and what they want is blood! Geez, and you thought your neighborhood had rules.

Phil and the rest of the town, led by the satanic Lady Zellis (Blanche Baker, daughter of actress Caroll Baker), simply perform blood sacrifices so the Isolates don't kill them. A goat or two will usually keep them at bay. Michael is not going kill anything. He's ready to leave this crazy town, but Cristine, now pregnant with their second child, wants to stay and have her baby de-

296 CREEPY CONNECTICUT

Deep in the Darkness shooting in Johnsonville. (Courtesy Colin Theys)

livered by Lady Zellis, with whom, we will discover, she has made a pact. Michael just can't catch a break. The Isolates kidnap him, forcing him to deliver one of their creatures. (One would think you would need to bill extra for that.)

Phil is sickened after the Isolates kill Rosy, leaving only her eyeballs behind in a Ziploc bag on his bed stand. Michael goes to the cave with Phil to confront them, where he is then forced to kill Phil, whom they quickly devour. Michael manages to fend off the Isolates by injecting them with some bubonic plague he just happened to have lying around in his lab, but just as he is about to get his wife and daughter Jessica (Athena Grant) out of Ashborough, he returns home to find Cristine, with the help of Lady Zellis, delivering their baby. Out of her loins comes, in all its bloody splendor, an Isolate! The film ends with Michael screaming, and the promise of a sequel, but to this day that has not happened.

Some scenes from *Deep in the Darkness* were filmed in what was once called Johnsonville Village, an 1800s mill community located in East Haddam, Connecticut. The surrounding area of Moodus and East Haddam is filled with beautiful and historic buildings and mills. Johnsonville was famous for manufacturing carpet warp and twine. In 1965, Raymond Schmitt purchased the town known as Johnsonville, which included the Neptune Mill, surrounding properties, and the Emory Johnson Homestead. He

CONNECTICUT IN THE MOVIES 297

Moodus, Connecticut, was once called the "Twine Capital of America," with twelve mills in operation. The area around the mills which housed workers was called Johnsonville. The Emory Johnson Homestead in Johnsonville was built in 1842 in the Italianate style. The house was used again for a horror short entitled *Nacht Der Damonen* (2015), directed by Patrick Linberg and written by Linberg and Brendan Pike.

purchased and brought in other vintage buildings, and towed a sternwheeler down the Connecticut River to have it moored at Johnson Pond. Johnsonville became a tourist attraction for years. It was especially picturesque at Christmas. In 1994, after a dispute with the town, Schmitt shuttered his attraction. Schmitt died in 1998 and the buildings were sold off. For many years Johnsonville was abandoned, a ghost town. A church group purchased the properties in recent years, but it is said that there remains one ghost—Raymond Schmitt—who still haunts his former town.

WE NEED TO TALK ABOUT KEVIN (2011)

We Need to Talk About Kevin (2011) is a psychological horror film based on the 2003 novel by Lionel Shriver about a mother coming to terms with her violent son. The setting for the film is an affluent suburb in Stamford.

After a brief but intense courtship with Franklin Plaskett (John C. Reilly), Eva Khatchadourian (Tilda Swinton) finds herself pregnant. They get married and settle into a beautiful country home in

Tilda Swinton and John C. Reilly in *We Need to Talk About Kevin*. Scenes were shot at Cove Marina Mini Golf at 44 Calf Pasture Beach Road in Norwalk, as well as their "dream house." (Photofest)

Stamford, but Connecticut is once again a place where very bad things are about to happen. Their mid-century modern house has lots of glass and looks out on bucolic scenes of nature, but when Eva looks out the window, she has a mother's intuition that something is off with her pregnancy.

Scottish director Lynne Ramsay, who uses images of the ordinariness of perfect suburbia to convey that all is not perfect with Eva and her family. The sets and production design are predominantly flat, with muted colors, set off by occasional bursts of red which foretell the coming bloodletting.

Eva knows for sure something is very wrong with Kevin. He grows into a disturbed and angry young man. Kevin (Ezra Miller) is an extremely introverted and troubled kid whose actions are becoming more and more violent and antisocial. Mother and son share a secret and intense mutual dislike for each other. She tries to tell Franklin of her fears, but he refuses to believe that Kevin is responsible for all the things Eva tells him about; instead, he blames her for simply not loving him enough.

In an attempt to counteract Kevin, Eva decides to have another baby. The angelic little girl, named Celia (Ashley Gerasimovich), proves to be Eva's undoing. To torment Eva, Kevin punishes the girl relentlessly. After Celia is hurt badly at Kevin's hands, Eva decides she and Franklin can no longer live together as man and wife, and she moves out. Kevin eventually goes on a killing spree, targeting first his family, then his classmates. He leaves his mother alive, and she must bear the responsibility for her son's actions.

We Need to Talk About Kevin is an extremely disturbing film because it tries to trace the origins of violence in boys. Was Kevin born as an unreachable, unsalvageable sociopath? Or were there signs that "we needed to talk about Kevin"? Could he have been "fixed," or was he born that way?

After Kevin's school massacre, he is arrested, but he cannot even articulate why he did it. An added layer to the horror is a mother's anguish that a child she bore could grow up to be a monster. Eva lives with the guilt that she might have been able to stop him. The film lets us ponder: Is Eva culpable, or is Kevin just evil? Are parents helplessly waiting for the next "Kevin" to be born, to follow the same path? Or maybe they just shouldn't have moved to Connecticut?

Rachel, Rachel (1968). Joanne Woodward with director and husband Paul Newman. (Photofest)

CHAPTER 14
THE CHANGING LANDSCAPE AND A SEARCH FOR IDENTITY

A variety of films set in Connecticut, starting in the late 1960s and continuing through to the present, have dealt with the subject of identity. Connecticut's search for identity is a complicated affair. Who are we? Are we uptight Puritans, standing in judgment of anyone who is different? Are we folksy New Englanders whose small-town values and common sense transform cynical city dwellers? Are we escaping the rat race and moving to Connecticut? Or are we escaping closed-minded Connecticut? For a small state, we certainly have a lot of identities. The struggle to know, and to accept, who we are is reflected in all of these films.

RACHEL, RACHEL (1968)

Rachel, Rachel (1968), filmed in Danbury, is a woman's coming-of-age story—a tale of sexual awakening and independence in a small Connecticut town. What stands out about *Rachel, Rachel* is that it's a sensitive woman's picture produced and directed by one of the most famous "guy's guys" there is: Paul Newman. What Danbury locals remember most about watching the acting couple, Connecticut's most celebrated residents, filming in their town was Newman's unassuming presence, wearing a beat-up polo shirt and shorts, drinking beer, and walking around barefoot.

Rachel, Rachel has the same laid-back style. A few avant-garde camera angles and fantasy sequences remind you it's the 1960s. Other than those flourishes, however, the film is shot very simply, with a lot of handheld camera work that gives it a quiet sense of intimacy. The New Wave–style ed-

Joanne Woodward in *Rachel, Rachel* (1968). The film began shooting in August of 1967. The gymnasium on Osborne Street in Danbury became a makeshift studio for cast and crew. Other Danbury locations included the Green Hotel and Shababb's Confectionary on Main Street. The pharmacist in the scene with Joanne Woodward was an actual pharmacist in Danbury at the time. The funeral home seen in the film was actually the Bouton Funeral Home in Georgetown, Connecticut. Scenes were also shot at Grassy Plain School in Bethel. (Photofest)

iting is courtesy of Dede Allen. Allen's input was crucial to Newman, who was directing for the first time. She edited *The Hustler* (1961), in which Newman had starred, and later revolutionized film editing with *Bonnie and Clyde* (1967), winning an Academy Award for her work on that film.

Newman kept the focus on Joanne Woodward. He captured a woman not only exploring her sexuality, but owning it. Scenes of a woman pleasuring herself, experiencing her first sexual encounter, or having casual conversations about abortions were not common at the time. The honest—at times provocative—depiction of female sensuality predates the personal films John Cassavetes made with his wife, Gena Rowlands, such as *A Woman Under the Influence* (1974), and Paul Mazursky's collaboration with Jill Clayburgh in *An Unmarried Woman* (1978). *Rachel, Rachel* is so female-driven you have to remind yourself that a man directed the film, and not just any man, but the man who starred in such odes to masculinity as *Hud* (1963), *Cool Hand Luke* (1967), *Butch Cassidy and the Sundance Kid* (1969), and *Slap Shot* (1977).

Not only is *Rachel, Rachel* a character study of a woman, it's also a character study of an artistic partnership: a love letter from a husband to his extraordinarily talented actress-wife. Paul Newman described what it was like to direct Joanne Woodward: "She is sitting on a set and appears to be doing absolutely nothing, but there is something—some strange method that we fellas don't understand. I would be watching her, and I would literally have to turn away from the camera because it would get to me."

Summer plays an important part in *Rachel, Rachel*. As another school year ends, Rachel, a teacher, says good-bye to her students. Her friend and colleague, Calla (Estelle Parsons), celebrates by releasing a caged pet canary through her classroom window. The bird is free. Calla and Rachel are not.

Rachel confides to Calla that she is thirty-five, and "this is my last ascending summer." There are no far-off journeys that will take her away from Manawaka, Connecticut. The only trip she'll take is walking the familiar streets back to the quarters she shares with her mother, May (Kate Harrington), above the funeral parlor business that her father, a mortician, once owned. After he died, they were forced to sell the business to Hector (Frank Corsaro), although he kindly let them stay there. Rachel's mother uses guilt to keep her daughter in servitude, warning her she'll have a heart attack if Rachel ever disobeys her.

Through flashbacks we learn that being the daughter of a mortician has had a profound effect on Rachel's psyche. In one scene, a young Rachel (Nell Potts) watches her father gently bathe and prepare the body of a dead child. She longs for the same loving touch. When her father discovers her there, he is furious, and he carries her outside, admonishing her never to step foot in there again. The trauma of rejection has caused Rachel to remain stuck in childhood, disconnected from the normal thoughts of a grown woman. Rachel fantasizes about morbid scenes of her own death. She daydreams about men, but she stifles any thoughts of real sex, considering herself too unattractive to be touched, or to be an object of desire.

Rachel admits to her friend Calla that she is sleepwalking through life but doesn't know what to do about it. Calla has filled her own loneliness with religion, and urges Rachel to do the same. The idea of two lonely women finding joy in the Lord smacks of desperation, even to Rachel, but for the sake of the friendship she agrees to try it out. On the eve of the revival meeting they plan to attend, she runs into her childhood friend Nick Kazlik (James Olson) at the malt shop, when she's buying a chocolate bar for her mother. Nick, who is also a schoolteacher, has come back to town to help out his elderly parents. He mistakes Rachel's friendly banter for flirting and asks her out on a date. Rachel gets skittish. (Apparently, she's unaware that a sexual revolution is occurring—this was 1967, after all.) When Nick suggests he's "looking for a little action," and "thought you were too," Rachel

Joanne Woodward, James Olson, and Paul Newman, on the set of *Rachel, Rachel*. Woodward discovered the novel *A Jest of God* by Canadian author Margaret Laurence and brought it to her husband, Paul Newman, to direct. The screenplay was adapted by Stewart Stern. Stern's screen credits include *Rebel Without a Cause* (1955) and *Sybil* (1976). He relocated the story to Connecticut to accommodate the Newmans. Newman chose Danbury to stand in for the fictional Manawaka, partly for its rural atmosphere, but mostly because it was an easy commute from their home in Westport. Shooting in their backyard also meant there was no studio interference from Warner Bros., who gave them a relatively small budget of $780,000. Newman would employ the same method on his second collaboration with Woodward, shooting *The Effect of Gamma Rays on Man-in-the-Moon Marigolds* (1972) in Bridgeport because it was only seventeen minutes from their home in Westport. Both films costarred their daughter, Nell Potts. She appears as young Rachel in *Rachel, Rachel*. Her blue eyes are unmistakable. (Photofest)

stammers that she already has plans for the evening.

Those plans also take an eventful turn. The revival meeting run by Reverend Wood (Geraldine Fitzgerald) is, as Rachel expected, filled with lonely hearts and fellow spinsters, but it offers a decidedly 1960s version of an EST awareness vibe. As fellow parishioners surround and touch her, a rush of emotion and desire floods her body, and she screams out, "Love me!" She goes outside to regain her composure and Calla runs after her, to try to comfort her.

Calla's caresses turn sexual, and she begins kissing Rachel, revealing her true feelings for her. Rachel at first lets herself be kissed, but then dramatically pushes her away. The women stand apart, looking at each other, awkward and exposed. Calla had previously chided Rachel for her lack of courage by saying, "Every time we go for ice cream, you only order vanilla," but now that she has revealed she's gay, she is terrified Rachel will no longer want to be her friend. Estelle Parsons, fresh off her Oscar win in *Bonnie and Clyde*, is superb here.

Rachel, Rachel shows the damage that can be done not only by repressing your sexuality, but also by keeping your sexuality a secret. Calla's fears are realized when Rachel does run off, and after that night, keeps her distance from her.

It's midsummer, and with her friendship with Calla now at loose ends, Rachel takes a long walk in the woods, contemplating what to do next. The Connecticut landscape gives us time to breathe and reflect along with Rachel. She walks through the fields, picking wildflowers. The montage also accentuates Rachel's connection to nature, to being a living, breathing thing.

A small miracle awaits her. When she comes out of the woods, she finds herself right in front of Nick's parents' farm. When Nick again asks her on a date, this time she accepts. He takes her to a movie, but is barely interested in the film. He finishes a beer he snuck in, asks her if she wants to "go somewhere," and Rachel nods.

After they leave the theater, Nick drives Rachel to the edge of town. He lays out a blanket, takes off his clothes, and waits for Rachel to do the same. There is a resoluteness to Rachel as she prepares for her first sexual encounter, which plays out like a bad prom night experience. She tries to share with Nick that she is a virgin, but he doesn't realize, or even care. The lonely sound of a passing train's whistle is all that marks the occasion for her. After that, Nick invites her to "play house," as his parents are away for the weekend. She has a vague hope the relationship will last and tells Nick she loves him, but that scares him. Nick lies to her, saying he's married, and then leaves for New York without even telling her.

Rachel is disappointed but somehow not crushed. The experience has made her grow up a bit. She suddenly sees a world of options and possibilities; she may even be pregnant. She musters the courage to call on Calla to share her news. They discuss her options: to have the baby or obtain an abortion. Rachel is pleased, saying, "I never thought anything alive could grow in me." A trip to the doctor reveals Rachel is not pregnant—it's just a cyst—but the experience has put into motion the idea of change.

Calla secures a teaching post in Oregon for Rachel, which Calla calls the first decision she's ever made that shows respect for herself. Rachel's last ascending summer has come to an end, and she must say good-bye not only to Manawaka, but to her friend, as well. It's bittersweet. Calla, although happy for Rachel, still can't feel free to be her true self. Rachel admits, "I will be afraid always." And then, like the caged canary at the beginning of the story, she spreads her wings and flies.

Grace, the character Woodward plays in *Rally 'Round the Flag, Boys!* (1958) (see chapter 5), is the polar opposite of the woman she would portray in *Rachel, Rachel*. After winning an Academy Award in 1957 for *The Three Faces of Eve*, Woodward had been stuck playing what she called a string of vapid glamour girls. *Rachel, Rachel* was made during the women's liberation movement and spoke to women who were demanding to be seen and heard and felt. It represented the shift in cinema away from glamour girls and happy housewives who seemingly had no inner emotional lives. *Rachel, Rachel* became a surprise hit and was nominated for Best Picture, Best Actress for Woodward, Best Supporting Actress for Estelle Parsons, Best Screenplay for Stewart Stern, and Best Director for Newman. Newman *did* receive the New York Film Critics Circle Award for directing.

ONE SUMMER LOVE (1976)

Director Gilbert Cates was not afraid to tackle serious subjects. In his first film, he took on the topic of aging with *I Never Sang for My Father* (1970). In *Summer Wishes, Winter Dreams* (1973), a mother comes to terms with her son's homosexuality. His third film, *One Summer Love* (1976), was a low-budget film made entirely on location in Connecticut that dealt with mental health in an era when there were few options for patients recently released from mental institutions.

A young adult, Jesse (Beau Bridges), returns to his hometown in Danbury after being institutionalized since he was a child. The circumstances of his being committed are murky, and he wants to try to get his family to explain just why he was put there. Soon after his release, though, he discovers he is not equipped to deal with the outside world. The traumas he has suffered revisit, and he begins to act out, fearing he will once again be committed.

When he meets the free-spirited Chloe (Susan Sarandon), who works at a movie theater, there is a hope that he can put the past behind him and heal. Chloe loves him unconditionally; she's a little kooky herself, and she truly wants to help him, but his emotional outbursts, the result of being committed in a mental institution against his will, are wounds that can't be healed by love, and keep them from having a real future. It is through their love affair, however, that Jesse begins to come

Susan Sarandon as Chloe tries to help Jesse (Beau Bridges) deal with mental health issues in *One Summer Love* (1976). Some of the notable Danbury locations in *One Summer Love* (1976) include the Palace Theatre, the Danbury Public Library, and the Danbury Railyard (now the Danbury Railway Museum). (Photofest)

to terms with his past and recognize his mental illness. Chloe accepts Jesse, but he cannot yet accept himself. Jesse is a lost soul; without help from a doctor, or his family, we can only hope the fragile love between Jesse and Chloe will survive.

This sensitive drama was a surprise from AIP (American International Pictures), known for releasing the exploitation films of Roger Corman. *One Summer Love* (also known as *Dragonfly*) showcases a young Susan Sarandon in one of the quirky Earth Mother roles for which she would become famous. Beau Bridges (son of Lloyd, and brother to actor Jeff Bridges) began his career as a child actor. *The Landlord* (1970) was one of his first leading roles as an adult; *One Summer Love*, which came out not long after, is rarely even mentioned in his body of work. He has always chosen interesting films and roles, and his performance, along with glimpses of Danbury, are worth a second look.

CONNECTICUT IN THE MOVIES

WHEN EVERY DAY WAS THE FOURTH OF JULY (1978)

Dan Curtis drew from his own Bridgeport childhood when he wrote, produced, and directed *When Every Day Was the Fourth of July* (1978), starring Dean Jones. Curtis hoped this story of the lessons learned when a young girl befriends a troubled war vet in 1930s Bridgeport would serve as a possible pilot for a TV series, but it was not picked up. The storyline is similar to the plot of *To Kill a Mockingbird*, with a principled lawyer (Jones) accepting a case to defend a man wrongly accused of a crime. This was a heavy dramatic role for Jones, known for his work in Disney comedy classics such as *That Darn Cat* (1965) and *The Love Bug* (1968). Jones was also in the original Broadway cast of the Stephen Sondheim musical, *Company*. Dan Curtis later produced and directed a sequel, *The Long Days of Summer* (1980), which also starred Dean Jones.

When Every Day Was the Fourth of July was a film way ahead of its time. The subject matter of traumatic brain injuries and veterans' disabilities was highly unusual, and seldom even discussed. Curtis opens the film with narration: "It seems as if a thousand summers have come and gone since then . . . [It was] a time of innocence and adventure, when life was yet to be lived, and every day was the Fourth of July."

Nine-year-old Sarah Cooper (Katy Kurtzman) is a tomboy who knocks about with the boys. She gets upset when the local kids tease a mentally challenged war vet, Albert Cavanaugh (Geoffrey Lewis), by calling him "Snowman." She doesn't

Bridgeport native Dan Curtis was associated primarily with the horror genre when he made *When Every Day Was the Fourth of July* (1978). He was the creator, executive producer, and occasional director of the gothic pop culture cult TV series *Dark Shadows* (1966–1971). He also directed two feature film versions of his show, *House of Dark Shadows* and *Night of Dark Shadows*, as well as the classic horror film *Burnt Offerings* (1976).

know that he is suffering from a brain injury. Although Snowman keeps to himself, he is known as the town weirdo. Prolific character actor Geoffrey Lewis began his career in television and was later known for his costarring roles with Clint Eastwood (*High Plains Drifter*, 1973; *Every Which Way But Loose*, 1978; *Pink Cadillac*, 1989). He was also the father of actress Juliette Lewis (*Cape Fear*, 1991).

When a local druggist, Mr. Najarian (Michael Pataki), is found killed, Snowman becomes a likely suspect. Sarah wants her father, Ed Cooper (Dean Jones), a high-profile lawyer, to defend Albert. Ed has taught Sarah to stand up for what she believes in, so he is compelled to take the case, even though he is certain he will lose because of the town's prejudice against Albert.

During the trial in Fairfield, a psychiatrist explains to the jury that Albert suffers from passive resignation, the result of a brain injury, and couldn't possibly kill anyone. A motive is established by prosecutor Joseph Antonelli (Harris Yulin) when Albert is connected to an anarchist group he may have unknowingly joined. Sarah tries to help Albert, but her testimony backfires and Albert is found guilty. Then Mrs. Najarian (Ronnie Claire Edwards) steps forward, revealing that her husband was a bookmaker, and implicating Officer Doyle (Scott Brady) as the real killer. Albert is released in time to celebrate the Fourth of July and is reunited with Sarah and the other children, who have gained a newfound understanding of Albert's mental illness.

PROMISES IN THE DARK (1979)

A doctor must decide whether to honor her sacred oath to save lives or a secret promise to let a patient die with dignity. Dr. Alexandra Kendall (Marsha Mason) takes an assignment in West Hartford to work under Dr. Walter McInerny (Donald Moffat) at his clinic. The hospital scenes were shot at Manchester Memorial Hospital in Manchester, Connecticut, and doctors within the hospital appeared on camera in supporting roles.

Just getting over a divorce, Dr. Kendall decides to immerse herself in her work, putting off advances from Dr. Jim Sandman (Michael Brandon). While McInerny is out of town, a seventeen-year-old girl named Buffy (Kathleen Beller) comes in with a simple leg fracture. Kendall thinks there is something more to the injury. After ordering tests and X-rays, they learn Buffy has a malignant tumor in her leg. Buffy's parents, Fran and Bud (Susan Clark and Ned Beatty), are caught off guard by the diagnosis, having been so busy working that they have spent little time with Buffy. She's not resentful, but they aren't close.

Fran has a difficult time accepting what is happening to her daughter, and thinks somehow that "happy thoughts" can save her. Bud shuts down from grief and just can't face talking about Buffy's prognosis with Fran. Buffy is scared and needs someone to be honest with her. Dr. Kendall becomes more than a doctor to her; she becomes a mother figure, and an ally in her care.

Buffy's leg is amputated to stave off the disease. Dr. Kendall, who is perceived by her coworker, Dr. Sandman, as having a hardened exterior, is devastated when she learns that Buffy's cancer, even with the amputation, has begun to spread, and is terminal. At night she goes back to her apartment and breaks down in tears. McInerny warns her not to become so personally and emotionally involved, but it's too late. Her heart cries out for Buffy, and she does everything she can to be with her, even though she knows it is hopeless. Buffy's friends do their best to rally around her, but she begins to separate herself from them. They are alive, after all, and she must prepare for death.

Marsha Mason is a recently divorced doctor starting over in Hartford in *Promises in the Dark* (1979). Kathleen Beller plays her patient, Buffy, who is battling cancer.

Buffy even tells her boyfriend Gerry (Paul Clemens) to go away and not come back. It is only to Dr. Kendall she tearfully explains that not being able to consummate their love is too much for her to bear. This hits home with Kendall, who has been unable to be intimate with Jim because she's not over the painful breakup of her marriage. She realizes how lucky she is to be alive, and she and Jim begin a relationship in earnest.

Buffy pleads with Dr. Kendall to promise that if she ever goes into a coma, Dr. Kendall will not let her lie in a vegetative state—that she will terminate her life support. Despite the wishes of Buffy's parents, Kendall secretly keeps that promise.

GOOD FENCES (2003)

As a cinematographer, Ernest Dickerson might be best known for his frequent collaborations with Spike Lee (*She's Gotta Have It*, 1986; *Do the Right Thing*, 1989). He transitioned to directing in 1990, and Showtime's *Good Fences* (2003) was one of his earliest major directorial efforts. Since then, Dickerson has gone on to great acclaim in television series such as *The Wire*, *Dexter*, and *House of Cards*.

Good Fences is a about a different, more challenging search for identity. It's a thought-provoking and very dark comedy about an upwardly mobile Black family that moves to Hamden, Connecticut, in the 1970s. *Good Fences* would have benefited by being made in Connecticut, since it's where the novel and film are set, but it was made entirely in Toronto, Ontario, Canada. It's a period film, and while the clothing is accurate, some of the production elements meant to reflect Connecticut suburbia are lacking. That being said, I would watch Whoopi Goldberg in pretty much anything, and she and Danny Glover—reunited here nearly two decades after *The Color Purple* (1985)—work very well together.

Tom Spader (Danny Glover) wants to move his family to Connecticut, hoping to give them a step up in life. He's an attorney who has worked much harder for his success than his white counterparts at a law firm. After getting a high-profile case, he's able to move his family to the affluent white suburb of Greenwich. Tom begins pressuring his wife, Mabel (Whoopi Goldberg), to acclimate, but she struggles to find an identity of her own in bland suburbia. She's conflicted about being herself, embracing her own roots as a Black woman, or assimilating into what Tom wants her to be.

Some of my favorite moments are watching Mabel after she has moved to Connecticut and is trying to fit in with her stuffy neighbors. Whoopi has a wonderful way of telegraphing her discomfort. I think we've all been in that situation where we're meeting people for the first time and thinking, who are these Martians? As the housewives discuss how great life in suburbia is, Mabel almost turns her face to the camera as if to ask us, you see what I'm seeing, right?

Things change when another Black family, headed by the audacious Ruth Crisp (Mo'Nique), a recent lottery jackpot winner, moves in next door. Ruth is loud and proud, and Mabel is happy she will have a friend with whom she can be herself. Tom is not happy, though, feeling Ruth and her family are not the "right" kind of Black family. He fears that this "ghetto invasion" will have a negative effect on how he and his family are perceived by their white neighbors.

Tom instructs Mabel not to have anything to do with Ruth. At first Mabel agrees, confiding in her best friend, "As long as I trust in Tom, I'll be fine." It's painful for Mabel to reject Ruth; she knows she has hurt her friend deeply. Tom's desire to make it, as he says, "in a white man's world," eventually leads him and his family into madness.

THE LIFE BEFORE HER EYES (2007)

Though this film (released in 2007) is about an event like the 1999 Columbine school shooting, which occurred long before the deadly Sandy Hook shooting in 2012, it's hard not to also associate it with the tragic events that occurred there, as the film is set in Connecticut.

The focus of *The Life Before Her Eyes* is not the school shooting itself, but the story of how a young girl's life would have turned out if she had survived. The central concept is that it's a fantasy—a wish made by a sixteen-year-old girl in the final moments she is alive as a student at Briar Hill School. (The filming location was the Mauro-Sheridan Interdistrict Magnet School in New Haven.)

Diana (Evan Rachel Wood) is rebellious and neglectful of her schoolwork but trying to turn her life around. She finds solace and friendship with her best friend, Maureen (Eva Amurri), who is deeply religious. The girls have different personalities—Diana is a bad girl, Maureen is good—but they share a bond: They both dream of escaping their working-class mothers' lives. They live in a run-down section of town in fictional Briar Hill, Connecticut. (Locations here include New Haven and a great walk-by at the Palace Theatre in Stamford.)

Evan Rachel Wood is an actress who possesses immense power and presence and is able to go to very dark places and make it seem effortless.

The Life Before Her Eyes (2007), a thought-provoking film starring Uma Thurman as a survivor of a school shooting. (Photofest)

312   THE CHANGING LANDSCAPE AND A SEARCH FOR IDENTITY

Here she portrays a girl we would like to watch grow up and achieve her dream of becoming a teacher, or having a country house with a porch, or growing old with Maureen. In the final days of school, while in the girls' washroom, Diana and Maureen are confronted by a school shooter, Michael (John Magaro), in the midst of a mass shooting. He forces the best friends to choose which one of them he is going to kill. In that fleeting minute both girls relive the highlights of their past few months together. One of the girls does not survive, but you don't know which one it is until the end of the film.

The film shifts fifteen years into the future, to the anniversary of the school shooting. Grown-up Diana (Uma Thurman) has a seemingly perfect life but suffers from survivor's guilt. She stayed in town and married a professor, has a beautiful child, and became a teacher. She's even fulfilled her dream of having a house with a porch.

St. Basil's Ukrainian Catholic Seminary at 195 Glenbrook Road in Stamford provides a spooky gothic backdrop in the present-day scenes, but it's not until the final moments of the film that we realize it's Diana who sacrificed her life—which she didn't think was worth much—so Maureen could live. *The Life Before Her Eyes* forces the viewer to examine the random cruelty of one child's survival over another's.

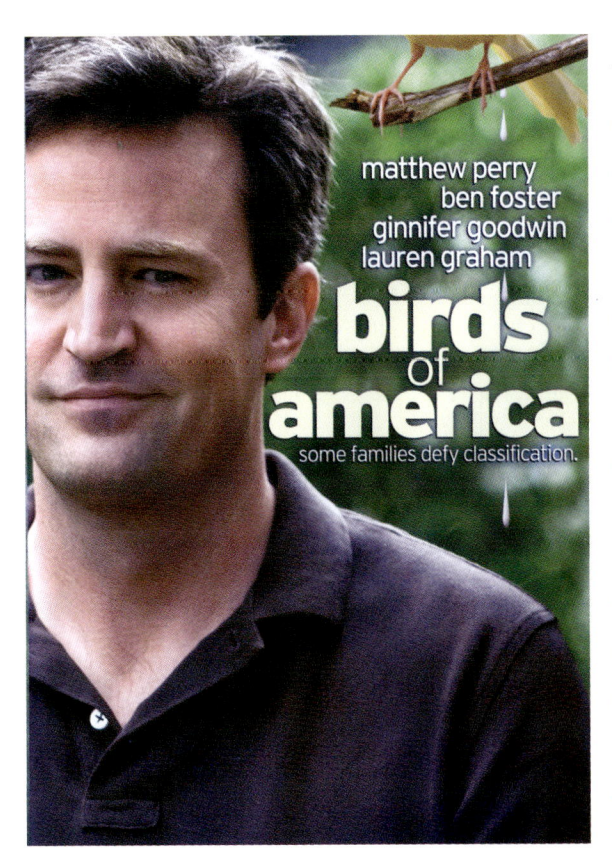

BIRDS OF AMERICA (2008)

Three siblings who have drifted apart search for meaning in their lives after returning to their childhood home in Norwalk, Connecticut. Morrie (Matthew Perry) has emotionally and psychically shut down after his eccentric father committed suicide and his mother died of cancer. Still living in his family's ramshackle Victorian house, he has tenure as a schoolteacher and a plan for his future, but that plan is upended when his siblings, Jay (Ben Foster) and Ida (Ginnifer Goodwin), arrive unexpectedly and move in with him and his wife, Betty (Lauren Graham). Betty wants them out, but Morrie hopes that having them there will bring healing to all three.

Jay is the colorful hippie brother. He has dealt with his grief in his own way—he tries to

CONNECTICUT IN THE MOVIES

break down people's boundaries. His exterior "be cool" attitude hides a lot of sadness. Ida acts out sexually and drinks too much. She claims she is living life to the fullest, but this has led her down a dark path. She looks up an old boyfriend who is now married and tries to entice him into getting involved with her.

Jay's antics finally cross the line, and Morrie must decide which comes first—his teaching career, or his family. While Morrie's brother and sister bring chaos to his life, he realizes they also bring him happiness. He comes to terms with his father's death, and accepts his life with all of its flaws.

THE BIG BAD SWIM (2006)

The Big Bad Swim (2007), filmed in Uncasville, Old Lyme, and Groton.

In a small Connecticut town, a group of unlikely strangers gets to know each other during a weekly adult swim class. The swimming scenes in *The Big Bad Swim* (2006) were filmed at the Charles B. Luce Field House at Connecticut College.

The adults come from all walks of life and social spheres and are all going through big emotional shifts in their lives. Amy (Paget Brewster) is a math teacher at Old Lyme High School. She is going through a divorce and trying to regain her confidence about the dating scene. Jordan (Jess Weixler) is working as a stripper—at a club that's now the Mynx Cabaret in Groton—and part-time dealer at Mohegan Sun in Uncasville (with lots of scenes inside the casino). Even their swim instructor has issues. Noah (Jeff Branson) is trying to overcome depression since missing an opportunity to compete in the Olympics as a diver.

As the group faces their fears about learning how to swim, they conquer other fears that may be holding them back in life. Amy gets a second chance at romance, and even though the relationship ends, she reclaims her identity as a vital, sexy, older woman . . . who can now swim!

PEEPLES (2013)

Craig Robinson and Kerry Washington shooting *Peeples* in Greenwich. Scenes were also filmed in Rowayton, Connecticut.

Peeples is a sweet little fish-out-of-water comedy that showcases the talented Craig Robinson as Wade Walker, a children's entertainer trying to get up the nerve to propose to his wealthy and upwardly mobile girlfriend, Grace (Kerry Washington). After visiting Grace at her family's mansion in Sag Harbor (this house is located in Greenwich), and witnessing her lavish lifestyle, he gets cold feet. Grace's parents, especially her uptight father, Judge Virgil Peeples (David Alan Grier), disapprove of Wade. He's not the "right" type of man for Grace. Wade gets in one awkward situation after another, and even Grace begins to have doubts that he will fit in.

Grace has to decide if she will stand up to her overprotective father or lose Wade. The likability and talent of the cast (including a cameo by Diahann Carroll) help carry the thin *Meet the Parents*–type premise. The comedy set pieces rest on the shoulders of two gifted comic actors. Craig

Robinson's ability to combine vulnerability and humor is always appealing. He's able to mine laughs with things that have nothing to do with the story, such as a dead-on Michael Jackson "Thriller" dance and amazing piano riffs. David Alan Grier's sheer commitment to making the viewer laugh eventually succeeds because he's just so enjoyable to watch. In the end, Judge Virgil comes to accept Wade for who he is, once Wade accepts himself.

HELLO I MUST BE GOING (2012)

After a big Sundance Film Festival premiere, *Hello I Must Be Going* somehow got lost, and it really deserves a second look. The awkward mother–daughter relationship of Blythe Danner (*I'll See You in my Dreams*, 2015) and Melanie Lynskey (*Yellowjackets*, 2021), and their journey toward a newfound understanding of each other, is deeply touching.

Hello I Must Be Going (2012) was written by a Westport native, Sarah Koskoff, the daughter of Michael Koskoff, co-writer of *Marshall* (2014) (see chapter 11). In an interview in *Connecticut* magazine in 2012, Koskoff said she and her husband, director Todd Louiso, wanted to shoot the film in Westport because, having grown up there, she had certain locations in mind. She observed, "Westport is a very stratified world, and there is an emphasis on status. You grow up here and you have a conception of the world that isn't accurate. So, it has the right feeling of upper-class containment I wanted, but it's also ultra-sophisticated, too." Koskoff felt the Westport setting "added to [Amy] feeling trapped. She was in a place that's so beautiful, but when you're that depressed, you really can't appreciate it."

Thirty-something Amy (Melanie Lynskey) is taking time to reflect and reexamine her life after her husband, David (Dan Futterman), a successful Wall Street trader, has dumped her. Feeling like she's had the rug pulled out from under her and looking for stability, she moves back in with her parents, empty nesters living in upscale Westport.

Amy has mixed feelings about being

Hello I Must Be Going (2021) marks Melanie Lynskey's second time filming in Connecticut, after briefly appearing in *Away We Go* (2009), which was shot in New Haven.

back home. On a date, she sarcastically says about Westport's penchant for quaintness, "There's even a quaint little inn so people from New York can experience quaintness for $500 a night." Amy's attitude is the opposite of that of her parents, Ruth and Stan (Blythe Danner and John Rubinstein), who thrive in Connecticut. They live comfortably, in an ultramodern house that Ruth endlessly redecorates. Ruth is more interested in her expensive designer lamps, and is too self-involved to notice that Amy is in a major depression. Her priorities revolve around money, appearances, and Stan's early retirement, so they can go on an around-the-world cruise. Ruth pushes her husband to succeed while her own ambitions remain stifled so they can maintain an affluent lifestyle in Westport, and this has left her bitter and anxious.

You get the feeling that Ruth doesn't really like Amy, or thinks she's just got the blues. Really, it's because Amy's return shifts the focus off of Ruth. She fears that Amy coming home to try to figure out her vocation might mean putting her own dreams on hold once again.

Amy is a dabbler. She has drifted since college. She was once a literature major; now she is trying her hand at photography. Will this take, or will she find a new hobby to dabble in? Her one enjoyment comes from watching old Marx Brothers movies—hence the title *Hello I Must be Going*, from a song made famous by Groucho Marx in *Animal Crackers* (1930). Other than that, she spends her time sleeping, feeling like a failure, unable to cope with her newfound reality.

Looking for some kind of connection, Amy begins an affair with the nineteen-year-old son of one of her father's colleagues, Jeremy (Christopher Abbott), a handsome budding actor. Despite their big age difference, they share an emotional connection because neither has been brave enough to pursue what they want out of life. Though she is the adult in the relationship, Jeremy accuses her of being a child and a coward for abruptly breaking it off with him after they are discovered by the parents.

"Where the fuck is 'bottom'?" Amy asks herself, but it's through her relationship with Jeremy that Amy regains a belief in herself. When Stan backs out of his retirement, and the cruise, Ruth is heartbroken, but Amy, having gained new insight into her mother, decides to go in his place so mother and daughter can finally get to know each other.

HOPE SPRINGS (2012)

Change is hard, and it's even harder for old dogs. In addition to glimpses of the seaside community of Stonington, *Hope Springs* (2012) is worth watching because of the unforgettable performances of two veteran actors, Meryl Streep and Tommy Lee Jones, as an older married couple, Kay and Arnold Soames, trying to find their way back to intimacy after thirty years of marriage. These two Oscar-winning actors are not afraid to veer into extreme vulnerability to play the truth of the scene, and the result is some brave and beautiful stuff. This seldom-seen film also benefits from the romantic Stonington setting, where the "Maine" scenes were all shot.

The story follows an older woman, Kay, who feels she has lost her identity now that her children are grown. She feels unattractive to her husband; they barely speak over dinner, and he falls asleep in front of the TV. One day Kay reads about a crash course in couples therapy with a marriage guru, Dr. Bernie Feld (Steve Carrell), held in "Great Hope Springs," Maine. Hoping it will be like a second honeymoon, she pushes Arnold to attend, but he balks at the idea. Hurt, Kay decides to go on her own, and Arnold grudgingly follows her.

Meryl Streep and Tommy Lee Jones in *Hope Springs*, in Stonington, Connecticut. Stonington was an easy trek for Meryl Streep, who has been a resident of Salisbury for many years. Streep attended Yale School of Drama in New Haven. (Photofest)

Once there, neither of them can relax, and it is anything but romantic. Old resentments arise, and they discover it might be harder to reconnect than they first thought. Kay is on the brink of leaving the marriage when Arnold, broken down by one of the emotional exercises, is finally able to understand why he has become so distant. They leave the weekend with a better understanding of each other and a commitment to make their marriage stronger.

Streep and Jones were longtime fans of each other's work, and director David Frankel joked that Streep was always pushing Jones to "steal every scene." The best line in *Hope Springs* is when Jones quips, in reference to the quaintness of the inn where they are staying, "Is there a building in this place that does not have shutters? The whole town looks like it was built by Hansel and Gretel." He's referring to the Inn at Stonington, called "Captain Jack's Inn" in the movie. Streep and Jones later dine at Noah's Restaurant, which for the movie became the Nor'easter Diner. A large mural of two lobsters painted on the side of the building for shooting remains there today.

AND SO IT GOES (2014)

And So It Goes (2014) has three things going for it: Michael Douglas, Diane Keaton, and Connecticut. It features the seaside community of Black Rock in Bridgeport and a whole lot of Lake Compounce in Bristol. (The latter is "the oldest operating amusement park in North America.")

Oren Little (Michael Douglas) plays a high-profile Fairfield realtor about to retire. He needs to sell his Southport mansion so he can downsize in style at his beachside cottage fourplex in Black Rock—a gentrified section of Bridgeport—close to but on the other side of (and less pricey) than Southport. Oren is a widower who just wants to be left alone, but his plans are interrupted when his son goes to prison on a drug charge, and he's forced to watch over his granddaughter, Sarah (Sterling Jerins), until her father gets out. At his cottage, his bothersome—and yes, very quirky—neighbor Leah (Diane Keaton) offers to babysit young Sarah. Though their personalities clash—he's high-class, she's boho—you guessed it, they soon realize opposites attract. We now get to the best part of the film.

Oren and Leah take young Sarah out to visit Lake Compounce theme park in Bristol (in the film it's called "Bristol Park"). Nothing more fun than watching Keaton and Douglas ride the Scrambler. It's so rare that senior actors get to play the leads in a romantic comedy that I forgive the implausible story. Douglas has gotten into a comfortable groove playing this fussy, overly sophisticated, leave-me-alone-with-my-martini type, and Keaton, playing an aspiring chanteuse à la Annie Hall, manages to be adorable in her late sixties. (The Long Ridge Tavern in Stamford—called the "Oaks Bistro" in the film—is where Leah has a lounge act.) Oren and Leah are a comic mismatch but realize they are made for each other, which would have been a better title.

Michael Douglas and Diane Keaton are having a "senior moment" in *And So It Goes* (2014) from director Rob Reiner. Here's Douglas and Keaton at Lake Compounce in Bristol.

CONNECTICUT IN THE MOVIES

My mom serving her homemade apple tart to the cast of *The Green* at the Guilford Community Center.

CHAPTER 15
COMING HOME

THE GREEN (2011)

In movies, establishing shots are meant to paint a picture of the world we are about to enter. In *The Green* (2011), the establishing shots depict a town steeped in history, the beautiful shoreline community of Guilford, Connecticut. Guilford is known for its many historic seventeenth- and eighteenth-century homes, its quaint antiques shops and art galleries, and its famous tree-lined town green, where I have witnessed many the Yankee muster over the years.

In Connecticut, the town green was essential because it was where the townspeople met and gathered news, where they felt a sense of community. Of the ninety or so Connecticut films I have written about, *The Green* is the only one that uses its town green to tell its story. Located in New Haven County, Guilford is a nexus between two large cities, New York and Boston. This means it attracts many weekenders from both who own country houses there. Like much of Connecticut, the town delicately combines these two cultures. Natives who live and work here are suspicious of outsiders. "Look at those New York plates," my mom would say.

Guilford was very familiar to *The Green*'s screenwriter and producer, Paul Marcarelli, who was born and raised in North Haven. (He now lives in Litchfield.) Marcarelli is best known as the "Can you hear me now?" guy from the Verizon commercials, but he also had ambitions to make films. When his contract with Verizon ended in 2011, he used the money he had made to set up a produc-

Jason Butler Harner crosses the Guilford Green in *The Green* (2011), the only film to directly involve a town green.

tion company. He also purchased a country house in Guilford and found himself feeling more like one of those interloping New Yorkers.

Marcarelli grew up as a gay kid in an era before being openly gay was widely accepted. He describes it as "growing up in a place where you never felt you belonged." One day, after buying the weekend getaway in Guilford, the random thought occurred to him: "What would it take for the entire town to turn on me?" That idea evolved into a collaboration with director and fellow producer Steven Williford and his production company, Table Ten Films, to develop *The Green*.

When my offer for *The Green* came by telephone from a New York casting director, I barely let him finish the description of my character before I screamed yes! I had always wanted to make a film in Connecticut, and the queer storyline—a gay schoolteacher accused of inappropriate behavior and the townspeople who make him an outcast before they know the facts—sounded intriguing. At that time, queer cinema was still evolving, and it was common to have straight actors "playing gay." Paul was committed to casting gay actors—Jason Butler Harner as Michael and Cheyenne Jackson as Daniel—in the leading roles. In that summer, filming a gay movie with gay actors, a gay producer, gay director, and a gay storyline in Connecticut was a novelty. The *New Haven Register* ran a story about the making of the film with this headline: "Guilford's Verizon Guy Makes Film about Being Gay in Connecticut."

I recently reminisced with Paul about the experience of filming *The Green*. Before we got to that, he reminded me that most days my mother insisted on driving me to the set, then would drive back at lunchtime with my bagged lunch. These were no ordinary sack lunches; she'd have turkey meatloaf, or chicken salad on a baguette. She made an apple tart for the cast and distributed her homemade baked biscotti, so we can forgive her for the day she arrived with my lunch and literally drove

The Green was the first LGBTQ film made in Connecticut. I was very proud to come home to be a part of it. It was a close-knit cast brought together by mutual respect for the screenwriter, Paul Marcarelli. A Connecticut native, Marcarelli, writer and producer of *The Green*, chose Guilford, where he was also living, as the setting of his first produced feature. "It was a statement of identity, and it has made me more comfortable in the place I call home." The story follows a lawyer (Julia Ormond) who must defend a schoolteacher, Michael (Jason Butler Harner), against a false accusation. Cheyenne Jackson plays Michael's partner, Daniel. I play his best friend, a fellow schoolteacher. Locations include State Street, the Catering Company, Guilford Harbor, and Guilford Marina. One critic wrote that *The Green* was a human movie, not a gay movie.

through a scene we were filming. We were outside at the police station set (across from the Morgan School in Clinton), and as she approached in her silver Passat station wagon, the assistant director was frantically waving his arms to try to get her to stop driving forward. Somehow my mom thought this was a signal to keep going. Oh, well, can't get mad at someone bringing lasagna to one of the lead actresses.

When I spoke to Paul about why he chose Connecticut to make his film, he said:

> *The idea of shooting in my hometown was so appealing. The high school we shot in—North Haven School—was where I went to high school. Also, the low-budget nature of the film meant having to wear many hats and call in lots of favors. In the end, we were able to make a more-expensive-looking film because everyone in the town of Guilford helped out. Locals worked as extras. The Guilford Community Center housed the entire production so actors could get ready in the morning, with hair and makeup and wardrobe. When we needed rain for a rain scene, the fire department volunteered to stand with hoses just off camera to create an instant rainstorm for us. The house that Julia Ormond's character, Karen, lives in, which is on Fair Street, was donated to us by the parents of one of the actor's stand-ins after a previous location fell through, just ten hours before shooting [began].*

CONNECTICUT IN THE MOVIES

Cheyenne Jackson and me goofing around on the Guilford Green.

I always prefer shooting in an actual location because it gives it a certain reality, but in *The Green*, we were shooting at someone's house, and they would be coming in and out of the kitchen, getting a snack. Everyone was so nice that Paul worried how the final film would be received. I remember when we were going to screen the film for the first time, I was concerned that the town, which had been so generous in helping, would perceive its depiction as unfair because of the storyline, but people were so supportive. We set aside tickets, thinking maybe two hundred people at most would sign up to watch the film at the Community Center. Over five hundred people signed up! We had to change the venue to accommodate everyone. There was another successful screening at The Kate, the Katharine Hepburn Cultural Arts Center in Old Saybrook, and then *The Green* went on to be a big hit on the indie festival circuit. It won Best Feature Film at the Connecticut Film Festival, Best Feature at the Connecticut Gay and Lesbian Film Festival, and numerous individual awards for acting for Jason Butler Harner, Cheyenne Jackson, and myself.

Michael Gavin (Jason Butler Harner) and his partner, Daniel (Cheyenne Jackson), are New

York transplants who have recently moved to Guilford. Michael is a budding novelist working as a drama teacher at a private high school, and Daniel is beginning to make a name for himself as a local caterer. They are doing their best to fit in but still don't feel entirely accepted as gay men with a gay lifestyle.

Michael has been trying to help a troubled young teen in his class named Jason (Chris Bert). His friend and fellow teacher, Trish (Illeana Douglas), who has recently dealt with a bout of cancer, politely suggests it doesn't look right for a gay man to take such an interest in the young boy. Though they are close, Michael is surprised by Trish's provincial attitude, which he thinks verges on homophobia. In leaving New York for New England, Michael has discovered not only a clash of cultures, but also the repressive atmosphere of the small New England town. This atmosphere forces Michael to project an image at school that he is "normal," so parents feel comfortable that their children are safe. Michael and Daniel are busy renovating their turn-of-the-century house. Like the house, their relationship is a work in progress.

At the time *The Green* was made, Connecticut was only the second state to legalize gay marriage, and the film addresses the reality that this newfound freedom was not for everyone. Michael does not believe in marriage, which has caused him and Daniel to question their love for each other. The relationship is further tested when Jason's mother, Janette (Karen Young), and her live-in boyfriend, Leo (Bill Sage), make a complaint against Michael after witnessing the two having a heated argument. The appearance of impropriety is backed up by witnesses who saw Jason push Michael off him when he tried to intercede on Jason's behalf when kids at school were picking on him. A formal accusation of inappropriate behavior is made. Michael is at first suspended, and later arrested. Trish's husband, Phillip (Boris McGiver), who is a local lawyer, intercedes, but no longer feels he can represent Michael when he discovers Michael had a prior arrest for solicitation in a New York bathroom many years ago.

When I spoke to Marcarelli, he said he included this revelation about Michael (based on an incident a friend of his was involved in) because he "wanted to express that Michael feels this intense shame for what he did, and it's this shame that keeps Michael from being wholly a part of the community where he lives." The arrest muddies the waters for everyone involved, and now even loyal friends like Trish are suspicious about why he concealed the earlier arrest from them.

Daniel feels the most betrayed. He seeks out a high-profile lesbian attorney, Karen, who is used to defending these kinds of cases. She happens to also be happily married to her partner, a fact not lost on Michael and Daniel. While Trish and her husband remain loyal to the two men, there is a strain on the friendship. Trish's cancer returns, and Michael becomes distant. This was supposed to be a retreat from the big, bad city, but Michael soon finds that without Trish, he is an outcast.

Michael is told by his contractor, George (Tom Bloom), that his wife won't let him work for him anymore. Next, Daniel begins losing high-profile catering jobs. At a meeting at Karen's house, she explains to Michael that the only way to win the case is by fighting back and accusing Jason and his mother of exploiting the incident to get money out of the school. Michael's hesitancy further erodes Daniel's belief in his innocence, which leads to Daniel's moving out.

On a stormy summer night, Jason shows up outside Michael's house to try to explain himself, but he gets frightened and runs away. Michael chases after him, following him back to his mother's house, where Jason reveals with anguish that it is his mother's boyfriend, Leo, who has actually been molesting him. The townspeople, who had rushed to judgment against Michael, now give him their full support, and he is cleared of all the charges. He goes back to working on his beloved house, and his contractor returns, but his relationship with Daniel is not so easily fixed.

Though there is still love between them as they sit side by side on the dock at the Guilford marina, they realize they must go their separate ways. After they say good-bye, Michael makes his way across the town green so he can accompany Trish to her final chemotherapy session. As he strides toward his destination, he comes to the realization that there, in Connecticut, he has finally found a home.

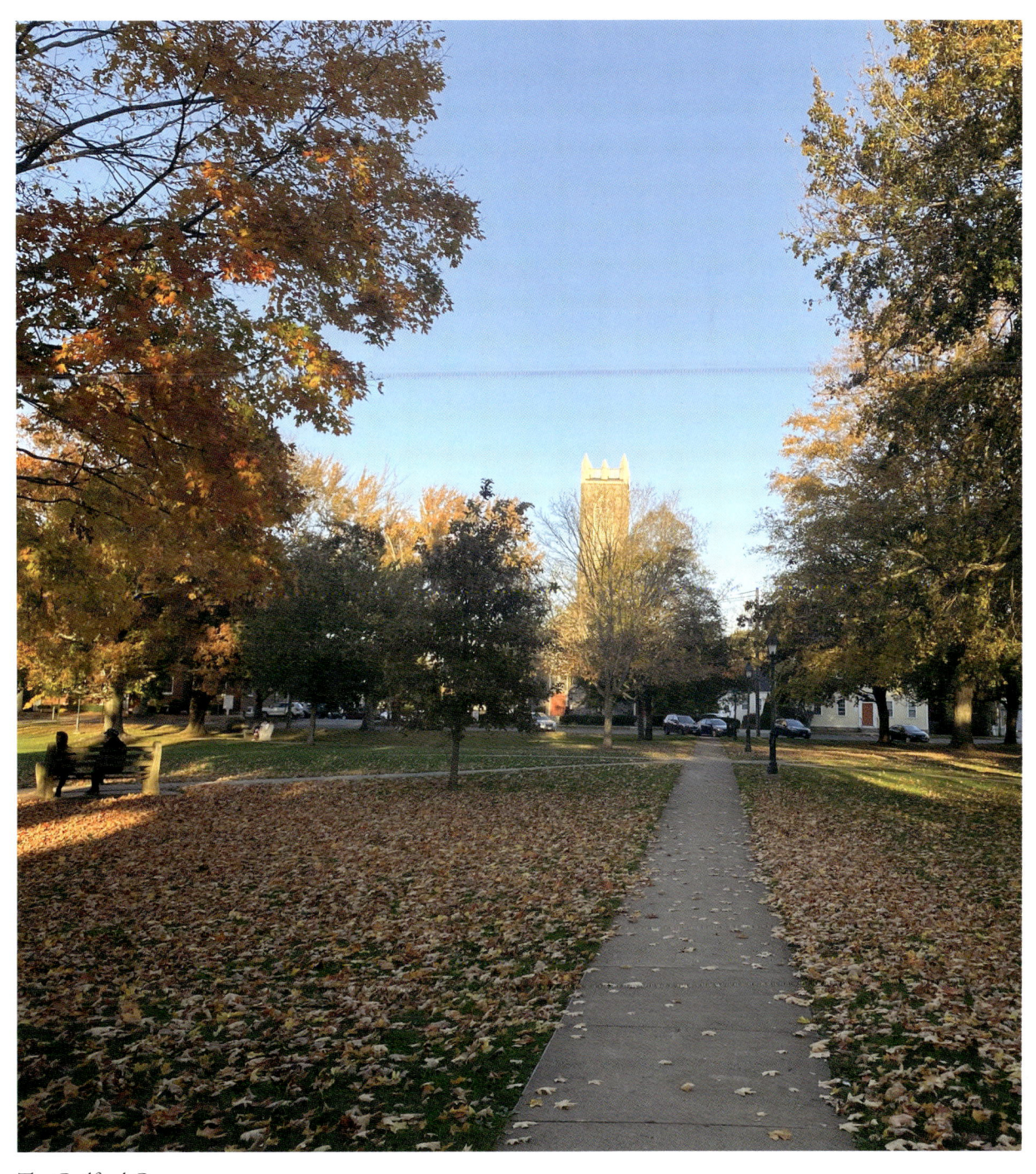

The Guilford Green.

ACKNOWLEDGMENTS

I want to start by thanking Rick Rinehart, executive editor at Globe Pequot Press, whose guidance from the beginning has meant the world to me. It's been a pleasure to work with the talented team at Globe Pequot, including copy editor Melissa J. Hayes and designer Amy Rinehart.

Thanks as always to my attorney and friend, Bill Soble, for his guidance, and to my attorney John Tishbi, for his legal expertise. To my manager, Lee Kernis—thanks for listening, and for your support and friendship. Thanks to Barbara Rey for keeping me pointed in the right direction. Thank you to my publicist, Danny Deraney, for your professional help and guidance. Thanks to Betty Ahmadi for your service. Thanks as always to my friend and lifeline, Father Michael Cooper. Speaking of lifelines, I send a special thank-you to my fellow *Trailers From Hell* guru, the writer extraordinaire, Josh Olson. It was Josh who convinced me—in a parking lot in the Valley in LA—that a book about movies made in Connecticut was a worthwhile venture, and that I should pursue it.

Thanks to Dave Mirkin, for providing feedback on a couple of chapters early on. Special thanks to my friend and fellow artist, Ruthie Danzinger, who never got tired of me calling and asking, "Hey, can I read you something?" Her encouragement and notes were instrumental. Thanks to Alan K. Rode for his care packages and creative talks, and for our mutual love of all things Delmer Daves.

I could not have completed this book without the help of Steve Thompson, who did a meticulous job as researcher and copy editor, championing obscure horror films, and discovering fun facts to include.

I am honored to have Jeanine Basinger, whom I have long admired, provide a quote for the book. As the former chair of film studies at Wesleyan University and curator of their cinema archives, she *is* Connecticut cinema.

I am grateful to all the people who let me comb through archives and libraries, or provided photographs, including Robert Byrne and the San Francisco Silent Film Festival; Tracey Goessel and the Film Preservation Society LLC; the staff at the Eugene O'Neill Theater Center; Joan Miller at Wesleyan Cinema Archives; Sarah Lucey and the curators of Gillette's Castle in East Haddam; and the Chester, Greenwich, Old Saybrook, Roxbury, Simsbury, Southbury, and Windsor Historical Societies. Thank you to Howard Mandelbaum and Derek Davidson from Photofest, for going the extra mile.

Thank you to Sal and John Dominello, Dennis Haysbert, Amy Holden Jones, Paul Marcarelli, Penelope Ann Miller, Connie Stevens, and Colin Theys, for providing personal recollections. Tip of the hat and hugs and kisses to the friends and colleagues who have helped out in a thousand ways, including Allison Anders, Susan Arosteguy, Candi Cazou, Craig Chester, Beverly D'Angelo, Ronan Farrow, Wayne Federman, Danny Ferrington, Joely Fisher, Bruce Goldstein, Leonard Maltin, Ben Mankiewicz, Colin McEnroe, Michael McKean, Kliph Nesteroff, Matt Oswalt, Walter Painter, Bill Prudich, Steven Rogers, Phil and Monica Rosenthal, Adam Shartoff, Sydney Stern, Quentin Tarantino, Lawrence Trilling, Carrie Wick, and all of my friends at the Hallmark Channel.

A few key folks who have helped to make my actual Connecticut dream house possible must be acknowledged, including Linda O'Hara, Jack Morton, Joe Turnello, and the late Jesse Spencer—a true salt-of-the-earth New Englander, the plumber who, after one of my pipes burst, uttered the immortal words, "Hey, it's not everyone who can brag they have a swimming pool in their basement."

Finally, thank you to my family—my mom, my brother Erik, dearest Chauncey, and Saturnino Salas, who made all of this possible, who visits me when I need him to, and keeps sending me golf balls to remind me that I really am home.

ABOUT THE AUTHOR

Illeana Douglas is an Emmy-nominated actress, writer, producer, and director. She is known for playing fearless and outspoken characters in films like *Goodfellas*, *Cape Fear*, *To Die For*, *Grace of My Heart*, *Picture Perfect*, *Stir of Echoes*, and *Ghost World*, and on TV in *The Larry Sanders Show*, *Action*, *Six Feet Under*, *Entourage*, *Welcome to Sweden*, *Shrill*, and *Goliath*. She wrote, produced, starred, and frequently directed the multi-award-winning, first-ever branded web series, *Easy to Assemble*.

Illeana is the granddaughter of two-time Academy Award–winning actor Melvyn Douglas. As part of the Turner Classic Movies family, she's interviewed a pantheon of cinema greats, hosted *Funny Ladies* and *Trailblazing Women*, and participated in scores of film documentaries, including *CNN: The Movies*, *78/52*, *Greatest Cult Films of All Time*, *The True Adventures of Raoul Walsh*, and Kino Lorber's *Pioneers: First Women Filmmakers*, which she executive-produced and hosted. She's also a regular contributor to *Joe Dante's Trailers From Hell*.

Her first book, *I Blame Dennis Hopper: And Other Stories from a Life Lived In and Out of the Movies*, received a Kirkus review, and was named "Best Pop Culture Book of 2015" by *Entertainment Weekly* and one of the "Best New Books" (2015) by *People* magazine.

The author in Belltown, East Hampton, Connecticut.

CONNECTICUT IN THE MOVIES

APPENDIX: LIST OF FILMS WITH CREDITS

A CONNECTICUT YANKEE IN KING ARTHUR'S COURT (1949)
Paramount Pictures; directed by Tay Garnett; screenplay by Edmund Beloin, based on a novel by Mark Twain; produced by Robert Fellows; cinematography by Ray Rennahan; music by Victor Young, with songs by Jimmy Van Heusen and Johnny Burke; starring Bing Crosby, William Bendix, Rhonda Fleming.

A DEATH IN CANAAN (1978)
CBS; directed by Tony Richardson; written by Joan Barthel, Spencer Eastman, and Thomas Thompson, based on nonfiction book of the same name by Joan Barthel; produced by Robert W. Christiansen; starring Stefanie Powers, Paul Clemens, Brian Dennehy, Conchata Ferrell, and Jacqueline Brookes.

AH, WILDERNESS! (1935)
MGM; directed by Clarence Brown; screenplay by Albert Hackett and Frances Goodrich, based on a play by Eugene O'Neill; produced by Clarence Brown and Hunt Stromberg; cinematography by Clyde De Vinna; music by Herbert Stothart and Edward Ward; starring Wallace Beery, Mickey Rooney, Lionel Barrymore, Aline MacMahon.

ALL ABOUT EVE (1950)
Twentieth Century Fox; written, produced, and directed by Joseph L. Mankiewicz, based on a story by Mary Orr; produced by Darryl F. Zanuck; cinematography by Milton R, Krasner; music by Alfred Newman; starring Bette Davis, Anne Baxter, George Sanders, Marilyn Monroe.

ALL GOOD THINGS (2010)
Magnolia Pictures, the Weinstein Company; directed by Andrew Jarecki; screenplay by Marcus Hinchey, Marc Smerling; produced by Andrew Jarecki, Bruna Papendrea, Michael London, Marc Smerling; cinematography by Michael Seresin; music by Rob Simonsen; starring Ryan Gosling, Kirsten Dunst, Frank Langella, Phillip Baker Hall.

A MIGHTY WIND (2003)
Warner Bros. and Castle Rock Entertainment; directed by Christopher Guest; written by Christopher Guest and Eugene Levy; produced by Karen Murphy; cinematography by Arlene Nelson; music by Christopher Guest; starring Christopher Guest, Eugene Levy, Michael McKean, Catherine O'Hara.

AMISTAD (1997)
HBO Films, DreamWorks Pictures; directed by Steven Spielberg; screenplay by David Franzoni; produced by Steven Spielberg, Debbie Allen, Colin Wilson; cinematography by Janusz Kaminski; music by John Williams; starring Matthew McConaughey, Anthony Hopkins, Morgan Freeman, Nigel Hawthorne, Djimon Hounsou.

AND SO IT GOES (2014)
Castle Rock Entertainment, Foresight Unlimited, Envision Entertainment, Clarius Entertainment, Freestyle Releasing; directed by Rob Reiner; written by Marc Andrus; produced by Rob Reiner, Mark Damon, and Alan Greisman; cinematography by Reed Morano; music by Marc Shaiman; starring Michael Douglas, Diane Keaton, Sterling Jerins.

APRIL FOOLS, THE (1968)
National General Pictures, Cinema Center Films; directed by Stuart Rosenberg; written by Hal Dresner; produced by Gordon Carroll; music by Marvin Hamlisch; starring Jack Lemmon, Catherine Deneuve, Myrna Loy, Charles Boyer.

AUNTIE MAME (1958)
Warner Bros.; produced and directed by Morton DeCosta; screenplay by Betty Comden, Adolph Green, based on a novel by Patrick Dennis; cinematography by Harry Stradling; music by Bronislau Kaper; starring Rosalind Russell, Joanna Barnes, Roger Smith, Coral Browne.

AWAY WE GO (2009)
Focus Features, Neal Street Productions, Big Beach; directed by Sam Mendes; screenplay by Dave Eggers and Vendela Vida; produced by Edward Saxon, Marc Turtletaub, Vincent Landay; cinematography by Ellen Kuras; starring John Krasinski, Maya Rudolph, Jeff Daniels, Catherine O'Hara, Maggie Gyllenhaal, Allison Janney.

BIG BAD SWIM, THE (2006)
Echo Bridge Home Entertainment Production Companies, Four Act Films, Renart Films, Setton Sun Productions, Visit Films; directed by Ishai Setton; written by Daniel Schechter; produced by Chandra Simon and Ishai Setton; cinematography by Josh Silfen; music by Chad Kelly; starring Paget Brewster, Jeff Branson, Jess Wexler, Raviv Ullman, Avi Setton.

BIRDS OF AMERICA (2008)
Plum Pictures, Ideal Partners Film Fund, Myriad Pictures; directed by Craig Lucas; screenplay by Elyse Friedman; produced by Daniela Taplin Lundberg, Jana Edelbaum, Celine Rattray, Galt Niederhoffer; cinematography by Yaron Orbach; music by Ahrin Mishan; starring Matthew Perry, Ginnifer Goodwin, Ben Foster, Lauren Graham.

BOOMERANG! (1947)
Twentieth Century Fox; directed by Elia Kazan; screenplay by Richard Murphy, based on an article by Anthony Abbot; produced by Louis de Rochemont and Darryl F. Zanuck; cinematography by Norbert Brodine; music by David Buttolph; starring Dana Andrews, Jane Wyatt, Lee J. Cobb, Arthur Kennedy, Ed Begley, Karl Malden, Sam Levene, Arthur Miller.

BORN RICH (1924)
First National Pictures; directed by William Nigh; screenplay by Harriete Underhill and Walter DeLeon; produced by William Nigh; cinematography by George Folsey; starring Claire Windsor, Bert Lytell, Frank Morgan, Doris Kenyon.

BRINGING UP BABY (1938)
RKO Radio Pictures; directed by Howard Hawks; screenplay by Dudley Nichols and Hagar Wilde, from a story by Hagar Wilde; produced by Howard Hawks and Cliff Reid; cinematography by Russell Metty; music by Roy Webb; starring Cary Grant, Katharine Hepburn, Charles Ruggles, May Robson, Walter Catlett.

BRISTOL BOYS (2006)
Cult Movies and Fabrication Films; directed, written, and edited by Brandon David Cole; produced by Chris Clarke, Brandon David, Josh Mond; cinematography by Bill Winters; starring Thomas Guiry, Dean Winters, Max Casella, Kevin Toolen.

CANNONBALL RUN, THE (1981)
Twentieth Century Fox; directed by Hal Needham; written by Brock Yates; produced by Albert S. Ruddy; cinematography by Michael Butler; music by Al Capps; starring Burt Reynolds, Roger Moore, Farrah Fawcett, Dean Martin, Jackie Chan, Dom DeLuise, Jack Elam.

CHRISTMAS IN CONNECTICUT (1945)
Warner Bros.–First National; directed by Peter Godfrey; screenplay by Lionel Houser and Adele Comandini, from a story by Aileen Hamilton; cinematography by Carl E. Guthrie; music by Friedrich Hollaender; starring Barbara Stanwyck, Dennis Morgan, S. Z. Sakall, Sydney Greenstreet, Reginald Gardiner.

CINDERELLA (1914)
Famous Players, Paramount Pictures; directed by Joseph Kirkwood Sr.; produced by Daniel Frohman, Adolph Zukor; starring Mary Pickford, Owen Moore, Isabel Vernon.

COME TO THE STABLE (1949)
Twentieth Century Fox; directed by Henry Koster; screenplay by Oscar Millard and Sally Benson, based on a story by Clare Booth Luce; produced by Samuel G. Engel; cinematography by Joseph LaShelle; music by Cyril J. Mockridge; starring Loretta Young, Celeste Holm, Elsa Lanchester.

COUNTRY DOCTOR, THE (1909)
Biograph Studios; written and directed by D. W. Griffith; cinematography by G. W. "Billy" Bitzer; starring Kate Bruce, Mary Pickford, Adele DeGarde.

CURSE OF THE LIVING CORPSE, THE (1964)
Twentieth Century Fox, Deal Films, Iselin-Tenney Productions; directed, written, and produced by Del Tenney; cinematography by Richard Hilliard; music by William Holmes; starring Helen Warren, Margot Hartman, Roy Scheider.

DEEP IN THE DARKNESS (2014)
O'Brien; cinematography by Adrian Correia and Claudio Rietti; music by Matthew Llwellyn; starring Sean Patrick Thomas, Dean Stockwell, Blanche Baker.

DESIRE UNDER THE ELMS (1958)
Don Hartman Productions, Paramount Pictures; directed by Delbert Mann; screenplay by Irwin Shaw, based on a play by Eugene O'Neill; produced by Don Hartman; cinematography by Daniel L. Fapp; music by Elmer Bernstein; starring Sophia Loren, Anthony Perkins, Burl Ives, Pernell Roberts.

DRAGONWYCK (1946)
Twentieth Century Fox; written and directed by Joseph L. Mankiewicz; produced by Darryl F. Zanuck, Ernst Lubitsch; cinematography by Arthur C. Miller; music by Alfred Newman; starring Gene Tierney, Walter Huston, Vincent Price.

EVERYBODY WINS (1990)
MGM/Orion, Recorded Picture Company; directed by Karel Reisz; screenplay by Arthur Miller; produced by Jeremy Thomas; cinematography by Ian Baker; music by Mark Isham, with songs by Leon Redbone; starring Nick Nolte, Debra Winger, Jack Warden, Frank Converse.

EVERYBODY'S FINE (2009)
Radar Pictures, Hollywood Gang; distributed by Miramax Films, Buena Vista International; written and directed by Kirk Jones, based on the film *Everybody's Fine* by Giuseppe Tornatore; produced by Gianni Nunnari, Ted Field, Vittorio Cecchi Gori, and Glynis Murray; cinematography by Henry Braham; starring Robert De Niro, Drew Barrymore, Kate Beckinsale, and Sam Rockwell.

FAMILY STONE, THE (2005)
Twentieth Century Fox; written and directed by Thomas Bezucha; produced by Michael London; cinematography by Jonathan Brown; music by Michael Giacchino; starring Dermot Mulroney, Sarah Jessica Parker, Diane Keaton, Luke Wilson, Claire Danes.

FAR FROM HEAVEN (2002)
Focus Features; directed and written by Todd Haynes; produced by Jody Patton and Christine Vachon; cinematography by Edward Lachman; music by Elmer Bernstein; starring Julianne Moore, Dennis Haysbert, Dennis Quaid, Viola Davis.

FRIDAY THE 13TH PART 2 (1981)
Paramount Pictures; directed and produced by Steve Miner; written by Ron Kurz and Victor Miller, based on characters created by Sean S. Cunningham and Victor Miller; cinematography by Peter Stein; music by Harry Manfredini; starring Adrienne King, Amy Steel, John Furey, Steve Dash (aka, Steve Daskewisz).

GENTLEMAN'S AGREEMENT (1947)
Twentieth Century Fox; directed by Elia Kazan; screenplay by Moss Hart, with Elia Kazan, based on the novel by Laura Z. Hobson; produced by Darryl F. Zanuck; cinematography by Arthur C. Miller; music by Alfred Newman; starring Gregory Peck, Dorothy McGuire, John Garfield, Dean Stockwell, Albert Dekker, June Havoc.

GOOD FENCES (2003)
Showtime, 40 Acres and a Mule Filmworks; directed by Ernest R. Dickerson; screenplay by Trey Ellis, from a novel by Erika Ellis; produced by Danny Glover, Whoopi Goldberg, Armand Leo, Sam Kitt, Spike Lee; cinematography by Jonathan Freeman; music by George Duke; starring Danny Glover, Whoopi Goldberg, Mo'Nique.

GREEN, THE (2011)
Table Ten Films; directed by Steven Williford; screenplay by Paul Marcarelli, from a story by Steven Williford; produced by Steven Williford and Paul Marcarelli; cinematography by Ryan Samul; music by William Brittelle; starring Jason Butler Harner, Cheyenne Jackson, Illeana Douglas, Julia Ormond.

HAUNTING IN CONNECTICUT, THE (2009)
Gold Circle Films, Integrated Films, Lionsgate; directed by Peter Cornwell; screenplay by Adam Simon and Tim Metcalfe; produced by Paul Brooks, Andrew Trapani, Daniel Farrands, Wendy Rhoads; cinematography by Adam Swica; music by Robert J. Kral; starring Virginia Madsen, Kyle Gallner, Martin Donovan.

HELLO I MUST BE GOING (2012)
Skyscraper Content, Union Entertainment Group; directed by Todd Louiso; screenplay by Sarah Koskoff; produced by Hans Ritter, Mary Jane Skalski; cinematography by Julie Kirkwood; music by Laura Veirs; starring Melanie Lynskey, Blythe Danner, John Rubinstein, Sara Chase.

HOLIDAY INN (1942)
Paramount Pictures; directed and produced by Mark Sandrich; screenplay by Claude Binyon and Elmer Rice, based on an idea by Irving Berlin; cinematography by David Abel; songs by Irving Berlin, music by Robert Emmett Dolan; starring Bing Crosby, Fred Astaire, Marjorie Reynolds.

HOPE SPRINGS (2012)
Columbia Pictures, MGM, Mandate Pictures, Escape Artists, Film 360; directed by David Frankel; written by Vanessa Taylor; produced by Guymon Casady, Todd Black, Brian Bell; cinematography by Florian Ballhaus; music by Theodore Shapiro; starring Meryl Streep, Tommy Lee Jones, Steve Carell, Elisabeth Shue, Jean Smart.

HORROR OF PARTY BEACH, THE (1964)
Twentieth Century Fox; directed by Del Tenney; written by Richard Hilliard; produced by Del Tenney and Alan V. Iselin; cinematography by Richard Hilliard; music by the Del-Aires; starring John Scott, Alice Lyon, Eulabelle Moore.

ICE STORM, THE (1997)
Fox Searchlight, Good Machine; directed by Ang Lee; screenplay by James Schamus, based on a novel by Rick Moody; produced by Ted Hope, James Schamus, Ang Lee; cinematography by Frederick Elmes; music by Mychael Danna ; starring Kevin Kline, Joan Allen, Tobey Maguire, Christina Ricci, Elijah Wood, Sigourney Weaver.

INDIANA JONES AND THE KINGDOM OF THE CRYSTAL SKULL (2008)
Lucasfilm Ltd., Paramount Pictures; directed by Steven Spielberg; screenplay by David Koepp, from a story by George Lucas and Jeff Nathanson; produced by Frank Marshall; cinematography by Janusz Kaminski; music by John Williams; starring Harrison Ford, Cate Blanchett, Karen Allen, Shia LaBeouf.

IN NAME ONLY (1939)
Distributed by RKO Radio Pictures; directed by John Cromwell; screenplay by Richard Sherman, based on a novel by Bessie Breuer; produced by George Haight; cinematography by J. Roy Hunt; music by Roy Webb; starring Cary Grant, Carole Lombard, Kay Francis.

IT HAPPENED TO JANE (1959)
Columbia Pictures, Arwin Productions; directed by Richard Quine; written by Norman Katkov, from a story by Norman Katkov and Max Wilk; produced by Richard Quine and Martin Melcher; cinematography by Charles Lawton Jr.; music by George Duning; starring Doris Day, Jack Lemmon, Ernie Kovacs, Steve Forrest, Tim Rooney, Gina Gillespie, Max Showalter.

IT'S A WONDERFUL LIFE (1946)
Liberty Films, RKO Radio Pictures; directed and produced by Frank Capra; screenplay by Frances Goodrich, Albert Hackett, and Frank Capra, based on a story by Philip Van Doren Stern; cinematography by Joseph Walker and Joseph Biroc; music by Dimitri Tiomkin; starring James Stewart, Donna Reed, Henry Travers, Lionel Barrymore, Thomas Mitchell.

JACKNIFE (1989)
Kings Road Entertainment, Cineplex Odeon, Vestron Pictures; directed by David Jones; screenplay by Stephen Metcalfe, adapted from his play; produced by Carol Baum and Robert Schaffel; cinematography by Brian West; music by Bruce Broughton; starring Robert De Niro, Ed Harris, Kathy Baker, Charles S. Dutton.

LAND OF STEADY HABITS, THE (2018)
Likely Story; directed and written by Nicole Holofcener, based on a novel by Ted Thompson; produced by Stefanie Azpiazu, Anthony Bregman, and Nicole Holofcener; cinematography by Alar Kivilo; music by Marcelo Zarvos; starring Ben Mendelsohn, Edie Falco, Connie Britton, Thomas Mann.

LAST HOUSE ON THE LEFT, THE (1972)
Sean S. Cunningham Films, The Night Company, Lobster Enterprises, Hallmark Releasing, American International Pictures; written, directed, and edited by Wes Craven, based on an earlier screenplay by Ulla Isaksson; produced by Sean S. Cunningham; cinematography by Victor Hurwitz; music by David Hess; starring Sandra Peabody, Lucy Grantham, David Hess, Fred J. Lincoln, Jeramie Rain, Eleanor Shaw (credited as Cynthia Carr), Richard Towers (credited as Gaylord St. James).

LET'S SCARE JESSICA TO DEATH (1971)
Paramount Pictures, The Jessica Company; directed by John Hancock; written by John Hancock and Lee Kalcheim (as Ralph Rose and Norman Jonas), inspired by a story by J. Sheridan Le Fanu; produced by Charles B. Moss Jr. and William Badalato; cinematography by Robert M. Baldwin; music by Orville Stoeber; starring Zohra Lampert, Barton Heyman, Kevin O'Connor, Mariclare Costello, Gretchen Corbett.

LIFE BEFORE HER EYES, THE (2007)
Magnolia Pictures, 2929 Entertainment; directed by Vadim Perelman; screenplay by Emil Stern, based on a novel by Laura Kasischke; produced by Anthony Katagas, Vadim Perelman, Aimée Peyronnet, Mark Cuban; cinematography by Pawel Edelman; music by James Horner; starring Uma Thurman, Evan Rachel Wood, Eva Amurri, Gabrielle Brennan, Oscar Isaac, Brett Cullen.

LONG DAY'S JOURNEY INTO NIGHT (1962)
Embassy Pictures; directed by Sidney Lumet; play by Eugene O'Neill; produced by Ely Landau; cinematography by Boris Kaufman; music by André Previn; starring Katharine Hepburn, Jason Robards, Dean Stockwell, Ralph Richardson.

LOVING (1970)
Columbia Pictures, Brooks Ltd.; directed by Irvin Kershner; screenplay by Don Devlin, based on a novel by J. M. Ryan; produced by Don Devlin; cinematography by Gordon Willis; music by Bernardo Segall; starring George Segal, Eva Marie Saint, Keenan Wynn, Roy Scheider.

MAN IN THE GRAY FLANNEL SUIT, THE (1956)
Twentieth Century Fox; directed by Nunnally Johnson; screenplay by Nunnally Johnson, based on a novel by Sloan Wilson; produced by Darryl F. Zanuck; cinematography by Charles Clarke; music by Bernard Herrmann; starring Gregory Peck, Jennifer Jones, Fredric March, Lee J. Cobb, Keenan Wynn.

MAN IN THE NET, THE (1959)
United Artists; directed by Michael Curtiz; written by Reginald Rose, from a story by Hugh Wheeler; produced by Walter Mirisch, Alan Ladd; music by Hans J. Salter; starring Alan Ladd, Carolyn Jones, Charles McGraw, Michael McGreevey.

MAN ON A SWING (1974)
Paramount Pictures, Jaffilms, Inc.; directed by Frank Perry; written by David Zelag Goodman, based on a book by William Arthur Clark; produced by Howard B. Jaffe; cinematography by Adam Holender; music by Lalo Schifrin; starring Cliff Robertson, Joel Grey, Dorothy Tristan, Elizabeth Wilson, Peter Masterson.

MARSHALL (2017)
Open Road Films, Starlight Media, Chestnut Ridge Productions, Hudlin Entertainment; directed by Reginald Hudlin; written by Michael and Jacob Koskoff; produced by Paula Wagner, Reginald Hudlin, Jonathan Sanger; cinematography by Newton Thomas Sigel; music by Marcus Miller; starring Chadwick Boseman, Josh Gad, Sterling K. Brown, Kate Hudson.

MR. BLANDINGS BUILDS HIS DREAM HOUSE (1947)
RKO Radio Pictures, Selznick Releasing Organization; directed by H. C. Potter; written by Norman Panama and Melvin Frank, based on a novel by Eric Hodgins; produced by Dore Schary, Melvin Frank, and Norman Panama; cinematography by James Wong Howe; music by Leigh Harline; starring Cary Grant, Myrna Loy, Melvyn Douglas, Louise Beavers.

MY SIX LOVES (1963)
Paramount Pictures; directed by Gower Champion; screenplay by John Fante, Joseph Calvelli, and William Wood, based on a story by Peter V. K. Funk; produced by Gant Gaither; cinematography by Arthur E. Arling; music by Walter Scharf; starring Debbie Reynolds, Cliff Robertson, David Janssen, Eileen Heckart, Max Showalter, Alice Ghostley, John McGiver.

MY SOUL TO TAKE (2010)
Universal Pictures, Corvus Corax, Relativity Media, Rogue Pictures; directed and written by Wes Craven; produced by Wes Craven, Anthony Katagas, Iya Labunka; cinematography by Petra Korner; music by Marco Beltrami; starring Max Thieriot, John Magaro, Denzel Whitaker.

MYSTIC PIZZA (1988)
The Samuel Goldwyn Company; directed by Donald Petrie; screenplay by Amy Jones, Perry Howze, Randy Howze, and Alfred Uhry, based on a story by Amy Jones; produced by Mark Levinson and Scott Rosenfelt; cinematography by Tim Suhrstedt; music by David McHugh; starring Annabeth Gish, Julia Roberts, Lili Taylor, William R. Moses, Vincent D'Onofrio.

ONE SUMMER LOVE (AKA, DRAGONFLY) (1976)
American International Pictures; directed and produced by Gilbert Cates; written by N. Richard Nash; cinematography by Gerald Hirschfeld; music by Stephen Lawrence; starring Beau Bridges, Susan Sarandon, James Noble, Ann Wedgeworth.

OTHER, THE (1972)
Twentieth Century Fox; directed by Robert Mulligan; screenplay by Thomas Tryon, based on his book; produced by Robert Mulligan and Thomas Tryon; cinematography by Robert L. Surtees; music by Jerry Goldsmith; starring Uta Hagen, Chris and Martin Udvarnoky.

OTHER PEOPLE'S MONEY (1991)
Warner Bros.; directed by Norman Jewison; screenplay by Alvin Sargent, based on a play by Jerry Sterner; produced by Norman Jewison, Ric Kidney; cinematography by Haskell Wexler; music by David Newman; starring Danny DeVito, Gregory Peck, Penelope Ann Miller.

PARRISH (1961)
Warner Bros.; directed, written, and produced by Delmer Daves, based on a novel by Mildred Savage; cinematography by Harry Stradling Sr.; music by Max Steiner; starring Troy Donahue, Claudette Colbert, Karl Malden, Connie Stevens, Dean Jagger, Diane McBain, Sharon Hugueny.

PEEPLES (2013)
Lionsgate, 34th Street Films; directed and written by Tina Gordon Chism; produced by Tyler Perry, Paul Hall, Stephanie Allain, Ozzie Areu, and Matt Moore; cinematography by Alexander Gruszynski; music by Aaron Zigman; starring Craig Robinson, Kerry Washington, David Alan Grier, S. Epatha Merkerson, Diahann Carroll.

PRIVATE LIVES OF PIPPA LEE, THE (2009)
Plan B Entertainment, Screen Media Films; directed and written by Rebecca Miller, based on her novel; produced by Lemore Syvan; cinematography by Declan Quinn; music by Michael Rohatyn; starring Robin Wright, Alan Arkin, Winona Ryder, Keanu Reeves Blake Lively.

PROMISES IN THE DARK (1979)
Warner Bros., Orion Pictures; directed and produced by Jerome Hellman; written by Loring Mandel; cinematography by Adam Holender; music by Leonard Rosenman; starring Marsha Mason, Susan Clark, Michael Brandon, Kathleen Beller, Ned Beatty.

RACHEL GETTING MARRIED (2008)
Sony Pictures Classics; directed by Jonathan Demme; written by Jenny Lumet; produced by Jonathan Demme, Neda Armian, Marc E. Platt; cinematography by Declan Quinn; music by Donald Harrison Jr. and Zafer Tawil; starring Anne Hathaway, Rosemarie DeWitt, Debra Winger.

RACHEL, RACHEL (1968)
Warner Bros.–Seven Arts, Kayos Productions; directed and produced by Paul Newman; screenplay by Stewart Stern, based on a novel by Margaret Laurence; cinematography by Gayne Rescher; music by Jerome Moross; starring Joanne Woodward, Estelle Parsons, James Olson.

RALLY 'ROUND THE FLAG, BOYS! (1958)
Twentieth Century Fox; directed and produced by Leo McCarey; written by Claude Binyon and Leo McCarey, based on a novel by Max Shulman; cinematography by Leon Shamroy; music by Cyril J. Mockridge; starring Paul Newman, Joanne Woodward, Joan Collins.

REVOLUTIONARY ROAD (2008)
BBC Films, DreamWorks Pictures, Neal Street Productions, Evamere Entertainment; directed by Sam Mendes; screenplay by Justin Haythe, based on a novel by Richard Yates; produced by Sam Mendes, Bobby Cohen, Scott Rudin, John Hart; cinematography by Roger Deakins; music by Thomas Newman; starring Kate Winslet, Leonardo DiCaprio, Michael Shannon.

ROMEO AND JULIET (1916)
Metro Pictures, Quality Pictures Corporation; directed by John W. Noble; written by John Arthur, John W. Noble, and Rudolph De Cordova, based on a play by William Shakespeare; produced by Maxwell Karger; cinematography by R. J. Bergquist; starring Francis X. Bushman, Beverly Bayne, Fritz Leiber, Lawson Butt.

ROPE (1948)
Transatlantic Pictures; distributed by Warner Brothers; screenplay by Arthur Laurents, with story by Hume Cronyn, based on the play *Rope* (1929) by Patrick Hamilton; directed by Alfred Hitchcock; produced by Alfred Hitchcock and Sidney Bernstein; cinematography by Joseph A. Valentine and William V. Skall; starring James Stuart, John Dall, and Farley Granger.

SECRET LIFE OF AN AMERICAN WIFE, THE (1968)
Twentieth Century Fox; directed, written, and produced by George Axelrod; cinematography by Leon Shamroy; music by Billy May; starring Anne Jackson, Walter Matthau, Patrick O'Neal.

SHERLOCK HOLMES (1916)
Essanay Studios; directed by Arthur Berthelet; written by H. S. Sheldon, based on works by William Gillette and Arthur Conan Doyle; starring William Gillette, Edward Fielding.

STANLEY & IRIS (1990)
MGM, Lantana Productions, Star Partners II Ltd.; directed by Martin Ritt; screenplay by Harriet Frank Jr. and Irving Ravetch, based on a novel by Pat Barker; produced by Arlene Sellers and Alex Winitsky; cinematography by Donald McAlpine; music by John Williams; starring Jane Fonda, Robert De Niro, Swoosie Kurtz, Jamey Sheridan, Zohra Lampert.

STEPFORD WIVES, THE (1975)
Columbia Pictures; directed by Bryan Forbes; screenplay by William Goldman, based on a novel by Ira Levin; produced by Edgar J. Scherick; cinematography by Owen Roizman; music by Michael Small; starring Katharine Ross, Peter Masterson, Paula Prentiss, Patrick O'Neal.

STRANGER, THE (1946)
RKO Radio Pictures; directed by Orson Welles; screenplay by Anthony Veiller, with John Huston and Orson Welles, based on an adaptation by Decla Dunning and Victor Trivas of an original story by Victor Trivas; produced by Sam Spiegel; cinematography by Russell Metty; music by Bronisław Kaper; starring Edward G. Robinson, Loretta Young, Orson Welles.

STRANGERS ON A TRAIN (1951)
Warner Bros.; produced and directed by Alfred Hitchcock; screenplay by Raymond Chandler, Whitfield Cook, and Czenzi Ormonde, based on a book by Patricia Highsmith; cinematography by Robert Burks; music by Dimitri Tiomkin; starring Farley Granger, Robert Walker, Ruth Roman.

SWIMMER, THE (1968)
Columbia Pictures, Horizon Pictures; directed by Frank Perry; screenplay by Eleanor Perry, based on a story by John Cheever; produced by Frank Perry and Roger Lewis; cinematography by David L. Quaid; music by Marvin Hamlisch; starring Burt Lancaster, Janice Rule, Janet Landgard, Joan Rivers, Cornelia Otis Skinner.

THEODORA GOES WILD (1936)
Columbia Pictures; directed by Richard Boleslawski; screenplay by Sidney Buchman, from a story by Mary McCarthy; produced by Everett Riskin; cinematography by Joseph Walker; music by Arthur Morton and William Grant Still; starring Irene Dunne, Melvyn Douglas, Thomas Mitchell, Thurston Hall.

THOROUGHBREDS (2017)
Focus Features, June Pictures, B Story, Big Indie Pictures; directed and written by Cory Finley; produced by Andrew Duncan, Alex Saks, Kevin J. Walsh, Nat Faxon, Jim Rash; cinematography by Lyle Vincent; music by Erik Friedlander; starring Olivia Cooke, Anya Taylor-Joy, Anton Yelchin.

TUNNEL OF LOVE, THE (1958)
MGM; directed by Gene Kelly; written by Joseph Fields, based on plays and a novel by Joseph Fields, Peter DeVries, and Jerome Chodorov; produced by Martin Melcher and Joseph Fields; cinematography by Robert J. Bronner; starring Doris Day, Richard Widmark, Gig Young, Gia Scala, Elizabeth Wilson.

VIOLENT MIDNIGHT (1963)
Del Tenney Productions, Victoria Films; directed by Richard Hilliard; screenplay by Robin Miller and Mann Rubin (with Margot Hartman and Del Tenney, uncredited), based on a story by Richard Hilliard; cinematography by Louis McMahon; starring Lee Philips, Shepperd Strudwick, James Farentino, Jean Hale, Margot Hartman, Sylvia Miles, Dick Van Patten.

WANDA (1970)
Foundation for Filmmakers, Bard International Pictures; directed and written by Barbara Loden; produced by Harry Shuster and Barbara Loden; cinematography by Nicholas Proferes; music by Dave Mullaney; starring Barbara Loden, Michael Higgins, Jerome Thier.

WAY DOWN EAST (1920)
United Artists; directed and produced by D. W. Griffith; written by Anthony Paul Kelly, Joseph Grismer, and D. W. Griffith, based on a play by Lottie Blair Parker; cinematography by G. W. "Billy" Bitzer; starring Lillian Gish, Richard Barthelmess, Lowell Sherman.

WEDDING NIGHT, THE (1935)
Film Classics, Inc.; directed by King Vidor; screenplay by Edith Fitzgerald, based on a story by Edwin H. Knopf; produced by Samuel Goldwyn; cinematography by Gregg Toland; music by Alfred Newman; starring Gary Cooper, Anna Sten, Ralph Bellamy, Walter Brennan.

WE NEED TO TALK ABOUT KEVIN (2011)
BBC Productions, BBC Films, UK Film Council, Footprint Investment, Piccadilly Pictures, Lipsync Productions, Artina Films, Rockinghorse Films; distributed by Artificial Eye UK; directed by Lynne Ramsey; screenplay by Lynne Ramsey and Rory Stewart Kinnear, based on a novel by Lionel Shriver; produced by Jennifer Fox, Luc Roeg, Bob Salerno; cinematography by Seamus McGarvey; music by Jonny Greenwood; starring Tilda Swinton, John C. Reilly, Ezra Miller.

WHAT DAISY SAID (1916)
Biograph Company; written by Stanner E. V. Taylor; directed by D. W. Griffith; cinematography by G. W. Bitzer; starring Mary Pickford.

WHAT JUST HAPPENED (2008)
2929 Productions, TriBeCa Productions, Linson Films; distributed by Magnolia Pictures; written by Art Linson, based on his book of the same name; directed by Barry Levinson; produced by Art Linson, Robert De Niro, Jane Rosenthal, and Barry Levinson; cinematography by Stephane Fontaine; starring Robert De Niro, Sean Penn, Catherine Keener, Stanley Tucci, John Turturro, Bruce Willis, and Robin Wright.

WHEN EVERY DAY WAS THE FOURTH OF JULY (1978)
Dan Curtis Productions, NBC Television; directed by Dan Curtis; written by Dan Curtis, with Lee Hutson; produced by Dan Curtis and Stephen P. Reicher; cinematography by Frank Stanley; music by Walter Scharf; starring Dean Jones, Geoffrey Lewis, Katy Kurtzman, Louise Sorel.

WIVES AND LOVERS (1963)
Paramount Pictures; directed by John Rich; written by Edward Anhalt, based on a play by Jay Presson Allen; produced by Hal B. Wallis; cinematography by Lucien Ballard; music by Lyn Murray; starring Janet Leigh, Van Johnson, Shelley Winters, Jeremy Slate, Ray Walston, Martha Hyer, Claire Wilcox.